International Review
of Health Psychology

Editorial Board

International Review of Health Psychology

VOLUME 1

Edited by

S. Maes
Leiden University, The Netherlands

H. Leventhal
Rutgers University, USA

and

M. Johnston
University of St Andrews, Scotland

JOHN WILEY & SONS
Chichester · New York · Brisbane · Toronto · Singapore

Copyright ©1992 by John Wiley & Sons Ltd,
Baffins Lane, Chichester,
West Sussex PO19 1UD, England

Other Wiley Editorial Offices

John Wiley & Sons, Inc., 605 Third Avenue,
New York, NY 10158-0012, USA

Jacaranda Wiley Ltd, G.P.O. Box 859, Brisbane,
Queensland 4001, Australia

John Wiley & Sons (Canada) Ltd, 22 Worcester Road,
Rexdale, Ontario M9W 1L1, Canada

John Wiley & Sons (SEA) Pte Ltd, 37 Jalan Pemimpin #05-04.
Block B, Union Industrial Building, Singapore 2057

British Library Cataloguing in Publication Data

A catalogue record for this book is
available from the British Library.

ISBN 0-471-92754-6

Typeset in 10/12 pt Sabon by Dobbie Typesetting Limited, Tavistock, Devon
Printed and bound in Great Britain by Biddles Ltd, Guildford and King's Lynn

Contents

List of Contributors

Vincent J. Adesso
University of Wisconsin-Milwaukee, Milwaukee, USA

Veronika Brezinka
Leiden University, Leiden, The Netherlands

Christine Eiser
University of Exeter, Exeter, UK

Raymond Fleming
University of Wisconsin-Milwaukee, Milwaukee, USA

Ellen L. Idler
Rutgers University, New Brunswick, USA

Derek W. Johnston
St Andrews University, Scotland

Stanislav V. Kasl
School of Medicine, Yale University, New Haven, USA

Brian Oldenburg
University of Sydney, Sydney, Australia

Neville Owen
University of Adelaide, Adelaide, Australia

Karl Peltzer
Amani Counselling Society, Nairobi, Kenya

Diane M. Reddy
University of Wisconsin-Milwaukee, Milwaukee, USA

Seth Serxner
University of Hawaii at Manoa, Honolulu, USA

Helen R. Winefield
University of Adelaide, Adelaide, Australia

Preface

Writing a preface for the first volume of a new series is always a pleasure for an editor, since this marks the end of a long period of labour and the start of the public life of the series. For these reasons it is the appropriate moment to look both back and forward.

When John Wiley & Sons approached me more than three years ago with the idea of starting a new health psychology series, many questions entered my mind. For example, were there enough health psychologists? Were there substantial aspects of health psychology, which were not sufficiently covered by existing series and journals? And, if so, would there be enough potential contributors? And, last but not least, how much time and energy would it take to get such a new series going? The first question was easy to deal with. At that time (1989), it was obvious that health psychology was developing so rapidly that the number of potentially interested readers would not constitute a major problem. Within the United States alone the number of active health psychologists has been estimated at about 10 000, of which at least a quarter are members of the Health Psychology Division of the American Psychological Association. The American behavioral medicine movement, represented by the American Society for Behavioral Medicine, accounts for another large forum of potential readers. In Europe, the establishment of the European Health Psychology Society in 1986—which holds well attended annual European meetings—and of several national health psychology and/or behavioural medicine societies, illustrates that there is a growing number of European scientists and professionals who have become interested in the field of health and behaviour. Likewise, the number of health psychologists is growing in Australia and New Zealand and also in Japan, where, for a few years, there has also been a flourishing national health psychology society with several hundred members. Moreover, the establishment of the health psychology division of the International Association of Applied Psychology in 1984 and of the International Society of Behavioural Medicine in 1988 gave impetus to similar developments in other parts of the world.

Answering the second question was more complex. There were several internationally recognized journals covering the field; for example the APA journal *Health Psychology* (since 1982), the *Journal of Behavioural Medicine* (since 1978), *Psychology and Health* (since 1987) and at least a dozen other outstanding journals in related areas such as social science and medicine, psychosomatic medicine, medical, community and clinical psychology, public health, health promotion, disease prevention, and patient education and counselling, offering health psychologists numerous opportunities for publication and dissemination of their work and ideas. Going through copies of these journals with the eyes of a would-be-editor did not convince me that yet another series should be added to the list. One day, when I was skimming one of my favourite journals, namely the *Clinical Psychological Review*, it became clear to me what was lacking. That journal publishes excellent review type contributions, some of which go into clinical health psychology issues. If anything would supplement the existing journals, it would be review type chapters. They can inform the interested researcher, professional, or advanced student about the state of the art in a specific health psychology area. When I was thinking it over, I became convinced that unlike most of the existing journals, the new series should also truly reflect the actual international health psychology scene, implying a more important involvement of europeans, australians, asians and if possible africans and latin americans.

By then I had taken the decision to meet the challenge. I suggested to Wiley that we name the new publication *The International Review of Health Psychology* and obtain the support of two co-editors. In Howard Leventhal and Marie Johnston I found two outstanding health psychologists who were prepared to join me as editors. In addition to their professional qualities, I had good personal relations with both of them and knew I could rely on them to do the work, which was to be expected from them.

One of our first tasks was to decide how many issues per year would be published. In close contact with the publisher, it was decided to publish only one volume per year containing eight to ten review type chapters. This decision was taken, because for academic and marketing reasons we thought it wise to cover several themes in each volume. As a consequence, we also discussed whether it would be better to welcome any review type chapter on a diversity of topics or to solicit contributions around a specific theme. We thought that there was a danger at each side of this continuum, and decided that we would try to collect review chapters covering different areas. The four areas, which will be covered in each volume are:

   I. General Concepts and Methodology
  II. Health Behaviour and Health Promotion
 III. Illness Behaviour and Health Care
 IV. Practical and Professional Issues

The first area will be covered by chapters which present the current state of the art concerning general concepts such as gender, age, social class or ethnicity and health, as well as contributions on, for example, social support, coping, perceived control, compliance, stress or pain, as well as chapters on methodological issues related to measurement and research in health psychology and related disciplines. The second, health behaviour and health promotion, area will contain chapters on various behaviours which are related to health (such as smoking, physical exercise, weight, eating and nutrition habits, use of alcohol, sleeping habits or safety) and especially on interventions related to these behaviours carried out in various settings (including total community, health care, school, worksite, leisure and family settings). The third, illness behaviour and health care, area will contain review type contributions concerning psychosocial consequences and psychological interventions in various groups of patients (including cardiovascular, cancer, AIDS and diabetes patients as well as patients suffering from rheumatic or chronic obstructive pulmonary diseases), together with chapters concerning psychological aspects of, and psychological interventions relevant to, medical examinations (e.g. vaginal examination or pre-natal diagnosis) and procedures (e.g. various forms of surgery). In addition, we also aim to publish within this area contributions related to the health care system, including studies on health care processes (e.g. patient–provider interaction), treatment settings (e.g. health–care organization) and health careers (e.g. stresses of health carers or training of health professionals). Within the fourth area we will try to give special attention to practical and professional issues, related to health psychology research, practice and training in different parts of the world, as well as to the relationships between health psychologists and other health professionals.

With this structure in mind, we approached several distinguished scientists from different parts of the world and asked them to join the editorial board and to assist us in recruiting potential authors and in taking the manuscripts through the review process. Thanks to their support, the first volume reflects what we were aiming for: high quality review papers from different parts of the world which cover all four areas. As such the first area, Part I, is covered by the contributions of Diane Reddy, Raymond Fleming and Vincent Adesso on 'Gender and health' and the one by Ellen Idler on 'Self-assessed health and mortality'; the second area, Part II, by Derek Johnston's contribution on 'The management of stress in the prevention of coronary heart disease', Veronika Brezinka's review on 'Conservative treatment of childhood obesity' and the one by Stan Kasl and Seth Serxner on 'Health promotion at the worksite'. The papers by Christine Eiser on, 'Psychological consequences of chronic diseases in children' and by Helen Winefield on 'Doctor–patient communication' fit into the third or illness behaviour and health care, area (Part III). Finally, in Part IV, the chapters by Karl Peltzer on 'Health psychology in Africa' and by Neville Owen and Brian Oldenburg on 'Australian health psychology' are representative of the last area on practical and professional issues. In addition, the selection of chapters also represents the international perspective, since three are from the US, three from Europe, two from Australia and one from Africa.

While we will go on inviting people from different parts of the world to write chapters which fit into one of the four areas, we would also like to encourage people to submit chapters spontaneously and/or to send us comments on previously published chapters. It is however advisable that people who intend to submit a review chapter contact me at an early stage in order to avoid overlap. All manuscripts will go through the same review process and at least two independent reviewers will evaluate each manuscript.

Also, in the name of my co-editors, I would like to express my gratitude to the members of the editorial board and the authors, who have devoted much time to reviewing or preparing and rewriting chapters. Special thanks go to Karen Belk, who has been my indefatigable and loyal secretary for many years. She supported me for the last time while preparing this volume for press, as personal reasons require her competence elsewhere in the future. I sincerely hope that this first volume will be welcomed as the first of an authoritative, useful and well-regarded serial work in the important field of health psychology and behavioural medicine.

Stan Maes
Principal Editor

Part I

GENERAL CONCEPTS AND METHODOLOGY

1 Gender and Health

DIANE M. REDDY, RAYMOND FLEMING,
VINCENT J. ADESSO
*Dept of Psychology, University of Wisconsin-Milwaukee, PO Box 413,
Milwaukee 53201, USA*

Gender is a socially constructed variable that affects many aspects of the self. Our aspirations, choices, self-concepts, and identities are but a few examples. Gender also influences health in tangible and significant ways. The extent to which we consult physicians, practice unhealthy and risky behaviors, engage in health-promoting behviors, and even how long we are likely to live and what we are likely to die from are influenced by gender.

The topic of gender and health is broad and complex. Both physical and mental health are impacted by gender and many potential explanatory variables are involved (eg differences in illness behavior, reporting behavior, inherent vulnerabilities to disease, and physical risks of illness; Verbrugge, 1979). Consequently, we emphasize some topics over others in this chapter and focus our review on gender differences in physical health. We do not discuss gender differences in health by age, race, socioeconomic status or marital status due to space limitations. Age, race and other variables such as personality, social support and cultural norms have an important influence on health, too.

Gender differences in physical health are discussed throughout this chapter from the perspective of why men are different from women (eg we discuss why men die earlier than women rather than why women live longer than men). We do this to provoke critical thought on why men are always viewed as the "standard" in research and as the "standard" for health. There is after all no prototypical person, yet empirical evidence shows that for some clinicians the healthy male is synonymous with the healthy adult (Broverman et al., 1970). Moreover, male subjects are less likely than female subjects to have their gender identified in research, and findings based on all male samples are more likely than findings based on all female samples to be generalized and reported as relevant to all people (Levy & Richey, 1988).

By writing this chapter as if women were the "standard" for health and science in general, we hope to challenge the fundamental assumption of male "normality". This tactic is more than a political statement or subtle matter of semantics; it has very important implications for the interpretation of research on gender and health and for public policy stemming from such research.

International Review of Health Psychology. Edited by S. Maes, H. Leventhal and M. Johnston
©1992 John Wiley & Sons Ltd

Take, for example, the gender difference in life expectancy which is discussed in subsequent sections of this chapter. From the perspective advocated in this chapter, the critical question is, "What is it about being male that causes men to die earlier than they should (ie earlier than women)?" One implication of this question is that shorter life expectancy in men is problematic, and to the extent that modifiable risk factors relate to this, public policy should focus on health promotion and risk prevention. From the typical perspective viewing men as the standard for health, the fact that women live longer than men has little bearing on male life expectancy. Researchers can, therefore, continue to justify excluding women as subjects in investigations of disease. Moreover, from the typical perspective viewing men as the standard for health, hormones and other biologically based factors rather than behaviors are seen as primarily responsible for women's longer life expectancy. Consequently, policymakers will continue to have trouble understanding why funds comparable to those for research on disease treatment should be allocated for basic research on health promotion and risk prevention. The first part of this chapter reviews current gender differences in major indicators of health status and proposed artifacts accounting for lower morbidity rates in males than females. Possible explanations for the gender difference in life expectancy and mortality are then reviewed in the second part of this chapter.

GENDER DIFFERENCES IN HEALTH STATUS

Up-to-date estimates of health status in the United States come from the National Center for Health Statistics. One source of data this center uses to obtain information on health status is the National Health Interview Survey. The National Health Interview Survey is a nationwide survey of the civilian, noninstitutionalized population in the United States. This survey has been conducted continuously in the United States since 1956 and over the years has achieved response rates between 95 and 98%.

Each week, probability samples of participants are drawn, participants are notified of their selection, and personnel from the US Bureau of the Census conduct household interviews. Efforts are made to have all household members over the age of 19 respond for themselves. However, this is not always possible and proxy respondents are allowed to respond for those absent the day of the interview. Proxy respondents are required for all children and any person who cannot respond for him or herself. Consequently, some of the data from the survey are based on respondents' reports of other people's health rather than self-reports. Information is obtained on the demographic characteristics of respondents and three major indicators of health status: respondent-assessed health, morbidity, and utilization of medical services.[1] Population estimates of

---

1. Utilization of medical services is not actually an indicator of health status. These data are subsumed under the heading "Gender differences in health status" and are discussed as such because they partially reflect gender differences in health and are relevant to the discussion included in this section on errors and biases potentially contributing to morbidity differences.

life expectancy and mortality are also published by the National Center for Health Statistics. All five of these indicators of health status show gender differences to varying degrees.

Respondent-assessed health

Respondent-assessed health was measured in the 1988 National Health Interview Survey by asking respondents to assess their own health or that of a household member as "excellent", "very good", "good", "fair", or "poor". The results showed that the health of the majority of respondents (66.9%) was assessed as "excellent" or "very good" (National Center for Health Statistics, 1989c). However, more males (69.6%) were given this assessment than females (64.3%) (National Center for Health Statistics, 1989c). Conversely, fewer males (8.9%) than females (10.9%) were assessed in "fair" or "poor" health (National Center for Health Statistics, 1989c). The direction of the gender difference in respondent-assessed health is consistent with morbidity and medical service utilization differences.

Morbidity

Data from the 1988 National Health Interview Survey on the incidence rate of acute conditions and the prevalence rate of reported chronic conditions were selected to illustrate differences between males and females in morbidity.

Acute conditions

To be considered an acute condition in the 1988 National Health Interview Survey, three criteria had to be met. First, the condition's duration had to be less than three months. Second, respondents had to have first noticed the condition within three months of the interview. Finally, the condition had to either result in a physician consultation or a reduction in usual activity for at least a half a day. The estimated incidence rate for all acute conditions combined (excluding disorders of menstruation, other disorders of the female genital tract, delivery and other conditions of pregnancy and the puerperium) was lower for males than for females (161.5 versus 182.3 acute conditions per 100 persons per year). Some of the gender difference observed for acute conditions might be due to the shorter life expectancy of men, that is, age is confounded.

Figure 1.1 shows the estimated rate of five categories of acute conditions per year in 1988 for males and females in the United States. The estimated incidence rate was lower for males than for females for infectious and parasitic diseases (eg intestinal virus, common childhood diseases, viral infection), respiratory conditions (eg the common cold, upper respiratory infection, pneumonia, acute bronchitis), digestive system conditions (eg indigestion, nausea, vomiting) and "other" assorted acute conditions (eg acute urinary, skin, and musculoskeletal

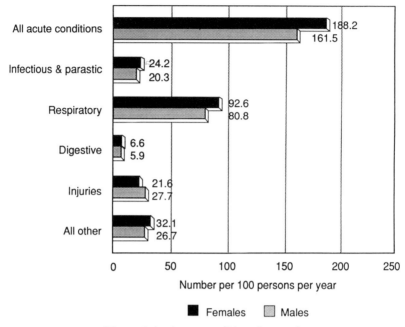

Figure 1.1. Acute conditions by gender

conditions). Only in the case of injuries was the incidence rate higher for males than for females. The largest gender difference was for respiratory conditions. Differences between males and females in the incidence rate of influenza, upper respiratory infection, and the common cold appear to account for this (data not shown).

Chronic conditions

To be considered a chronic condition in the 1988 National Health Interview Survey, the condition either had to belong to a group of conditions considered chronic (eg heart disease) or have been first noticed three months or more from the time of the interview. The results showed that the prevalence rate estimates for males were lower than those for females in 45 of the 63 chronic conditions or 71% of the nongender-specific cases presented in Current Estimates from the National Health Interview Survey, 1988 (National Center for Health Statistics, 1989). A Sign test indicated that this result was highly significant, $p < 0.001$.

Table 1.1 shows the estimated prevalence rate and prevalence rate ratio of males to females for the chronic conditions in the United States with the largest gender difference in prevalence. As can be seen, males had substantially lower prevalence rates than females for chronic sinusitis, arthritis, migraine headache,

Table 1.1. Rate and gender ratio of selected chronic conditions showing the largest gender differences in prevalence, USA 1988

Chronic condition	Rate per 1000 persons		Ratio of male to female rates
	Male	Female	
Color blindness	22.06	1.85	11.94
Absence of extremities	11.10	1.78	6.24
Gout, including gouty arthritis	12.51	4.72	2.65
Emphysema	11.18	4.79	2.34
Hearing impairment	106.24	76.18	1.40
Chronic sinusitis	116.11	161.94	0.72
Arthritis	92.50	165.05	0.56
Tachycardia or rapid heart	4.65	9.51	0.49
Migraine headache	21.85	53.73	0.41
Disorders of the bone or cartilage	3.48	8.71	0.39
Varicose veins of lower extremities	13.31	48.90	0.27
Anemias	6.50	26.04	0.25
Spastic colon	2.28	9.30	0.24
Bladder disorders	4.76	20.32	0.23
Goiter or other disorders of the thyroid	3.73	28.83	0.13
Frequent constipation	10.98	104.94	0.11
Trouble with bunions	3.12	78.71	0.04

Source: National Center for Health Statistics (1989c).

varicose veins of the lower extremities, frequent constipation, and trouble with bunions, the chronic condition with the largest gender difference based on the ratio of male to female prevalence rates. The estimates were substantially higher for males than females for hearing impairment through color blindness. These data are not age-standardized. Consequently, the gender difference for hearing impairment and color blindness might be underestimated, while the other gender differences might be overestimated.

The two types of morbidity data reviewed in this section are congruent with one another. As in the case of acute conditions, fewer chronic conditions were revealed for males than for females. Taken together, these data suggest that males either have proportionately fewer symptoms, illnesses, and diseases than females or tend to report proportionately fewer symptoms, illnesses, and diseases. The answer to this question cannot be determined from the data we abstracted or analyzed for this chapter. In any case, the gender difference in morbidity has a direct bearing on differences between males and females in use of medical services. These differences are reviewed in the next section.

Utilization of medical services

As in the case of the other indicators of health status reviewed thus far, we selected information on utilization of medical services from Current Estimates from the National Health Interview Survey, 1988 (National Center for Health

Statistics, 1989c) because this information is current. However, physician contacts for gender-specific care (eg prenatal and postnatal care) are not excluded from the relevant data in this publication. Consequently, we also present data from the 1985 National Ambulatory Medical Care Survey, a probability sample survey of office-based physicians that was last conducted in the United States in 1985. This source reports data on the number of physician visits by gender and principal diagnosis. Accordingly, current differences between males and females in physician contacts can be more accurately gauged from examining relevant data from both sources.

Physician contacts

National Health Interview Survey, 1988, data indicate that males (with 4.5 contacts) had a lower rate of physician contacts per person per year than females (with 6.2 contacts). As noted earlier, these rates do not exclude physician contacts for gender-specific care. As such, this gender difference may be somewhat inflated. This assertion is corroborated by the fact that the rates of physician contacts for males and females were most divergent in the peak reproductive age bracket (the 18–44 age group). Males in this age group had 3.4 physician contacts per person per year compared to 6.2 in same age females. However, the rate of physician contacts was also lower for males (with 5.2 contacts) than females (with 6.9 contacts) in the 45–64 age group and for males (8.5 contacts) than females (8.8 contacts) in the 65 and older age group. The physician contact rates for males and females under the age of 18 were about the same (4.5 versus 4.4 contacts for males and females, respectively). The National Ambulatory Medical Care Survey, 1985 data (National Center for

Table 1.2. Numbr of physician office visits for selected principal diagnoses, USA 1985

Principal diagnosis (number of visits in thousands)	Male	Female
Infections and parasitic diseases	10 774	14 095
Endocrine, nutritional, and metabolic diseases and immunity disorders	7 554	14 926
Diseases of the nervous system and sense organs	29 144	40 708
Disease of the circulatory system	25 132	30 821
Diseases of the respiratory system	33 433	43 575
Diseases of the digestive system	12 207	15 015
Diseases of the skin and subcutaneous tissue	15 960	20 235
Diseases of the musculoskeletal system and connective tissue	17 833	27 231
Symptoms, signs, and ill-defined conditions	8 897	13 592
Injury and poisoning	27 637	25 106

Source: National Center for Health Statistics (1989b).

Health Statistics, 1989a) on office visits for nongender-specific principal diagnoses support a gender difference in the use of medical services.

Table 1.2 shows that in the United States in 1985 males had a smaller number of office visits than females to ambulatory care physicians for all selected nongender-specific principal diagnoses except injury and poisoning. Because age and the number of men and women in the general population are not controlled for in these data, the gender difference for injury and poisoning may be underestimated, while the other gender differences may be overestimated. Weaker evidence for a gender difference in utilization of medical services is also found in an examination of the number of short-stay hospitalizations for males and females in the United States in 1988. These data are presented next.

Hospitalizations

National Health Interview Survey (1988) respondents were asked to report the number of times they were hospitalized for at least one night during the year preceding the interview. The results showed a small gender difference in the number of short-stay hospitalizations during the previous year for all reasons excluding deliveries. The percentage of living males in the United States with one or more short-stay hospitalizations was 6.7 compared to 7.1 in females (National Center for Health Statistics, 1989c). Taken together, findings from the National Health Interview Survey, 1988 (National Center for Health Statistics, 1989c) and the National Ambulatory Medical Care Survey, 1985 (National Center for Health Statistics, 1989a) suggest that males and females in the United States differ in medical service utilization.

Life expectancy and mortality

Gender differences in life expectancy and mortality also exist. However, in contrast to all the health status indicators reviewed so far, males fare worse than females in life expectancy and mortality. Data from *Newsweek*, a United States news magazine (*Newsweek*, 5 March, 1990) and the Advance Report of Final Mortality Statistics, 1987 (National Center for Health Statistics, 1989c) are abstracted to illustrate this point.

Life expectancy

As alluded to earlier, males (as a group) do not live as long as females (as a group). This difference exists in all technologically based countries and is present at birth through senescence (National Center for Health Statistics, 1989b). The life expectancy for a male child born in the United States in 1990 is 76.1 years (*Newsweek*, 5 March, 1990). His female counterpart can expect to live an additional 7.3 years, dying at the age of 83.4 years (*Newsweek*, 5 March, 1990). As this male child and this female child reach subsequent birthdays their life

Table 1.3. Expectation for life at birth for males and females from selected countries: latest available year

Country (ordered by size of difference)	Year	Males	Females	Differences
USSR	1985–86	64.15	73.27	– 9.12
Poland	1987	66.81	75.20	– 8.39
France	1987	72.03	80.27	– 8.24
Finland	1986	70.49	78.72	– 8.23
Netherlands	1985–86	72.95	79.55	– 6.60
Australia	1986	72.77	79.13	– 6.36
United Kingdom	1984–87	71.22	77.51	– 6.29
New Zealand	1986–88	71.03	77.27	– 6.24
Sweden	1987	74.16	80.15	– 5.99
Denmark	1986–87	71.80	77.60	– 5.80
Japan	1987	75.61	81.39	– 5.78
China	1985–90	67.98	70.94	– 2.96
Papua New Guinea	1985–90	53.18	54.84	– 1.66

Source: Demographic Yearbook 1988 (United Nations, 1990), pp. 178–184.

expectancies will increase and as they age the differential in the expected age of their death will decrease, but will never disappear (National Center for Health Statistics, 1989b; *Newsweek*, 5 March, 1990).

Table 1.3 shows the life expectancy at birth for males and females from 13 selected nations other than the United States. Countries not listed lack statistics of national scope, lack recent data, or were omitted due to space limitations.

Mortality

In 1987 in the United States the age-adjusted death rate for all causes of mortality in males was 1.7 times higher than that for females (National Center for Health Statistics, 1989b).

Table 1.4 shows that the male to female ratio of age-adjusted death rates for the top 15 causes of death in the United States in 1989. As can be seen, males had a higher rate of mortality than females for each of the 15 causes of death listed. The largest gender difference was for human immunodeficiency virus infection, the etiological agent for acquired immune deficiency syndrome (AIDS). The first four listed causes of mortality in Table 1.4 (heart disease, malignant neoplasms, cerebrovascular disease, and accidents and adverse effects) account for 75% of the deaths among males and females in the United States in 1987. The remaining 11 causes of mortality listed in Table 1.4 account for another 12% of the deaths in the United States in 1987.

Discussion

In the previous section, we reviewed current data on health status in the United States. This review showed that gender differences exist for all major health

Table 1.4. Gender ratio of age-adjusted death rates for the top 15 causes of death, USA, 1987

Cause	Male to female ratio
1. Heart disease	1.89
2. Malignant neoplasms	1.47
3. Cerebrovascular diseases	1.16
4. Accidents and adverse effects	2.72
5. Chronic obstructive pulmonary disease and allied conditions	2.04
6. Pneumonia and influenza	1.77
7. Diabetes mellitus	1.11
8. Suicide	3.90
9. Chronic liver disease and cirrhosis	2.32
10. Atherosclerosis	1.28
11. Nephritis, nephrotic syndrome and nephrosis	1.54
12. Homicide and legal intervention	3.22
13. Septicemia	1.36
14. Certain conditions originating in the prenatal period	1.28
15. Human immunodeficiency virus infection	9.09

Note: Causes are rank ordered based on number of deaths.
Source: National Center for Health Statistics (1989b).

status indicators: subjective assessments of health, indices of morbidity, measures of medical service utilization as well as life expectancy and mortality. These findings are largely consistent with what has been observed in previous years in the United States and are generally consistent with health status data from other Western, technologically based countries (National Center for Health Statistics, 1989a; Preston, 1976; Waldron, 1983a). Gender reversals have been found in rates of physician contacts, reports of certain symptoms, and subjective assessments of health in Western countries (Preston, 1976; Waldron, 1983a). Gender reversals have also occurred historically in life expectancy and mortality in many countries and in nonaffluent regions (eg areas of Bangladesh and India) in contemporary times (Preston, 1976). Cultural norms preventing females from receiving basic health care and adequate nutrition are thought to be responsible for these reversals (Preston, 1976).

As shown in the previous section, men appear to have better health than women on morbidity-related indicators of health status. They assess their health more positively, contact physicians less often, are hospitalized fewer times, and report fewer symptoms, conditions, illnesses, and diseases than women. But, as also was shown in the previous review, men die earlier than women and have higher mortality rates from all the major causes of death, suggesting that they have poorer health. This discrepancy has, in part, sparked debate over whether gender differences in morbidity-related data are real or artifactual.

Although many criticisms have been raised and numerous sources of error have been hypothesized to account for the morbidity-related data, relatively few attempts have been made to actually test the validity of the proposed confounds. The errors that have been proposed can be organized into three categories: health practitioner biases, reporting biases, and illness appraisal biases. The first category of biases reflects societal influences on the "gatekeepers" of health services. The remaining two categories of biases reflect societal influences on the person and are not as conceptually distinct as the first category.

Health practitioner biases

The argument has been advanced that health practitioners differentially interpret, diagnose, and treat identical symptoms in males and females. Sexism in society in general and in medical and other graduate training nurtures this bias. Thus, women are medicated more often than men, have procedures performed on them more often than men, wind up in doctors' offices and hospitals more often than men, and eventually come to believe that the symptoms and physiological events they are experiencing are actually indicative of illness or disease. While this hypothesis is intriguing, there is little direct evidence supporting its validity.

Verbrugge (1980), in an analysis of 1975 National Ambulatory Health Care Survey data, found only a few findings suggesting that health practitioner bias might contribute to lower morbidity rates in males than females. Men who complained of urinary and eye or ear problems were diagnosed as "not sick" more often than women who presented with these complaints. To a lesser extent, physicians also assigned "not sick" diagnoses more often to men than women who presented with skin or hair and musculoskeletal complaints. However, Verbrugge (1980) found no evidence that physicians diagnose women as sick when in fact they are not or give them more diagnoses per complaint than men.

Other less direct evidence supporting the thesis that health practitioner bias might account for or inflate morbidity differences between males and females is found in the mental health literature. For example, Kaplan (1983) has criticized the Diagnostic and Statistical Manual of Mental Disorders III (DSM-III), an official classification scheme of mental disorders used worldwide, for gender bias in certain diagnostic categories. Extreme passivity and dependence, aspects of traditionally ascribed femininity, result in a mental disorder classification, while extreme aspects of traditionally ascribed masculinity do not (Travis, 1988).

Content analyses of drug advertisements placed in medical journals reveal that females are more often depicted as patients than males, especially in psychotropic drug advertisements (Prather & Fidell, 1975; Seidenberg, 1971). The preponderance of females in such advertisements may foster a belief among physicians that men are healthier than women and this belief may result in differential treatment of male and female patients contributing to the lower rates of morbidity found for men. Admittedly, this last point on drug advertisement is more of an explanation of why health practitioner bias might exist than evidence for it.

Reporting biases

Many types of reporting biases have been offered to account for the lower rates of morbidity found in men. It has been argued, for example, that rates of morbidity for men are lower artifactually than those for women because men are apt to be unavailable to respond for themselves in health surveys. This argument is based on the fact that there are proportionately more men than women in the paid work force. Moreover, it has been argued that men's illnesses fail to be recorded officially because taking time off from work to recuperate or to seek medical care poses a greater financial loss for men than women. This argument is also based on fact. Inferior pay is accorded to "female" jobs and to women in the paid work force in general. Finally, it has been argued that societal norms socialize men to be less concerned than women with pleasing others, and socialize men to be more stoical in expressing pain and other discomforts. Because of this, "big boys don't cry". They "stand up and take it like a man" and naysay questions posed by health interview surveyors about problems.

While all of these reporting biases are well reasoned, there are few data to back them up. (We found no information on the percentage of proxy respondents for males and females in the health status data we reviewed earlier.) As in the case of health practitioner biases, reporting biases have not been given much empirical attention. Nonetheless, Glynn & Leventhal (1990) found, in a study of juvenile illness behavior, that boys decreased in reactivity to illness and pain to a greater extent than girls as they aged. This suggests that the hypothesized gender difference in reporting illness emerges because of changes that occur over time in boys' reporting behavior.

Marcus & Siegel (1982) found that controlling for effects of employment status reduced the gender differential in medical service utilization. This finding supports the notion that male morbidity rates may be lower than those of females because of differences in the number of men and women in the paid work force.

Verbrugge (1980) found a number of differences in the manner in which men and women reported illnesses and injuries in the 1975 National Ambulatory Medical Care Study. Symptomatic men reported fewer complaints to physicians than symptomatic women, suggesting that men are less likely to elaborate on their health problems. In addition, men were more likely than women to present physical or mental symptoms rather than a combination of both. Men also tended to report a smaller variety of illnesses and injuries than women. How these differences contribute to the lower morbidity rates for males is unclear, especially since the men in this study were just as likely as the women to report a symptom to physicians and to get a diagnosis that concurred with their complaint. Thus, there was no evidence that men's illnesses fail to get counted because men describe their symptoms or illnesses less accurately or clearly than women.

Finally, Gove and colleagues (Clancy & Gove, 1974; Gove & Geerken, 1977; Gove et al., 1976) investigated gender differences in the tendency to yeasay or naysay in reporting psychiatric symptoms and found no support for this artifact as an explanation for the lower rates of reports of psychiatric symptoms among men.

Illness appraisal biases

It has been argued that differences in the manner in which men and women perceive symptoms and respond to them are responsible for the gender differential in morbidity. Men may pay less attention to symptoms and accord them less significance. Men may not seek out information about symptoms or engage in social comparison processes as readily as women. Men may also be more likely than women to deny symptoms. All of these appraisal behaviors could contribute to the lower rate of morbidity observed among men, but support for them is quite limited.

Verbrugge (1980) found that more men who were visiting physicians for "not sick" reasons (eg therapy, advice) were diagnosed as sick than comparable women. This finding could be taken as support for the hypothesis that men are more likely than women to deny symptoms and less likely than women to attend to symptoms and to accord them significance. Alternatively, these findings suggest that men may be more reticent about admitting to symptoms or have more asymptomatic problems that are uncovered during visits than women (Verbrugge, 1980). However Verbrugge points out an "anomaly" to this overall pattern of findings that muddles interpretation. Women who consulted physicians for two types of "not sick" reasons (exams or medications only) were diagnosed as sick more often than men. Thus, all the data in Verbrugge's (1980) report do not support illness appraisal biases in men.

Verbrugge (1980) also found that more men than women in the 1975 National Ambulatory Medical Care Survey had their problems assessed by physicians as "very serious" or "serious", suggesting that men are more likely than women to delay seeking diagnosis and care for symptoms. However, Marshall, Gregorio & Walsh (1982) found that men did not delay any longer than women in seeking medical care for symptoms of life-threatening diseases (ie cancer). Consistent with this, few gender differences in stage of cancer diagnosis have been observed (Marcus & Siegel, 1982).[2] These findings seem to discredit the interpretation that men are less likely than women to pay attention to symptoms, recognize their significance, and seek care for them when they arise. These data, however, leave open the possibility that men and women respond differently to ambiguous symptoms that are less clearly indicative of serious disease.

---

2. Malignant melanoma, the leading cause of skin cancer death, is an exception (Levy, 1984). Males typically present with more advanced stages than females due to a more rapid progression of disease in them. It is unclear what accounts for this (Carey, 1982).

Wallen, Waitzkin & Stoeckle (1979) in an analysis of doctor–patient interactions found that women ask more questions than men during exams. Consistent with this finding, Suchman (1965) found that women were more informed than men about health matters in general and about symptoms of disease. These findings provide some support for the idea that women seek out information about symptoms more often than men and, therefore, may be better able to accord significance to ambiguous and unambiguous symptoms of disease.

As shown in this overview of possible biases, the assertion that men have lower rates of morbidity than women has been challenged on many grounds. To a substantial extent, the empirical evidence to support (or refute) these biases is lacking. Based on the current data, one cannot conclude whether the lower rates of morbidity for men reflect real or artifactual differences. From the perspective that the differences in morbidity are real, one must then focus on how meaningful the differences actually are. In this regard, the majority of the respondents in the 1987 National Health Interview Survey indicated that their health was "excellent" or "very good". The largest gender difference in subjective assessments of health was, in fact, for these responses, and the percentages for males and females differed by only about 5%. At perhaps the more meaningful end of the response continuum, the percentages for males and females indicating their health was "fair" or "poor" differed by even less (2%). Can we meaningfully conclude on the basis of these data that men are healthier than women? We think not. Even though 2% represents a lot of people, it is not the case that the majority of men assessed their health any differently than the majority of women. What about the findings for other specific indicators of morbidity reviewed earlier? Even though these gender differences in the incidence rate of acute conditions and the prevalence rate of chronic conditions appear to be larger than the gender difference in subjective assessments of health, there is no basis to construe these more "objective" indicators of health status as closer to the truth or any more meaningful than people's global assessments of their health. Given these considerations and the discrepancy in interpretation based on morbidity-related indices of health versus life expectancy and mortality indicators of health, we chose to focus the next section of this chapter on explanations for the life expectancy and mortality findings, which seem less refutable than the morbidity findings.

EXPLANATIONS FOR THE GENDER DIFFERENCE IN LIFE EXPECTANCY AND MORTALITY

Numerous factors have been suggested to account for the shorter life expectancy of males and their excess mortality from most major causes of death. These factors can be sorted into three broad categories: genetic factors, behavioral factors, and psychophysiological factors. Substantial evidence demonstrates that genetic factors and behavioral factors play an important role in health and disease. Psychophysiological factors may also significantly influence health and disease although the evidence at this time is less than conclusive.

Genetic factors

Genetic factors have been implicated in the shorter life expectancy and higher rates of mortality for men. Infant mortality data show that boys have higher rates of death than girls from most major causes of mortality (Hammond, 1965). However, greater male infant mortality appears to contribute only minimally in the excess in male mortality. As shown in Table 1.4, the causes of death with the largest gender differentials (human immunodeficiency virus infection, suicide, homicide and legal intervention, and accidents and adverse effects) relate to behaviors rather than genetics. Moreover, the leading causes of death (heart disease and malignant neoplasms) are by and large chronic diseases of adults, not infants.

Greater male vulnerability to infectious diseases has also been noted, especially for males under the age of one and over the age of 40 (Preston, 1976). This gender difference might contribute moderately to the higher rates of male mortality in that at least 5 of the 15 leading causes of mortality may relate to infectious agents. Lower serum level of immunoglobulin M (IgM) in males might contribute to this. However, IgM differences between males and females are absent from infancy until about age 5 and again absent after age 65. Males still have higher infectious disease rates than females under the age of 5 and over 65. So, other immunologically related factors must be contributing to the lower male resistance to infectious diseases.

The contribution of sex hormones to the excess in male mortality has also been examined, especially in relation to coronary heart disease risk. Limited support exists for the detrimental function of testosterone in coronary heart disease risk. Animal research has shown that the administration of testosterone tends to speed blood clot formation, while the administration of estrogen tends to slow blood clot formation (Amos, Odake & Ambrus, 1969; Johnson, Ramey & Ramwell, 1977). Consistent findings have been reported in human clot formation and platelet aggregation studies (Johnson, Ramey & Ramwell, 1975). However, differences in platelet aggregation have not been found in all human studies (Kelton et al., 1980).

Stronger support exists for the protective function of estrogen in coronary heart disease risk. First, coronary heart disease risk increases with age in women, paralleling the gradual decrease in ovarian estrogen secretion (Gordon et al., 1978; Kannel et al., 1976). Second, increases in coronary heart disease risk following oophorectomy (surgical removal of the ovaries) and early natural menopause have been observed in some studies (Gordon et al., 1978). Third, combined estrogen–progestin replacement therapy has been shown in some work to lower cardiovascular disease rates in treated women compared to controls (Hammond & Maxson, 1982). Reductions in total cholesterol levels and increases in levels of high-density lipoproteins (which are negatively related to coronary heart disease) have also been found following estrogen replacement therapy (Barrett-Connor et al., 1979).

While these observations support the role of estrogen in the lower rate of female coronary heart disease mortality, the research literature is not in complete agreement on this point. Some studies have failed to find increases in coronary heart disease risk following oophorectomy or early natural menopause (McGill & Stern, 1979). Other investigators have found increases in coronary heart disease risk for women who underwent hysterectomies without oophorectomy (Gordon et al., 1978). The increase in coronary heart disease risk shown for these women, who had no diminution in ovarian hormone output, was the same as that shown for women who had undergone natural menopause or bilateral or unilateral oophorectomy.

In conclusion, genetically based gender differences in vulnerability to infectious diseases and infant mortality exist. In addition, the gender difference in rate of mortality for coronary heart disease appears to result, in part, from the protective effects of estrogen in women. These three genetic factors play an important, but quantitatively undetermined, role in the gender differential in mortality. Cultural and environmental factors significantly modulate the contribution of genetic factors to mortality (Waldron, 1983b).

Behavioral factors

Men and women have been found to differ in behavioral factors that have been shown to influence health and disease, and differences between men and women in these behaviors appear to contribute to gender differences in life expectancy and mortality (Waldron, 1986). In general, men tend to engage in more negative health-related behaviors than women. For example, more men than women drink alcohol and use illicit drugs such as crack, cocaine and heroin (Hall, in press; Mercer & Khavari, 1990). And, until recently, more men than women smoked cigarettes (Hall, in press). Moreover, men traditionally have been more likely than women to be heavier users of these substances (Hall, in press; Mercer & Khavari, 1990). Complementing this tendency, fewer men than women engage in positive health-related behaviors such as eating breakfast and taking vitamins (Moss et al., 1989). These dual health-related tendencies may stem from the ascribed "appropriateness" of the relevant behaviors for men and women.

Traditional sex roles dictate that men should be less nurturant, less person-oriented, and less concerned with family well-being than women. The relative deemphasis for men than women on caring may extend to health matters, contributing to fewer health promotion practices in men. Similarly, views of women as life-givers and moral guardians have led to more extensive and negative reactions to substance use in women than men, which may reflect on the current lower use of illicit drugs in women and their lower rate of alcoholism (Marsh, Colten & Tucker, 1982; Gomberg, 1982). Even cigarette smoking was considered unacceptable for "ladies" not that long ago, as one cigarette manufacturer reminds us with the slogan, "You've come a long way, baby!" If a woman in the early 1900s smoked, she typically did not begin smoking regularly until she was in her thirties. In contrast, her male counterpart began to smoke regularly before his twentieth birthday (Harris, 1983).

Reflecting the current acceptability of cigarette smoking in women, males and females initiate and regularly use cigarettes at about the same ages (Glynn, Leventhal & Hirschman, 1986). Intoxication and addiction to illicit drugs like heroin are another matter. These behaviors are still viewed as more reprehensible in women than men. This double standard appears to stem from two sources (Gomberg, 1982). First, observers may perceive that a drunk woman or female addict high on drugs has irresponsibly impaired her ability to function as a nurturer, a primary role exclusively assigned to women. Second, observers may conceptually link female drunkenness, female alcoholism, and female illicit drug addiction with sexual vulnerability and promiscuity. In any case, even though health behaviors predict each other only modestly, research suggests that men and women do differ in health practices and, as noted, these differences may result from current societal norms.

Data from the 1985 National Health Interview Survey of Health Promotion and Disease Prevention (National Center for Health Statistics, 1989a) show that men and women in the United States tend to differ in health-related behaviors and these behaviors were shown in studies performed in Alameda County, California to relate to mortality (Belloc & Breslow, 1972; Wiley & Camacho, 1980). In contrast to other National Health Interview Survey data reviewed earlier, self-responses were required in this survey. Overall, the age-adjusted findings showed that men tend to have less healthy lifestyles than women. More men (39.6%) than women (37.4%) snacked daily, slept six hours or less per day (22.8% versus 21.6%), and never ate breakfast (24.8% versus 24.0%). Men (25.6%) were also more likely than women (22.7%) to be overweight (ie 20% or more above desirable weight) as defined by 1983 Metropolitan Life Insurance Company standards. Other evidence shows that men are less flexible in their food choices and less aware of the role of dietary factors in health and disease (Hollis et al., 1986). While gender differences in dietary practices have not been systematically studied, such differences may contribute to the shorter life expectancy and higher rates of mortality shown in men. Overweight individuals are more likely to develop cardiovascular disease than individuals at desirable weight (Bennett & Gurin, 1982). This appears to be due to relationships between obesity and other disease risk factors such as high serum cholesterol, essential hypertension, and lack of exercise (Bennett & Gurin, 1982). Dietary factors such as the consumption of fish (Kromhout, Bosschieter & de Lezenne Coulander, 1985) and cod-liver oil supplements (Weiner et al., 1986) have been linked to lower coronary heart disease risk. Moreover, nutritional factors have been implicated in the development of at least 16 forms of malignant neoplasm (Simone, 1983). Overall, it has been estimated that poor dietary practices contribute to 40% of all cancers in men and 60% of all cancers in women (Simone, 1983).

Data from the 1985 National Health Interview Survey of Health Promotion and Disease Prevention (National Center for Health Statistics, 1989a) also showed that more than four times as many men (13.1%) as women (3.0%) were classified as heavier drinkers. A heavier drinker was defined according to the National Institute on Alcohol Abuse and Alcoholism measure as a person who consumed an average of one ounce of ethanol (two drinks) or more per day during the two-week period prior to the interview. Consistent with the higher proportion of men classified as heavier drinkers using this definition, more men (20.5%) than women (4.6%) were found to consume 5 or more drinks on at least 10 days during the 12 months prior to the interview (National Center for Health Statistics, 1989a). Prolonged consumption of five or more drinks per day has been shown to result in chronic liver disease and cirrhosis (Eckhardt et al., 1981). Chronic liver disease and cirrhosis was the ninth leading cause of death in the United States in 1987 and as shown in Table 1.4, with more than two times as many men than women dying from this cause. Cardiovascular and neural damage (Eckhardt et al., 1981) and stomach cancer (Gordon & Kannel, 1984) have also been linked to heavy, prolonged, alcohol consumption.

Alcohol is also involved in two-thirds of homicides (Mayfield, 1976), one-third of suicide attempts (Eckhardt et al., 1981) and one-third of all traffic fatalities (Perrine, Waller & Harris, 1977). As shown in Table 1.4, accidents and adverse effects, suicide, and homicide and legal intervention were, respectively, the fourth, seventh, and twelfth ranked causes of death in the United States in 1987. For each of these causes of death, males outnumbered females by a factor of two to one or greater. Overall, alcoholism increases the mortality rate for men by a factor from 2 to 3 and the mortality rate for women by a factor from 2.7 to 7 (Kilbey & Sobeck, 1988). Besides the heavier use of alcohol in men than women other differences in behavior contribute to the higher rates of mortality in men from homicide and legal intervention and accidents and adverse effects. For example, the general tendency among males to engage in riskier activities than females, including the use of guns and employment in hazardous jobs, contributes to fatalities from these causes.

Until recently, more men than women smoked cigarettes in the United States and, as in the case of alcohol, male consumption is heavier (ie men smoke more cigarettes per day than women and more men than women inhale deeply). Also, fewer men than women smoke low-tar and nicotine cigarettes. Gender-targeted advertisements suggesting the inappropriateness of "light" cigarettes for men, reduced health concerns about cigarette smoking, and the absence of unwanted side effects from "heavier" yield brands may explain lower use of low-tar and nicotine cigarettes among men (Silverstein, Feld & Kozlowski, 1980).

On the basis of mortality data for nonsmokers and total population samples, Waldron (1986) estimated that between 40 and 60% of the gender difference in total mortality across the adult lifespan is attributable to smoking. Waldron's analysis demonstrates that cigarette smoking is a major cause of excess mortality in men, although this estimate may be inflated by the univariate approach used.

Cigarette smoking is the major cause of lung cancer, and lung cancer has been the leading cause of death from malignant neoplasm for men and women in the United States since 1985. Many more men than women, however, die from lung cancer and approximately 90% of this mortality differential is attributable to smoking (Waldron, 1986). Aside from lung cancer, cigarette smoking is a major cause of heart disease, the leading cause of death in the United States for both men and women. As shown in Table 1.4, more men than women died from heart disease in 1987 and approximately 50% of this mortality difference is due to smoking (Waldron, 1986). Cigarette smoking may also contribute to excess male mortality as a cause of malignant neoplasms of the larynx, oral cavity, and esophagus and as a contributor to malignant neoplasms of the bladder, pancreas, and kidney.

On the positive side, data from the 1985 National Health Interview Survey of Health Promotion and Disease Prevention (National Center for Health Statistics, 1989a) indicated that men tend to be more physically active than women, based on self-perceptions of activity as well as energy expenditure in leisure activities. In the latter case, respondents were asked to report their participation in 23 leisure activities (eg walking, jogging, gardening) and their participation was converted into total kilocalories of energy expended over a two-week period. Subjects were classified as sedentary if they expended 0.0–1.4 kilocalories per kilogram per day on leisure activity. The results showed that fewer men (51.0%) than women (61.8%) were classified as sedentary. In addition, fewer men (15.7%) than women (21.9%) perceived themselves as less physically active. Investigations of the health effects of exercise have shown that exercise is inversely related to heart disease in both men and women (Dawber, 1980; Kramsch et al., 1981; Paffenbarger et al., 1984) and directly related to longevity (ie 2000 kilocalories or more energy expenditure per week was found to increase life expectancy in men by about two years; no women were included in this study; Paffenbarger et al.,1986).

The gender reversal for physical activity does not weaken the argument that men (as a group) tend to be less health conscientious than women (as a group). This is because most individuals with spotless records of health probably perform the vast majority of so-called "health" actions for reasons other than health. Take, for example, tooth brushing. Fewer men than women brush their teeth (Verbrugge, 1982). This gender difference does not help build a strong case for greater health conscientiousness in women than men. While most women (and men) without dental health problems would probably say that they brush their teeth to prevent dental caries and/or periodontal disease, we suspect that habit, the attractiveness of a bright smile, and the elimination of bad breath, caught food particles, unpleasant mouth tastes, and viscous tooth film have more to do with this action than disease prevention. There are healthy individuals who engage in positive health-related behaviors for health reasons, but these individuals may be in the minority. If differences between men and women are still found in health actions mainly performed for health reasons, then it can be concluded with greater confidence that a true gender difference in health conscientiousness exists.

To pursue this line of reasoning, we identified two classes of behaviors that are mainly performed for health reasons in healthy people: self-examinations for cancer detection and consumption of self-prescribed dietary supplements. We were able to find relevant current data on the use of dietary supplements only. The source of data was the 1986 National Health Interview Survey (Moss et al., 1989). As part of this survey, one adult and one child between the ages of two and six were selected from each family interviewed between January and July of 1986 to receive a vitamin and mineral supplement questionnaire. Respondents indicated whether they had taken any vitamin, mineral, or fluoride product during the two-week period preceding the interview. Those who responded affirmatively were asked to get the product container so additional information about the product could be recorded (eg manufacturer, nutrient composition). Supplements taken by pregnant and lactating women and all prescribed products were excluded from the survey. The results showed that 36% of the adult United States population in 1986 used at least one nonprescription vitamin or mineral supplement.

Figure 1.2 shows gender differences in the percentage of adults using nonprescription vitamin and mineral products in the United States in 1986.

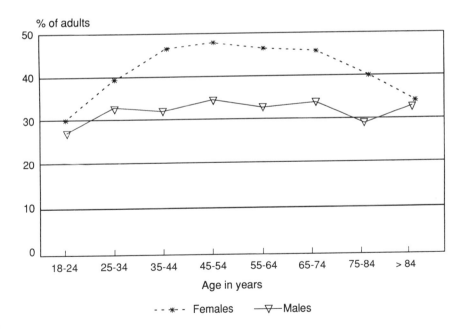

Figure 1.2. Use of vitamin and mineral products, United States 1986

As can be seen, men were less likely than women to use these products across most of the adult lifespan. Healthier individuals were more likely than those who assessed themselves as less healthy to use vitamins and mineral supplements (38 versus 31%). The data for children showed that more boys (44.7%) than girls (42.2%) between the ages of two and six took nonprescription vitamins and mineral supplements in the United States in 1986.

In conclusion, while it can be legitimately argued whether vitamin and mineral supplementation is a positive health behavior, millions of people in the United States apparently think so. A clear gender difference in adults exists. This behavior is related not only to gender, but also to education and income. People with more money and education are more likely to use vitamins and mineral supplements than those with less education and money.

For conceptual clarity, individual health practices have been discussed as if they occur in isolation from other health behaviors. This, of course, is not the case. There is a strong association between cigarette smoking, use of alcohol, and use of caffeine (Carmody et al., 1985; Istvan & Matarazzo, 1984). Consequently, it is possible that the excess in male mortality may result, in part, from the synergistic effects of interacting health habits. Occupationally related carcinogen exposure also may act synergistically with health habits (eg cigarette smoking) to produce health consequences in men that contribute to their greater rates of mortality. This not only applies to males working in hazardous occupations (eg construction), but also to males employed in "nonhazardous" jobs. For example, teachers have been exposed to asbestos fibers and dust in older school buildings; janitors have been exposed to vinyl chloride monomer, a discontinued propellant in cleaning products (Stellman & Stellman, 1981).

Differences in illness appraisal behaviors could also conceivably contribute to the higher rates of mortality in men than women. However, as reviewed earlier, men do not delay any longer than women in seeking diagnosis or care for symptoms of life-threatening diseases. Moreover, they have similar prognoses for most major causes of disease. Thus, differences in perception and response to serious symptoms probably do not play a big role in the excess in male mortality.

It is also possible that psychological variables covary with gender and contribute to the excess in male mortality and life expectancy (Matthews, 1989). Sex role socialization may cause males more often than women to develop coping strategies (eg Type A, hostility) that place them at risk for disease. In this regard, hostility has been linked to mortality in general and death due to coronary heart disease in men (Barefoot, Dahlstrom & Williams, 1983; Cook & Medley, 1954; Shekelle et al., 1983). Moreover, research has found that the Type A behavior pattern, which has been linked to increased risk for coronary heart disease, is more prevalent in men than in women in the United States (Baker et al., 1984).

The foregoing review of gender differences in behavioral factors indicates that being male is associated with many excesses that have been implicated in disease. Cigarette smoking stands out among these excesses as the major contributor to the shorter life expectancy of men compared to women. This is because cigarette smoking markedly alters risk for coronary heart disease, killing many men (and women). Moreover, most deaths from lung cancer and a sizeable proportion of deaths from malignant neoplasms of the mouth, throat, esophagus, stomach, bladder, urinary tract, and kidneys needlessly result from smoking cigarettes (Fielding, 1985). These facts have earned cigarette smoking the epitaph of the leading cause of preventable death in the United States and other Western or developed nations.

The evidence regarding an association between being female and greater health conscientiousness is not definitive because, as discussed, there are multiple reasons for practicing most health-enhancing or health-protecting behaviors. Nonetheless, the bulk of available data do support relationships between being female and engaging in positive health practices and avoiding negative health practices.

Psychophysiological factors

Gender differences in psychophysiological reactivity to stress might also contribute to the excess in male mortality. This may be particularly relevant to the gender differential in coronary heart disease. In a series of studies, Frankenhaeuser and colleagues (Frankenhaeuser, in press) found striking gender differences in catecholamine responses to a variety of cognitive achievement stressors (eg intelligence tests, color–word conflict tests, high school graduation examinations). When challenged, males showed consistent marked increases in epinephrine excretion and to a lesser extent norepinephrine increases. In contrast, females consistently showed no psychoendocrine response to cognitive achievement stressors or only slight increases. This gender difference was found not only in adults, but also in adolescents and young children (Lundberg, 1983). Differential performance was eliminated as an explanation for the differential psychophysiological reactivity exhibited since males and females performed equivalently. Interactions between sex hormones and stress hormones also do not appear to account for this gender difference. Collins et al. (1982) showed that the psychophysiological reactivity of postmenopausal women did not change before and after combined estrogen–progestin replacement therapy. This finding suggests that estrogen does not have inhibitory effects on catecholamine secretion. In addition, Lundberg et al. (1984) demonstrated that the psychophysiological reactivity of women with disorders related to excess androgens (hirsutism and oligomenorrhea) did not change before and after anti-androgen therapy. This finding suggests that androgens do not have a facilitory effect on catecholamine secretion. In other research, Frankenhaeuser and coworkers (Frankenhaeuser, in press) found increases in epinephrine and norepinephrine secretion to cognitive achievement stressors similar to those observed among men for women employed in traditional occupations. Complementing this finding, Lundberg et al. (1981) found lower epinephrine increases in men than women in a traditional female sphere (ie interpersonal relations). Fathers showed less of an increase than mothers in the interpersonally demanding context of bringing their three-year-old child to a hospital for a physical examination.

Taken together, these findings suggest that psychoendocrine differences between males and females may be a learned coping response. To the extent that cultural and social role expectations teach males to cope with most stressors in an excessively competitive and achievement-oriented fashion, the psychoneuroendocrine concomitants of this style of coping may contribute alone or in conjunction with known risk factors (eg cigarette smoking) to the excess in male coronary heart disease risk and mortality. It should be noted, however, that the urinary catecholamine increases observed in Frankenhaeuser's research over the past two decades have been of a modest size and it is not known whether catecholamine increases of this magnitude actually have a deleterious effect on cardiovascular health (Frankenhaeuser, in press).

Aside from the gender differences in catecholamine output to stressors, other gender differences in psychophysiological parameters have been found that may explain the greater risk among males for coronary heart disease. Stoney et al. (1988), in an investigation of gender differences in lipid, lipoprotein, cardiovascular, and neuroendocrine responses to acute stress, found that men showed larger low-density lipoprotein–cholesterol and systolic and diastolic blood pressure increases than women during all stressors (serial subtraction, a videotaped speech about a hypothetical embarrassing situation, self-evaluation of the videotaped speech). Women had larger heart rate responses than men to the videotaped speech delivery only. This study is the first demonstration of gender differences in low-density lipoprotein–cholesterol responses to acute stress. The larger systolic and diastolic blood pressure responses to acute stress exhibited by men in this study are consistent with past work (Matthews & Stoney, 1988), although all studies have not found support for gender differences in diastolic blood pressure reactivity (Stoney, Davis & Matthews, 1987). As in the case of catecholamine reactivity to acute stress, it is not known to what extent acute stress-related increases in low-density lipoprotein–cholesterol and blood pressure relate to disease. However, high blood pressure and high levels of low-density lipoprotein–cholesterol at rest are associated with increased risk of heart disease (Blackburn, 1979).

In a study of gender differences in peripheral vascular response to adrenergic agonists (ie clonidine, isoproterenol, and phenylephrine), Freedman, Sabharwal & Desai (1987) found that men were far more reactive than women to these adrenergic agonists, but were not any more reactive than women to compounds (ie nitroglycerin, digoxin, and tyramine) and procedures (ie reactive hyperemia and rapid cooling of the neck) that do not operate through adrenergic receptor pathways. These findings demonstrate that gender differences in vascular physiology exist. The peripheral vascular adrenergic receptors in males may be denser and/or more sensitive to stimulation. This finding offers an explanation for why men may be more reactive to circulating catecholamines than women.

In conclusion, gender differences in peripheral vascular adrenergic receptor reactivity and stress-induced lipoprotein, blood pressure, and catecholamine responses have been demonstrated. These gender differences are consistent with one another in that they suggest that men are more psychophysiologically reactive than women. It is not known to what extent these observed differences are biologically determined or a product of sociocultural influences as suggested by Frankenhaeuser's work.

SUMMARY AND CONCLUSIONS

Many differences between males and females have more to do with the social construction of gender than they do with genetic and hormonal factors related to sex. This is not only true for differences between males and females in behavior, but is also true for differences between men and women in health.

We argue that men are viewed as the standard for health and that this has a detrimental effect on science, theory, public policy, and the health of males and females. This perspective has justified the exclusion of women in research, contributed to the myth of women's "specialness" and "uniqueness", focused attention on sex steroids and other genetic factors as the determinants of differences in life expectancy and mortality rates between males and females, and discouraged policy formation and funding for disease prevention and health promotion. Because of the important ramifications stemming from the "male" perspective, we urge others to follow our example in future work and discuss gender differences as if females were the standard for health.

Up-to-date statistics of national scope were sought for inclusion in this review. In many cases, this necessitated using United States data to illustrate gender differences in health status that are present in most nations of the world. Our review showed that males are assessed as being in better health by themselves or a household member. Males also report or experience a lower rate of nonsex-specific acute and chronic conditions and have a lower rate of medical service utilization. In contrast to the morbidity data reviewed which suggest a male advantage in health status, the life expectancy and mortality data reviewed suggest that men are at a relative disadvantage to women in health status. They have a shorter life expectancy and a higher rate of death from all major causes of mortality. Part of this discrepancy should come as no surprise since the reported or experienced conditions with the largest gender differentials (eg arthritis, frequent constipation, bunions) are not related to death. Another unquantified portion of this discrepancy is probably due to confounds that inflate gender differences in morbidity in a direction that favors males. In this regard, health practitioner biases, reporting biases, and illness appraisal biases were identified as three categories of error that could contribute to the discrepancy between life expectancy/mortality data and morbidity data. After reviewing relevant data, it became clear that any conclusions at this time are premature since the empirical base to support or refute these biases is lacking. Even assuming that the morbidity differences are entirely free of artifact, we raised the question of just how meaningful these differences are. The majority of men are not any different from the majority of women. Indeed, we would venture to guess that if we walked up to Elizabeth and Christian on the street and asked them to rank order the meaningfulness of data on the number of symptoms, conditions, and diseases men and women are likely to experience and the life expectancy and rates of mortality for men and women, the latter information would be identified as more important. Given these considerations, we focused the second part of this review on genetic, behavioral, and psychophysiological explanations for the gender difference in life expectancy and mortality.

We concluded that biologically based gender differences in vulnerability to infectious diseases exist. However, greater male infant mortality appears to contribute only minimally to the excess in male mortality. This is because the major causes of death with the largest gender differentials (human immunodeficiency virus, suicide, homicide and legal intervention, and accidents and adverse effects) relate to behaviors rather than to genetics and the leading causes of death (heart disease and malignant neoplasm) are, by and large, chronic diseases of adults, not infants. Greater male vulnerability to infectious diseases might contribute moderately to the higher rate of male mortality in that at least 5 of the 15 leading causes of death reviewed may relate to infectious diseases. Finally, the contribution of sex hormones to the excess in male mortality relates primarily to coronary heart disease risk. Limited support exists for the detrimental function of testosterone in coronary heart disease risk in males, whereas stronger support exists for the protective function of estrogen in coronary heart disease risk in women. While the gender differences in infant mortality, vulnerability to infectious disease, and the protective function of estrogen in coronary heart disease risk in women play an important, but quantitatively undetermined, role in the excess in male mortality, we point out, as others have, that cultural and environmental factors significantly modulate the contribution of genetic factors to mortality.

In our review of behavioral explanations we note that men and women differ in behavioral factors that have been shown to influence health and disease, and differences in these behaviors could contribute to gender differences in life expectancy and mortality. In general, the data indicate that men engage in more negative health-related behaviors and fewer positive health-related behaviors than women. We argue that these differences in behavior stem from the socially ascribed appropriateness of the relevant behaviors for males and females.

Compared to women, men are more likely to get fewer than six hours of sleep per day, snack daily, never eat breakfast, and be overweight. Men as a group also tend to be less flexible than women in their food choices and are less aware of the role of dietary factors in health and disease. Moreover, they are more likely to be classified as heavier drinkers than women and are more likely to consume 5 or more drinks on 10 days during the past year. Until recently, more men than women also smoked cigarettes and, consistent with data on alcohol consumption, men's consumption of cigarettes is heavier. Men are also less apt to smoke low-tar and nicotine cigarettes.

On the positive side, men are more physically active than women. This finding is based on self-perceptions of activity as well as energy expenditure in leisure activities. This long list of health-related behavioral differences between males and females seems to indicate a gender difference in health conscientiousness. However, we caution against such a conclusion because most healthy individuals perform "health actions" for multiple, nonhealth reasons. Thus, the "failure" on the part of women (as a group) to play racquetball, shovel snow, and mow grass as often as men (as a group) does not necessarily reflect weaker health conscientiousness on their part. Similarly, greater flexibility in food choices and sleeping six or more hours per day do not reflect greater health conscientiousness on the part of women. The gender difference in the use of nonprescription vitamins and mineral supplements among adults is, however, in line with the hypothesis of a gender difference in health conscientiousness.

The excess in male mortality may also result, in part, from the synergistic effects of interacting health habits. Occupationally related carcinogen exposure may also act synergistically with health habits to produce health consequences in men that contribute to greater rates of mortality. Differences in illness appraisal behaviors could conceivably contribute to greater rates of mortality in men. However, we concluded that illness appraisal behaviors do not play a big role in the excess in male mortality because men and women have similar prognoses for most major forms of cancer. Similarly, men do not delay any longer than women in seeking diagnosis or care for symptoms of life-threatening disease. Finally, psychological variables could covary with gender and contribute to the excess in male mortality. Likely candidates in this regard are the Type A behavior pattern and hostility. Of all the behavioral explanations reviewed, cigarette smoking stands out from the rest as the prime contributor to the gender differential in life expectancy and mortality.

In the last section of the chapter, we note that gender differences in psychophysiological reactivity to stress also might contribute to the excess in male mortality, especially in regard to coronary heart disease. Men in general show greater catecholamine (especially epinephrine) reactivity to stress than women, greater low-density lipoprotein–cholesterol reactivity to acute stress than women, greater blood pressure (in particular, systolic blood pressure) reactivity to stress than women, and greater responses to adrenergic receptor stimulation than women that presumably result from a greater density and/or sensitivity of adrenergic receptors. Research is needed to address whether reactivity to acute stress relates to disease and to what extent these observed differences are a product of socially constructed gender or genetic sex.

We end this chapter with a few points. First, the gender differential in life expectancy and mortality arises, in part, from the cumulative effects of the different social worlds that men and women experience from the moment of their birth. Consequently, the health status of men and women can be improved by modifying personal behaviors and societal conditions that promote health-damaging behaviors. More widespread and long-term results potentially could be achieved by societal modification than by personal health habit modification alone.

Second, by conceptualizing females as the "standard" for health and for research, the health of all people may be improved and science may be advanced. One consequence of this reconceptualization is that research attention and policy formation will focus on disease prevention and treatment rather than only on disease treatment. It will also have the effect of reducing gender bias in the selection of subjects, in the methods used and in the interpretation of data. Explanations for gender differences will not rely as much on the "specialness" of women, and stereotypes and myths concerning women's health will break down. Only then can we fulfill the promise of science, eradicate needless deaths for men and women, and increase the life expectancies of humankind.

ACKNOWLEDGMENTS

We thank Robyn Ridley-Johnson, Janice D. Yoder, and two anonymous reviewers for their helpful comments.

REFERENCES

Amos, S., Odake, K. & Ambrus, C. M. (1969). Effect of sex hormones on the serum-induced thrombosis phenomenon. *Proceedings of the National Academy of Science*, **62**, 150–154.

Baker, L., Dearborn, M., Hastings, J. E. & Hamberger, K. (1984). Type A behavior in women: A review. *Health Psychology*, **3**, 477–497.

Barefoot, I. C., Dahlstrom, G. & Williams, R. B. (1983). Hostility, CHD incidence, and total mortality: A 25-year follow-up study of 255 physicians. *Psychosomatic Medicine*, **45**, 59–63.

Barrett-Connor, E., Brown, W. V., Turner, J., Austin, M. & Criqui, M. H. (1979). Heart disease risk factors and hormone use in postmenopausal women. *Journal of American Medical Association*, **241**, 2167–2169.

Belloc, N. B. & Breslow, L. (1972). Relationship of physical health status and health practices. *Preventive Medicine*, **1**, 409–421.

Bennett, W. & Gurin, J. (1982). *The Dieter's Dilemma: Eating Less and Weighing More*. New York: Basic Books.

Blackburn, H. (1979). Workshop report: epidemiological section. Conference on the effects of blood lipids: optimal distributions for populations. *Preventive Medicine*, **8**, 612–678.

Broverman, I., Broverman, D., Clarkson, R., Rosenkrantz, P & Vogel, S. (1970). Sex role stereotypes and clinical judgments of mental health. *Journal of Consulting and Clinical Psychology*, **34**, 1–7.

Carey, T. (1982). Immunologic aspects of melanoma. *CRC Critical Reviews in Clinical Laboratory Sciences*, **18**, 141–182.

Carmody, T. P., Brischetto, C. S., Matarazzo, J. D., O'Donnell, R. P. & Conner, W. E. (1985). Co-occurrent use of cigarettes, alcohol, and coffee in healthy community-living men and women. *Health Psychology*, 4, 323–335.

Clancy, K. & Gove, W. R. (1974). Sex differences in respondents' reports of psychiatric symptoms: An analysis of response bias. *American Journal of Sociology*, 78, 205–244.

Collins, A., Hanson, U., Eneroth, P., Hagenfeldt, K., Lundberg, U. & Frankenhaeuser, M. (1982). Psychophysiological stress responses in postmenopausal women before and after hormonal replacement therapy. *Human Neurobiology*, 1, 153–159.

Cook, W. W. & Medley, D. M. (1954). Proposed hostility and pharisaic-virtue scales for the MMPI. *Journal of Applied Psychology*, 38, 414–418.

Dawber, T. R. (1980). *The Framingham Study: The Epidemiology of Atherosclerotic Disease*. Cambridge, MA: Harvard Press.

Eckhardt, M. J., Harford, T. C., Kaelber, C. T., Parker, E. S., Roisenthal, L. S., Ryback, R. S., Salmoiraghi, G. C., Venderveen, E. & Warren, K. R. (1981). Health hazards associated with alcohol consumption. *Journal of the American Medical Association*, 246, 648–666.

Fielding, J. E. (1985). Smoking: Health effects and control. *New England Journal of Medicine*, 313, 491–498, 555–561.

Frankenhaeuser, M. (in press). A biopsychosocial approach to stress in women and men. In V. J. Adesso, D. M. Reddy & R. Fleming (Eds), *Psychological Perspectives on Women's Health*. Washington, DC: Hemisphere.

Freedman, R. R., Sabharwal, S. C. & Desai, N. (1987). Sex differences in peripheral vascular adrenergic receptors. *Circulation Research*, 61, 581–585.

Glynn, K. & Leventhal, H. (1990). Dimensions of juvenile illness behavior: Effects of age, gender, and social adjustment. Unpublished manuscript.

Glynn, K., Leventhal, H. & Hirschmann, R. (1986). A cognitive developmental approach to smoking prevention. NIDA/RAUS Research Monograph Series.

Gomberg, E. S. L. (1982). Historical and political perspective: Women and drug use. *Journal of Social Issues*, 38, 9–23.

Gordon, T. & Kannel, W. B. (1984). Drinking and mortality: The Framingham Study. *American Journal of Epidemiology*, 120, 97–107.

Gordon, T., Kannel, W. B., Hjortland, M. C. & McNamara, P. M. (1978). Menopause and coronary heart disease: The Framingham Study. *Annals of Internal Medicine*, 89, 157–161.

Gove, W. R. & Geerken, M. (1977). Response bias in surveys of mental health: An empirical investigation. *American Journal of Sociology*, 82, 1289–1317.

Gove, W., McCorkel, J., Fain, T. & Hughes, M. (1976). Response bias in community surveys of mental health: Systematic bias or random noise? *Social Science and Medicine*, 10, 497–502.

Hall, S. M. (in press). Women and drugs. In Adesso, V. J., Reddy, D. M. & Fleming, R. (Eds), *Psychological Perspectives on Women's Health*. Washington, DC: Hemisphere.

Hammond, C. B. & Maxson, W. S. (1982). Current status of estrogen therapy for the menopause. *Fertility and Sterility*, 37, 15.

Hammond, E. G. (1965). Studies in fetal and infant mortality—II. Differentials in mortality by sex and race. *American Journal of Public Health*, 55, 1152–1163.

Harris, J. E. (1983). Cigarette smoking among successive birth cohorts of men and women in the United States during 1900–1980. *Journal of the National Cancer Institute*, 71, 473–479.

Hollis, J. F., Carmody, T. P., Connor, S. L., Fey, S. G. & Matarazzo, J. D. (1986). The Nutrition Attitude Survey: Associations with dietary habits, psychological and physical well-being, and coronary risk factors. *Health Psychology*, 5, 359–374.

Istvan, J. & Matarazzo, J. (1984). Tobacco, alcohol, and caffeine users: A review of their interrelationships. *Psychological Bulletin*, 95, 301–326.

Johnson, M., Ramey, E. & Ramwell, P. W. (1975). Sex and age differences in human platelet aggregation. *Nature*, 253, 355–357.

Johnson, M., Ramey, E. & Ramwell, P. W. (1977). Androgen mediated sensitivity in platelet aggregation. *American Journal of Physiology*, 232, 381–385.

Kannel, W. B., Hjortland, M. C., McNamara, P. M. & Gordon, T. (1976). Menopause and risk of cardiovascular disease: The Framingham Study. *Annals of Internal Medicine*, 85, 447–452.

Kaplan, M. (1983). The issue of sex bias in DSM-III. *American Psychologist*, 38, 802–803.

Kelton, J. G., Powers, P., Julian, J., Boland, V., Carter, C. J., Gent, M. & Hirsh, J. (1980). Sex-related differences in platelet aggregation: Influence of the Hematocrit. *Blood*, 56, 38–41.

Kilbey, M. M. & Sobeck, J. P. (1988). Epidemiology of alcoholism. In C. B. Travis (Ed.), *Women and Health Psychology: Mental Health Issues*, pp. 92–107. Hillsdale, NJ: Erlbaum.

Kramsch, D. M., Aspen, A. J., Abramowitz, B. M., Kreimendahl, T. & Hood, W. B., Jr. (1981). Reduction of coronary atherosclerosis by moderate conditioning exercise in monkeys on an atherogenic diet. *New England Journal of Medicine*, 305, 1483–1489.

Kromhout, D., Bosschieter, E. G. & de Lezenne Coulander, C. (1985). The inverse relation between fish consumption and 20-year mortality from coronary heart disease. *New England Journal of Medicine*, 312, 1205–1209.

Levy, R. L. & Richey, C. A. (1988). Measurement and research design. In E. A. Blechman & K. D. Brownell (Eds), *Handbook of Behavioral Medicine for Women*, pp. 421–438.

Levy, S. M. (1984). Behavior as a biological response modifier: Psychological variables and cancer prognosis. In B. L. Andersen (Ed.), *Women with Cancer: Psychological Perspectives*, pp. 289–306. New York: Springer-Verlag.

Lundberg, U. (1983). Sex differences in behavior pattern and catecholamine and cortisol excretion in 3–6 year old day-care children. *Biological Psychology*, 16, 109–117.

Lundberg, U., de Chateau, P., Winberg, J. & Frankenhaeuser, M. (1981). Catecholamine and cortisol excretion patterns in three year old children and their parents. *Journal of Human Stress*, 7, 3–11.

Lundberg, U., Hanson, U., Eneroth, P., Frankenhaeuser, M. & Hagenfeldt, K. (1984). Anti-androgen treatment of hirsute women: A study of stress responses. *Journal of Psychosomatic Obstetrical Gynecology*, 3, 79–92.

McGill, H. C. & Stern, M. P. (1979). Sex and atherosclerosis. *Atherosclerosis Review*, 4, 157–248.

Marcus, A. C. & Siegel, J. M. (1982). Sex differences in the use of physician services. *Journal of Health and Social Behavior*, 23, 186.

Marsh, J. C., Colten, M. E. & Tucker, M. B. (1982). Women's use of drugs and alcohol: New perspectives. *Journal of Social Issues*, 38, 1–8.

Marshall, J. R., Gregorio, D. I. & Walsh, D. (1982). Sex differences in illness behavior: Care seeking among cancer patients. *Journal of Health and Social Behavior*, 23, 197–204.

Matthews, K. A. (1989). Are sociodemographic variables markers for psychological determinants of health? *Health Psychology*, 8, 641–648.

Matthews, K. A. & Stoney, C. M. (1988). Influences of sex and age on cardiovascular responses during stress. *Psychosomatic Medicine*, 50, 46–56.

Mayfield, D. (1976). Alcoholism, alcohol intoxication, and assaultive behavior. *Diseases of the Nervous System*, 37, 228–291.

Mercer, P. W. & Khavari, K. A. (1990). Are women drinking more like men? An empirical examination of the convergence hypothesis. *Alcoholism: Clinical and Experimental Research*, 14, 461–466.

Moss, A. J., Levy, A. S., Kim, I. & Park, Y. K. (1989). Use of vitamin and mineral supplements in the United States: Current users, types of products, and nutrients. Advance data from *Vital and Health Statistics*, NO. 174. Hyattsville, MD: National Center for Health Statistics. DHHS Pub. No. (PHS) 89-1250.

National Center for Health Statistics (1988a). H. Koch: Utilization of psychotropic drugs in office-based ambulatory care, National Ambulatory Medical Care survey 1980 and 1981. Advance Data from *Vital and Health Statistics*, No. 90. DHHS Pub. No. (PHS) 83-1250. Public Health Service, Hyattsville, MD, June 1983.

National Center for Health Statistics (1988b). Hospital Care Statistics Branch, Division of Health Care Statistics: 1987 Summary: National Hospital Discharge Survey. Advance data from *Vital and Health Statistics*, No. 159, DHHS Pub. No. (PHS) 88-1250. US Department of Health and Human Services.

National Center for Health Statistics (1989a). Nelson, C. & McLemore, T.: The National Ambulatory Medical Care Survey: 1975–81 and 1985. *Vital and Health Statistics*, Series 13, No. 93, DHHS Pub. No. (PHS) 88-1754. US Department of Health and Human Services, Hyattsville, MD, June 1988.

National Center for Health Statistics (1989b). Advance report of final mortality statistics, 1987. *Monthly Vital Statistics Report*, Vol. 38, No. 5, Supplement, DHHS Pub. No. (PHS) 89-1120. US Department of Health and Human Services, Hyattsville, MD, September 1989.

National Center for Health Statistics (1989c). Adams, P. E. & Hardy, A. M.: Current estimates from the National Health Interview Survey, 1988. *Vital and Health Statistics*, Series 10, No. 173, US Department of Health and Human Services, Hyattsville, MD, October 1989.

Newsweek (5 March, 1990), p. 46.

Paffenbarger, R. S., Jr., Hyde, R. T., Wing, A. L. & Hsieh, C. (1986). Physical activity, all-cause mortality, and longevity of college alumni. *New England Journal of Medicine*, 314, 605–613.

Paffenbarger, R. S., Jr., Hyde, R. T., Wing, A. L. & Steinmetz, C. H. (1984). A natural history of athleticism and cardiovascular health. *Journal of the American Medical Association*, 252, 491–495.

Perrine, M. W., Waller, J. A. & Harris, L. S. (1971). *Alcohol and Highway Safety: Behavioral and Medical Aspects*. Report No. DOT HS-800 600. Washington, DC: National Highway Traffic Safety Administration.

Prather, P., Jr. & Fidell, S. (1975). Sex differences in the content and style of medical advertisements. *Social Science and Medicine*, 9, 23–26.

Preston, S. H. (1976). *Mortality Patterns in National Populations*. New York: Academic Press.

Seidenberg, R. (1971). Drug advertising and perception of mental illness. *Mental Hygiene*, 55, 21–31.

Shekelle, R. B., Gale, M., Ostfeld, A. M. & Paul, O. (1983). Hostility, risk of coronary heart disease, and mortality. *Psychosomatic Medicine*, 45, 109–114.

Silverstein, B., Feld, S. & Kozlowski, L. T. (1980). The availability of low nicotine cigarettes as a cause of cigarette smoking among teenage females. *Journal of Health and Social Behvior*, 21, 383–388.

Simone, C. G. (1983). *Cancer and Nutrition*. New York: McGraw-Hill.

Stellman, S. D. & Stellman, J. M. (1981). Women's occupations, smoking, and cancer and other diseases. *Cancer*, 31, 29–43.

Stoney, C. M., Davis, M. C. & Matthews, K. A. (1987). Sex differences in physiological responses to stress and in coronary heart disease: a causal link? *Psychophysiology*, **24**, 127–131.

Stoney, C. M., Matthews, K. A., McDonald, R. H. & Johnson, C. A. (1988). Sex differences in lipid, lipoprotein, cardiovascular, and neuroendocrine responses to acute stress. *Psychophysiology*, **25**, 645–656.

Suchman, E. A. (1965). Social patterns of illness and medical care. *Journal of Health and Social Behavior*, **6**, 2–16.

Travis, C. (1988). Medical decision making: The case of hysterectomy. In C. B. Travis, *Women and Health Psychology*, pp. 32–53. Hillsdale, New Jersey: Lawrence Erlbaum Associates.

United Nations (1990). *Demographic Yearbook, 1988* (4th issue), Special Topic: Population Census Statistics. New York: Department of International, Economic, and Social Affairs, Statistical Office.

Verbrugge, L. M. (1979). Female illness rates and illness behavior: Testing hypotheses about sex differences in health. *Women and Health*, **4**(1), 61–75.

Verbrugge, L. M. (1980). Sex differences in complaints and diagnoses. *Journal of Behavioral Medicine*, **3**(4), 327–355.

Verbrugge, L. M. (1982). Sex differentials in health. *Prevention*, **97**, 417–437.

Waldron, I. (1983a). Sex differences in illness incidence, prognosis and mortality: Issues and evidence. *Social Science and Medicine*, **17**, 1107–1123.

Waldron, I. (1983b). Sex differences in human mortality: The role of genetic factors. *Social Science and Medicine*, **17**, 321–333.

Waldron, I. (1986). The contribution of smoking to sex differences in mortality. *Public Health Reports*, **101**, 163–173.

Wallen, J., Waitzkin, H. & Stoeckle, J. D. (1979). Physician stereotypes about female health and illness: A study of patient's sex and the information process during medical interviews. *Women and Health*, **4**, 135–146.

Weiner, B. H., Ockene, I. S., Levine, P. H., Cuenaud, H. F., Fisher, M., Johnson, B. F., Daoud, A. S., Jarmolych, J., Hosmer, D., Johnson, M. H., Natale, A., Vaudreuil, C. & Hoogasian, J. J. (1986). Inhibition of atherosclerosis by cod-liver oil in a hyperlipidemic swine model. *New England Journal of Medicine*, **315**, 841–846.

Wiley, J. A. & Camacho, T. C. (1980). Life-style and future health: Evidence from the Alameda County Study. *Preventive Medicine*, **9**, 1–21.

2 Self-Assessed Health and Mortality: A Review of Studies

ELLEN L. IDLER

Department of Sociology, Institute for Health, Health Care Policy, and Aging Research, Rutgers University, 30 College Avenue, New Brunswick, NJ 08903, USA

In 1982 a remarkable article appeared in the *American Journal of Public Health*, reporting convincing evidence of an association that had only been hinted at in previous studies. Two Canadian researchers, one working at Yale, published results of an analysis of the Manitoba Longitudinal Study on Aging which showed that their elderly respondents' self-assessments of health (the answers to the simple question "For your age, in general, would you say your health is excellent, good, fair, poor, or bad?") were much better predictors of their survival during the follow-up period than the very extensive data on their health available from the Canadian province's medical records (Mossey & Shapiro, 1982). There were two quite different measures of health status available in these data, one a longitudinal record of the respondent's use of medical care and diagnoses from their medical record (an external, objective measure), and the other a single measure of self-reported global health status (an internal, subjective measure). The multivariate analysis performed by the researchers showed that, regardless of their *objective* health status, respondents with poorer *subjective* health status experienced greater mortality throughout the seven years of the study period. This article was extremely exciting because it indicated that these self-reported survey responses, often considered vague or too prone to measurement error or response bias to be useful, had just had the most powerful kind of criterion validity extended to them. The finding conferred a retroactive significance on the large body of social scientific work done since the 1950s which showed that discrepancies between subjective reports of health and more objective measures of health were often associated with social and demographic factors, and implied that perceptions of health status were frequently influenced in some way by the respondent's social position. It was one more indication of the crucial role psychosocial factors play in determining health status.

This, then, is the subject of this review: the independent association between subjective, global assessments of health status made as survey responses, and subsequent mortality in follow-up studies. I begin by reviewing the evidence

International Review of Health Psychology. Edited by S. Maes, H. Leventhal and M. Johnston
©1992 John Wiley & Sons Ltd

for this association, then look more closely at the nature of the subjective and objective health status variables in these investigations, and end by suggesting some directions for studies which could improve our understanding of the important processes at work.

The word "independent" in the first sentence of the above paragraph defines the subset of studies to be included here. Considered by themselves, subjective assessments of health are unremarkable as predictors of mortality. Their unique qualities are revealed only when their considerable covariance with other measures of physical health status is removed. The more covariation that can be identified and eliminated, the more confidence one can have that what one is seeing is a real independent effect attributable to the unique vantage point the individual has for viewing his or her own health. Specifically, independence implies that the individual has access to internal data and can integrate those data in ways inaccessble to any external observer. The studies to be considered here all contain subjective evaluations of health status that were collected simultaneously with other, more objective measures of physical health status. They are also all large prospective studies of mortality in probability samples of adult or elderly populations, and they provide multivariate analyses of their data.

Several questions permeate the following discussion. First is the adequacy of the measures of objective health status as control variables; self-perceptions of health are interesting as predictors of mortality only if they seem to be tapping some source of health information that is not available to external observers and thus potentially "capturable" as an objective measure. The better these objective measures of health are, that is, the more they tap of the same information conveyed by the subjective global health measure, the more confident we can be that the remaining subjective data are truly unique. In a multivariate analysis we would see this as an independent effect of self-perceived health remaining after all possible measures of objective health status have been entered in the model. A second question derives from the first. If the subjective health perceptions do have independent effects, what are the source or sources of these perceptions? Are they based on information known only to the respondent, or are they the result of an idiosyncratic process of integration, or both? Third, what role do social and demographic factors play in affecting perceptions of health, and how do they affect the relationship between perceptions of health and mortality?

THE EVIDENCE

The six studies which fit the criteria above are described, in the order in which they were published, in Tables 2.1 and 2.2. The studies were performed with data from the Manitoba Longitudinal Study on Aging (Mossey & Shapiro, 1982), the Alameda County, California, Human Population Laboratory (Kaplan & Camacho, 1983), Kiryat Ono, Israel (Kaplan, Barell & Lusky, 1988), the Yale Health and Aging Project, Connecticut, and the 65 + Rural Health Study,

Iowa, both sites of the National Institute on Aging's Established Populations for the Epidemiologic Study of the Elderly (EPESE) (Idler, Kasl & Lemke, 1990), and the National Health and Nutrition Examination Survey I Epidemiologic Follow-up Study (NHEFS) (Idler & Angel, 1990b). Table 2.1 shows sample characteristics and measures used in each. One would have to say that the differences between these studies are as important as the similarities. Four are of US samples, one national and three regional (one each from the east coast, the west coast, and the midwest), one is Canadian and one is Israeli (both regional). The samples range in size from 1078 to 6928; four are of the elderly only, one is of younger adults only, and one contains both young adults and elderly. Follow-up periods range from 4 to 14 years; one study began as early as 1965. Mortality among sample members was highest in the Manitoba study, 28%, and lowest in Alameda County, California, where it was 10%. Other important differences in the studies concern the measurement of the subjective and objective health variables, and the inclusion of covariates, to be addressed below. Thus, although the number of studies is relatively small, their substantial differences allow us to place some confidence in the extraordinarily consistent results. A number of other studies, notably those of LaRue et al. (1979), Pfeiffer (1970), Singer et al. (1976) Taubman & Rosen (1982), and Heyman & Jeffers (1963), find a similar association between self-assessed health and mortality, but are not included in the tables because they failed to meet the criteria; some had small, nonrandom samples and others had insufficient controls for objective health status.

The findings of studies meeting the criteria are displayed in Table 2.2, which shows odds ratios from the final multivariate models as reported in each analysis, and the associated 95% confidence intervals. All of these analyses proceeded by treating the self-assessed health variable as a set of dummy variables in which "excellent" health was the omitted category; the estimated coefficients thus form a set of contrasts for respondents who reported poor versus excellent health, and good versus excellent health. Odds ratios for both the logistic and hazard models were computed by taking the antilog of the estimated coefficient (Teachman, 1983). The adjusted risk of mortality for those reporting poor as opposed to excellent health ranges from 1.5 for men in the NHEFS (Idler & Angel, 1990b) to 6.7 for men in the Yale Health and Aging Project (Idler & Kasl, 1991). The risk of mortality for those reporting the poorest health was significantly elevated in every group tested in every study, with the single exception of the women in the NHEFS sample. In most cases there are significant risks for those reporting fair and even (only) good health, when compared with the mortality experience of the group reporting excellent health. The risks by level of self-reported health array themselves in perfect linear fashion in nearly every case.

Several of the studies with longer follow-up periods examined the strength of the association over the entire period. In some cases this was done with hazard models and in others by examining the earlier and later years of the follow-up

Table 2.1. Studies reporting association between self-assessed health and mortality, samples and data

Study	Sample	Item eliciting self-assessment	Response categories	Source for objective health status controls	Other control variables
Mossey & Shapiro (1982)	Manitoba Longitudinal Study on Aging, Canada N = 3128 Ages 65 +	"For your age, in general, would you say your health is . . . ?"	Excellent Good Fair Poor Bad	Manitoba Health Services data: ICDA-8 diagnoses physician visits hospitalization Self-reports of conditions	Sociodemographics Life satisfaction
Kaplan & Camacho (1983)	Alameda County, California N = 6928 Ages 16–94	"All in all, would you say your health is . . . ?"	Excellent Good Fair Poor	Self-reports of: functional disability chronic conditions symptoms energy level	Sociodemographics Health practices Social networks Psychological functioning
Kaplan, Barell & Lusky (1988)	Kiryat Ono, Israel N = 1078 Ages 65 +	"Do you consider yourself a . . . . person?"	Healthy Fairly healthy Sick Very sick	Self-reports of: chronic conditions functional disability medications	Age Sex
Idler, Kasl & Lemke (1990)	Yale Health and Aging Project, Connecticut N = 2812 Ages 65 +	"How would you rate your health at the present time?"	Excellent Good Fair Poor Bad	Self-reports of: chronic conditions functional disability pain symptoms Interviewer-measured blood pressure Interviewer-observed prescription medications	Sociodemographics Health practices
	65 + Rural Health Survey, Iowa N = 3097 Ages 65 +	"Compared to other people your age, would you say that your general health is . . . ?"	Excellent Good Fair Poor Very poor		

Idler & Angel (1990b)	NHANES-I Epidemiologic Follow-up Study (NHEFS), USA N = 6440 Ages 25–74	"Would you say your health in general is . . . ?"	Excellent Very good Good Fair Poor	Physician observed: ICDA-8 diagnoses, weighted by severity	Sociodemographics Health practices
Idler & Kasl (1991)	Yale Health and Aging Project, Connecticut N = 2812 Ages 65 +	"How would you rate your health at the present time?"	Excellent Good Fair Poor Bad	Self-reports of: chronic conditions functional disability pain symptoms Interviewer-measured blood pressure Interviewer-observed prescription medications	Sociodemographics Health practices External resources Internal resources

Table 2.2. Studies reporting association between self-assessed health and mortality, results

Study	Follow-up period	Proportion surviving (%)	Multivariate analytic technique	Adjusted odds ratio, (excellent health as reference category)	95% Confidence interval
Mossey & Shapiro (1982)	1971–77	72.0	Logistic regression	(1971–73) Poor 2.9 Fair 2.0 Good 1.4 (1974–77) Poor 2.8 Fair 2.0 Good 1.4	1.8, 4.7 1.5, 2.8 1.2, 1.7 1.9, 3.9 1.2, 3.2 1.2, 1.6
Kaplan & Camacho (1983)	1965–74	89.7	Logistic regression	Poor 1.9	1.8, 2.1
Kaplan, Barell & Lusky (1988)	1978–83	72.2	Cox proportional hazards model	(males) Very sick 2.4 Sick 2.0 Fairly healthy 1.1 (females) Very sick 1.8 Sick 1.9 Fairly healthy 1.1	Not available
Idler, Kasl & Lemke (1990)	1982–86	77.8 (Yale) 85.9 (Iowa)	Logistic regression	(Yale males) Poor 5.3 Fair 3.2 Good 2.5 (Yale females) Poor 3.0 Fair 2.6 Good 2.3 (Iowa males) Poor 4.8 Fair 2.3 Good 1.5 (Iowa females) Poor 3.2 Fair 1.8 Good 1.5	1.9, 14.7 1.4, 7.2 1.1, 5.8 1.3, 6.9 1.3, 5.4 1.1, 4.6 2.2, 10.6 1.3, 4.0 0.9, 2.6 1.5, 6.7 1.0, 3.2 0.9, 2.6

Idler & Angel (1990b)	1971–84	87.1	Cox proportional hazards model	(all males) Poor 1.5	1.1, 2.2
				(males 45–64) Poor 2.8	1.5, 5.3
				Fair 2.2	1.2, 4.1
				Good 1.9	1.0, 3.7
Idler & Kasl (1991)	1982–86	77.8	Logistic regression Cox proportional hazards model	(males) Poor 6.7	2.0, 22.7
				Fair 4.1	1.7, 10.1
				Good 3.2	1.2, 8.1
				(females) Poor 3.1	1.3, 7.2
				Fair 2.8	1.4, 5.8
				Good 2.4	1.2, 4.8

separately. In every case, no differences in the strength of the association were found. Self-assessed health continued to predict mortality throughout follow-up periods of 7 (Mossey & Shapiro, 1982), 9 (Kaplan & Camacho, 1983), 14 (Idler & Angel, 1990b), and even 17 (cited in Kaplan et al., 1987) years. A truncation of the association after a brief follow-up period would indicate that objective health status was inadequately measured, and that the respondents were offering poor short-term prognoses. These very persistent associations, however, suggest that something much more fundamental contributes to these self-perceptions.

The study supplying the weakest evidence for the association is the analysis of the NHEFS data (Idler & Angel, 1990b). In this study an initial association of self-assessed health with mortality among women disappeared when demographic variables were entered into the model; a strong association is found only among the middle-aged men. The NHEFS data are alone among the six studies in having the results of a standardized physician's examination as a control for physical health status, but the analysis shows that these controls are not the reason the association is eliminated. Rather, it is the demographic variables, especially age, but also employment, marital status, and race, that diminish the association among men and eliminate it among women. The other characteristics that set this study apart are its national sample and the young ages (25–74) of the respondents. Self-assessed health, however, does remain a very powerful predictor of mortality for men aged 45–64; men in this age group who reported poor health were 2.8 times less likely to survive than men who reported excellent health, a risk comparable to that found in the other studies.

This, then, is a strong pattern of findings; given the diversity of samples, analytic techniques, covariables, and periods of follow-up, little doubt can remain about the existence of the association. It is its meaning which remains uncertain.

NATURE OF THE SUBJECTIVE HEALTH VARIABLE

Items on surveys which require individuals to evaluate their health and characterize it as excellent, good, fair, or poor are extremely common. It has been the most frequent method of measuring health in the economic literature, and is often the only measure of health, objective or subjective, available in studies of economic behavior such as retirement (Manning, Newhouse & Ware, 1982). For example, analyses of the Longitudinal Retirement History Survey (LRHS) of the Social Security Administration, frequently used in studies of the decision to take early retirement, usually employ only the excellent, good, fair, poor rating, or a question about whether the respondent's health limited his ability to work (Sickles & Taubman, 1986; Anderson & Burkhauser, 1985; Burtless, 1987). The obvious importance of the information being conveyed by these ratings, though, is matched by an uncertainty about what is really being measured, and these articles are filled with arguments about the bias and self-interest inherent in these measures. "No other single question provokes so much discussion among analysts" (Fienberg, Loftus & Tanur, 1985, p. 560).

Initial interest in the concept of self-assessments of health focused on the issue of their validity, or to what extent these easily gathered data could substitute for more objective health status information that was more expensive to collect. Numerous studies were undertaken to compare global assessments with the results of physicians' examinations (Friedsam & Martin, 1963; Heyman & Jeffers, 1963; LaRue et al., 1979; Maddox, 1962; Streib, Suchman & Phillips, 1958). These studies established that there were consistent but modest correlations between the two measures. For example, one longitudinal study with six repeated measures of self-assessments and physicians' examinations showed that cross-sectional correlations between the two ranged from 0.31 to 0.43, rather low correlations considering the amount of feedback information these subjects were receiving about their health (Maddox & Douglass, 1973). When differences between the two measures were analyzed, one consistent finding has been that respondents are more likely to overrate than to underrate their health; disagreements between self- and physician ratings produce substantially more "health optimists" than "health pessimists" (La Rue et al., 1979; Maddox, 1964). These perceptions also appear to be quite stable over time (Goldstein, Siegel & Boyer, 1984; Maddox & Douglass, 1973; Heyman & Jeffers, 1963). One review of these studies concludes that "'perceived health' constitutes an analytically distinct aspect of health" (Tissue, 1972). One interpretation is that the self-assessment of health is the end result of a complicated cognitive process in which respondents review the data available to them about their own health, select from it that which seems relevant, and then evaluate this information according to some set of criteria. Thus the survey response fuses information about the respondent's physical status with the respondent's judgment about what that physical status means. Fienberg, Loftus & Tanur (1985) speculate that the process of evaluation takes place by means of comparisons with the health of others who are similar to the respondent in other important characteristics, or the respondent may compare his or her current health with some period in the past. If this is an accurate representation of the process, then the survey items which explicitly prompt a comparison ("compared to other people your own age") should produce answers which are not different from those which do not, because the process of comparison is implicit in all of them. With respect to the prediction of mortality at least, this appears to be the case: Table 2.1 shows that three of the six studies used questions which asked directly for comparisons to others similar in age, or to earlier periods in the respondent's life, and three did not. There are no discernible differences in the results of these studies. We would note that there are fewer differences in the wording for the response categories.

One is forced to conclude that the concept of self-assessed health status is relatively insensitive to linguistic variations in the questions used to elicit it. It appears that respondents readily understand what is being asked, and are easily able to identify with one or another response category. After all, we practice this process whenever we answer the question, "How are you feeling today?" This is not to say, however, that no improvements in measurement could be made. The Rand Health Insurance Experiment contained multiple measures of general health perceptions (Brook et al., 1979) and produced scales from these items which are more reliable and multidimensional than the response to the single self-assessed health question (Manning, Newhouse & Ware, 1982).

NATURE OF THE OBJECTIVE HEALTH VARIABLE

First let us clarify the meaning of the term "objective". A quick inspection of Table 2.1 will show that most of the studies depend totally or in part on self-reports of conditions or disabilities for their "objective" health status controls. At first look this might appear problematic, if not actually contradictory. What is meant is that "objective" measures of health are objective and not subjective because they are, in principle, verifiable; that is, they could ultimately be proved right or wrong. Self-reports of conditions of arthritis or glaucoma could theoretically be checked against medical records or their presence verified by a physician. Reports of difficulty in activities of daily living could be substantiated by performance tests. Prescription drug use can be verified by checking bottles, dates, and amounts consumed. Reports of physician visits could be checked against office records. Thus self-reports of health states can be considered "objective" if they have the characteristic of observability, even if they are not actually observed.

This is clearly not a characteristic of "subjective" perceptions of health. Individuals who report themselves as being in excellent health, despite a physician's finding of multiple chronic conditions, cannot be said to be "wrong"; nor could a person who said they were unhappy after winning the lottery. We have no alternative but to accept reports of private feeling states such as distress, happiness, well-being, and evaluations of health at face value; they cannot be disproven because they do not refer to any external reality, and only the respondent has access to how he or she "really" feels (Angel & Gronfein, 1988). While the data on which the judgment is based are conceivably recoverable, the selective attention paid to it and the evaluations made of it remain entirely private.

Thus Table 2.1 contains a large array of measures of health status that the analyses used to remove the covariation of physical health with the self-assessments of it. All are objective in the sense specified above, but some are more the product of external observations than others. From a logical standpoint, the most "objective" measure of health status would be the results of a thorough physical examination conducted by a physician at the time of the administration of the survey. Such an examination would be standardized so that biases in reporting or health care utilization behaviors would be eliminated, and detailed enough that previously undiagnosed conditions could be discovered. An additional benefit of the medical examination is the potential for informed weighting of conditions by their clinical severity, a feature no self-reported data could accurately claim. This is exactly the methodology employed in the National Health and Nutrition Examination Survey I (NHANES-I), the purpose of which was to detect untreated, undiagnosed, and otherwise unreported conditions (Idler & Angel, 1990b).

The results of this analysis, however, do not show this medically-derived objective health measure to have any advantage over self-reported objective health measures as a control for physical health status, or as an independent predictor of mortality. Considerable variation in self-assessments of health remained when physical health status was controlled in this way; the weaker association of self-assessed health with mortality found in this study was not attributable to the presence of the physican examination variables as controls. This study, and that of Mossey & Shapiro (1982) who also used external observations in the form of health service utilization records, thus do not demonstrate any inherent superiority of a medical source for the "objective" health status variables in multivariate analyses.

At the other end of the spectrum among these objective measures of health status are symptom scales, self-reports of physical sensations or manifestations that the individual may currently be experiencing, or a rating of how often the individual has experienced them during the past week, month, or year. These symptom scales have been the object of a considerable body of recent work in health psychology which has demonstrated substantial inter-individual and intra-individual variability in reports of symptoms. Beginning with the work of Pennebaker (Pennebaker & Skelton, 1978; Pennebaker, 1982), numerous studies have demonstrated the dependence of symptom reports on such factors as the individual's focus of attention at the time of the report, the individual's interpretation of the meaning of the symptom, and his or her affect (positive or negative). Consistent findings are that people who are paying attention to their bodies, who are encouraged to think of their symptoms as painful, and who are in a sad or distressed mood are more likely to report symptoms. Most recently, attention has focused on the central role of negative affectivity (by which is meant neuroticism or trait anxiety) as a determinant of symptom reporting: Watson & Pennebaker (1989) and Vassend (1989) report on a series of studies which show that, while negative affectivity is not correlated with actual physical status, symptom reporting is correlated with both physical status and negative affectivity. Other researchers have established the influence of transient moods, or "state negative affectivity" on health complaints, finding that experimental induction (Salovey & Birnbaum, 1989; Croyle & Uretsky, 1987) or daily fluctuation (DeLongis, Folkman & Lazarus, 1988) of sad moods can elevate symptom reporting. In general, these studies conclude that reports of somatic complaints and psychological distress are similar, perhaps indistinguishable phenomena (see also Tessler & Mechanic, 1978).

One might conclude from this work that inclusion of symptom scales as measures of objective health in studies of the impact of global self-perceived health on mortality is inappropriate, given their apparently substantial subjective content. But we would make two points here. First, our knowledge of the relationship between global self-assessments of health, which have been shown to be quite stable over time (Goldstein, Siegel & Boyer, 1984; Maddox & Douglass, 1973) and symptom complaints, which appear to vary in response to moods and situational factors, is obviously incomplete. The work of Vassend (1989) suggests that complaints about some body systems may be more responsive to moods than others. Second, despite our uncertainty about the meaning of these measures, including them in studies of global perceived health and mortality carries little risk; to the extent that they share variation with global perceived health they will attenuate, not falsely inflate, its association with mortality.

So what is the optimal way to isolate the net effect of the subjective component in self-assessments of health? The easiest advice is that given by Manning, Newhouse & Ware (1982) in their examination of the role of health in estimating demand for health care: "one should use all the health status variables at hand" (p. 166). This may sound flip, but "the more, the better" is probably the best recommendation that could be made. If we use as a guide the World Health Organization's definition of health as "a state of complete physical, mental, and social well-being and not merely the absence of disease or infirmity", then the best controls for objective health status may be those which define health most broadly, and measure it in as many ways as possible. An optimal set of health status control variables, then, might contain measures of:

1. *Chronic conditions.* These could be derived from self-report, medical records, or physician examination. An advantage of the clinical sources would be the possibility of weighting for severity.
2. *Current symptoms of acute conditions.* While common acute conditions would not ordinarily be considered mortality risks, symptom checklists could pick up prodromal phases of undiagnosed chronic conditions.
3. *Current symptoms of chronic conditions.* Standard screening instruments are available for diagnosing disorders such as angina, bronchitis, intermittent claudication, arthritis, etc. This could be another opportunity for picking up undiagnosed disease.
4. *Functional ability.* Activities of daily living (ADL), instrumental activities of daily living (IADL), gross mobility, physical endurance, bed days, and days of work/normal activities lost or restricted should all be assessed. Observable physical performance measures could be added to these self-report measures.
5. *Direct physiological measurements*: blood pressure, serum cholesterol, single breath capacity, height and weight, hand grip strength, etc.
6. *Use of medical care,* such as prescription drug use, physician visits, hospitalizations, and nursing home stays. These could be derived from direct

observation (prescription medicines in use in the home could additionally be analyzed for compliance by collecting records of the date, dosage, and amount remaining in the container), medical records, or self-report.

Each of these measures is used in one or more of the studies under consideration here, but no study comes close to employing all of them. Some of these measures are perfectly "objective" (measurements of weight and height), and have the advantage of eliminating response bias altogether. Others are less available to external observation (reports of current symptoms), but provide information which could not easily be gained in any other way.

Are some of these measures better than others? In a sense this is strictly an empirical question. The best measure of objective health status is simply the one that shares the most variation with self-assessments of health and explains the greatest part of its association with mortality. These associations could easily vary from one study to another, and thus no definitive recommendation can be made. However, cross-sectional studies of the physical health correlates of self-assessments have established that functional ability plays a very important role in the formation of these perceptions (Liang, 1986; Martini & McDowell, 1976; Tissue, 1972; Linn & Linn, 1980). Functional ability indexes the severity of disease and the impact of multiple conditions; it is in effect a measure of the consequences of morbidity. Empirically, it is highly correlated with both self-assessments of health and mortality in those studies in which all three appear (Kaplan & Camacho, 1983; Kaplan, Barell & Lusky, 1988; Idler, Kasl & Lemke, 1990; Idler & Kasl, 1991). Functional status measures should be considered essential in future studies of this association, along with as many other measures suggested by the above list as possible. The best possible measurement of physical health status gains us two objectives. First, we confirm and narrow down the independent effect of self-perceived health on mortality because the maximum amount of its covariation with objective health has been factored out. Second, we learn more about the process by which individuals arrive at these self-perceptions by studying the shared variation between these objective and subjective measures because we learn which measures of objective health status are relevant to subjective perceptions and which are not.

Even if all of the measures in the above list were available, however, it is unlikely that complete agreement between objective physical health and the subjective assessments of it would ever be achieved. On the one hand, there are individuals who report symptoms in surveys, or present complaints in the clinical situation, for which no organic cause can be found. On the other, some individuals with demonstrable morbidity and functional limitations as a consequence report good health and do not seek medical care. These two "types", the hypochondriac and the health optimist, are both present in the clinical literature, especially in geriatric medicine (reviewed in Levkoff, Cleary & Wetle, 1987). The real relationship between objective and subjective health, however, is probably better represented, not by these extremes, but by the model of a continuum. While most respondents give subjective assessments of health that are relatively congruent with objective measures, discrepancies between the two can run in both directions: health optimism or pessimism can be mild or extreme. In studies using broad symptom scales (Costa & McCrae, 1985), and in detailed studies of single disease entities such as arthritis (Idler & Angel, 1990a; Butler et al., 1987), back pain (Mechanic & Angel, 1987), or functional disability (Nagi, 1969) similar patterns emerge: both "overreporting" and "underreporting" of symptoms are widespread tendencies in the populations studied, and there are "consistent and enduring individual differences in the perception, interpretation, and reporting of bodily symptoms" (Costa & McCrae, 1985, p. 20).

Self-assessments of health incorporate both objective and subjective information about the individual's health state. The more of the objective (in the sense of being observable or potentially observable) information that can be captured by a comprehensive set of physical health status measurements, the more reliable is the argument that the remaining independent effect of self-assessed health on mortality is due to the subjective component.

WHAT ELSE DO THESE ANALYSES TELL US?

Sociodemographic factors

The first observation to be made about the patterns that emerge from these analyses is that sociodemographic variables have an important impact on the self-assessed health–mortality association. Beginning with the earliest studies of self-assessments of health, it was clear that discrepancies between objective and subjective measures of health were associated with fundamental social categories: age, sex, race, ethnicity, income, and education all helped to explain the tendency to give incongruent optimistic or pessimistic assessments of health status (Haberman, 1969; Maddox, 1962). But the important point is that, in addition to their associations with subjective and objective health status, these sociodemographic factors also carry mortality risks of their own.

We can sort these factors into two groups. The most common case is that in which one of these factors has similar associations with both self-assessed health and mortality. Take education as an example. Individuals with less education tend to offer poorer self-assessments of health at any given level of objective health (Cockerham, Sharp & Wilcox, 1983; Ferraro, 1980; Idler & Angel, 1990a), and are also at greater risk for mortality (Taubman & Rosen, 1982); thus self-assessed health covaries with education and introducing education into the equation should reduce the effect of self-assessed health on mortality. The effect of education is thus important to control, but the observation of such a reduced effect also tells us something about self-assessed health and mortality: that one of the reasons people with optimistic self-assessments of health live longer is that they tend to have more education. Other variables that act in this way include: marital status (the unmarried have poorer self-assessed health and greater mortality risks (Taubman & Rosen, 1982; Pfeiffer, 1970)), race or ethnicity (nonwhites are also at risk in both ways (Maddox, 1962; Angel & Thoits, 1987)), income (those with lower income are also doubly at risk (Butler et al., 1987)), and in some causes, sex (being male) (Ferraro, 1980; Fillenbaum, 1979), and age (those who are older (Levkoff, Cleary & Wetle, 1987)). The introduction of any of these variables can be expected to reduce the independent effect of self-assessed health on mortality; in part, they "explain" the association. But because they are persistent social structural categories which carry known mortality risks, they should be considered as antecedent to self-assessments of current health; rather than explaining the association, they explain it away.

The other category is for variables which in some samples may have opposite associations with self-assessed health and mortality; this has sometimes been the case with both sex and age. Being older and being male present invariably higher mortality risks, but in some studies either or both have been associated with better, not poorer, self-assessed health (Prohaska et al., 1985; Linn & Linn, 1980; Cockerham, Sharp & Wilcox, 1983; Ferraro, 1980; Maddox, 1962; Heyman & Jeffers, 1963). In these cases, sex or age acts as a suppressor variable; when a variable of this type is omitted from a model, the positive relationship between self-assessed health and mortality is suppressed, or appears to be smaller than it actually is. For example, if the older people in a sample, who we know are at greater risk of mortality, are also inclined to give better self-assessments of health status (relative to their objective health) when compared with the younger people in the sample, then failing to control for age will produce a falsely low estimate for the effect of self-assessed health on mortality. The clearest example of this can be seen in the analysis of the Yale and Iowa data (Idler, Kasl & Lemke, 1990). These hierarchical models begin by entering self-assessed health and controlling for objective health status alone, and then add sociodemographic variables in a second step. The result, in each of the sex-specific models, from both samples, is a higher estimated coefficient for self-assessed health when age is controlled than when it is not. The oldest respondents in these elderly samples were evidently inclined to view their health positively, despite their obviously greater risk of mortality and higher levels of morbidity.

The recommendation here, as in the matter of objective health status controls, again belabors the obvious: sociodemographic variables are extremely important and must not be omitted from the analysis. These fundamental social categories form the context within which self-assessments of health are constructed, and they act simultaneously as powerful mortality risks. Thus their omission would be a serious fault in this type of analysis, but their inclusion offers an excellent opportunity to better understand the processes at work.

Health behaviors

A large assortment of other control and mediating variables are available in these six studies. The Alameda County, Yale, Iowa, and NHEFS data contain measures of health practices, including smoking, consumption of alcohol, and exercise. Controls for such health-related behaviors are important because, as with the sociodemographic variables, they are likely to be confounded with both mortality and self-assessments of health. That is, while they exert an independent influence on mortality, they are also likely to inform subjective assessments of health. People who smoke, for example, may evaluate a mild cough much more negatively than those who do not, because the health consequences of smoking are so well-known. So again, inclusion of these variables is necessary. Like the sociodemographic factors, these variables should be considered antecedent; as in the above example, self-assessed health may help us understand the effect of smoking, but smoking will probably not help us understand the effect of self-assessed health.

Psychosocial factors

The most innovative attempts to explain this association have come with the introduction of variables which could be said to mediate the effect of self-assessments of health on mortality. Unlike the sociodemographic or health behavior variables these psychosocial factors are conceptually similar to self-assessments of health; most have been shown to be associated with self-assessed health, or mortality, or both. They include social networks (Alameda County and Yale), life satisfaction (Manitoba), depression (Alameda County and Yale), religiousness (Yale), and optimism (Yale). The results of the investigations have been disappointing, however; despite their plausibility and attractiveness, these factors do not appear to act as intervening mechanisms, at least in the manner in which they have been operationalized in these studies. On the other hand, it is too early to rule anything out, and additional tests of these hypotheses would be welcome additions to the literature.

HOW CAN WE FIND OUT MORE?

Several strategies could be employed in further investigations of this association. Replications of the model are needed, with different populations and better measures of the concepts. But our understanding of the causal processes at work may be enhanced even more by a shift from these highly quantitative, population-level studies, to more quantitative, in-depth studies of smaller samples. Here are some specific recommendations.

1. *Begin studying outcomes other than mortality.* Morbidity outcomes that are also mortality risks would be of greatest interest: functional disability; recovery from cancer, stroke, myocardial infarction, hip fracture, trauma, etc.; hospital or nursing home admission; indeed, any of the measures of objective health status discussed above could be included here, as could outcomes which are health-related, but more social or behavioral in nature, such as illness behavior or entrance into the sick role. Such morbidity studies could be seen

as longitudinal extensions of the numerous cross-sectional studies comparing subjective and objective health status.

Building up a set of findings in this area could help us choose between two basic causal models (Idler & Kasl, 1991). The first is that self-assessed health predicts mortality because it alters the morbidity experience that follows the self-assessment but precedes mortality; optimistic or pessimistic perceptions of health status may affect the motivation necessary for recovery or rehabilitation. Support for this hypothesis would be found by identifying one or more morbidity outcomes to which self-assessed health is related, and then demonstrating that these intermediate outcomes intervene in the association.

The second model is that of an independent effect: if no effect on mortality through morbidity is observed, self-assessments would appear to be operating as direct predictions of survival periods. We might think of them as expressions of subjective life expectancy. This raises the question of what information the respondent is basing these subjective survival calculations on, an issue to be addressed below.

2. *Study the cognitive processes associated with these judgments of health status.* Several approaches may be taken here. One is to begin with the survey instrument itself and ask whether responses to the self-assessed health question are affected by the context in which it appears (Fienberg, Loftus & Tanur, 1985). Are responses to this question different when it appears after, rather than before, a symptom checklist, for example? This is not just a question about survey methodology; it raises the very important issue of whether judgments of overall health are primarily affected by the presence of conditions, or if the perception of conditions might not be affected by a more fundamental evaluation of underlying health status.

A second approach would be to study individual characteristics that are related to the cognitive process of health evaluation. Recent reports in the literature have demonstrated associations between better self-assessments of health and higher levels of intelligence (Perlmutter & Nyquist, 1990), optimism and coping ability (Scheier & Carver, 1985), distress (Tessler & Mechanic, 1978), and competence (Mechanic & Hansell, 1987). Together, these findings suggest that cognitive skills may play an important role in the evaluation of health states, possibly because of an ability to seek out and effectively use health information.

Another group of these individual characteristics are those related to the perception, interpretation, and reporting of symptoms. Higher levels of attention to the body and its functioning appear to be related to higher levels of symptom reporting and poorer self-assessments of health. This pattern of being preoccupied with the body was identified in some of the early Duke studies (Maddox, 1964) as "high body concern". More recently, investigators have linked greater "body awareness" to declines in self-assessed health over a period of one year (Hansell & Mechanic, 1991). More studies of this kind are needed, to establish the existence of this disposition and learn something about its origins, stability, and links to culture and social structure.

A fourth area of study with a cognitive emphasis would be an examination of the process by which reference-group comparisons are made. These comparisons, numerous authors have suggested, are at the heart of the self-assessment process (Fienberg, Loftus & Tanur, 1985; Angel & Thoits, 1987). The reference-group idea, in which people identify others by their membership in social categories and then compare themselves to these socially similar and dissimilar others, is especially powerful in this connection, because the basic social categories of gender, race, ethnicity, and class carry such different mortality (and morbidity) risks. We need to know a great deal more about common-sense epidemiology (Leventhal, Nerenz & Strauss, 1980; Jemmott, Croyle & Ditto, 1988), the extent to which these risks are known to respondents, and which groups, if any, are relevant to them in evaluating their own health.

In addition to these broad social categories, reference-group comparisons may also be based on personal and family history of disease. Certain diseases for which family history is a key risk factor, such as breast cancer, may create their own reference groups which influence self-assessments ("the women in my family have never had breast cancer, therefore my own risk is low"). Individuals may adopt these family patterns as elements in their own risk profile even when medical evidence for a genetic link is incomplete ("my family just tends to be heavy" or "we all have weak gallbladders"). These family histories may give an individual a sense of shared vulnerability (or resistance) that plays into evaluations of global health status even in the absence of symptoms or conditions.

In short, this set of proposed investigations of the cognitive processes involved in the evaluation of global health states has as its goal a better understanding of common-sense models of global health. The concept of common-sense models of illness (Meyer, Leventhal & Gutmann, 1985; Baumann & Leventhal, 1985) has been used successfully in the prediction of reactions to and compliance with medical regimens for particular illnesses. Expanding this approach to the level of global health would mean identifying for each individual a set of personal health threats, their causes, consequences, and duration (Leventhal, Nerenz & Steele, 1984); a schema or framework against which the transient perception of current health state is measured. Until we know something about the personal standards on which these calculations are based, the meaning of the answers that are derived will remain uncertain.

3. *Study health optimists and pessimists in more detail.* Even if the relationship between objective and subjective health forms a continuous spectrum from "persistent underreporting to frank hypochondriasis" (Costa & McCrae, 1985, p. 20), the opportunity still exists for studies of individuals at the extremes (Levkoff, Cleary & Wetle, 1987).

Health optimists, those who rate their health in positive terms despite the presence of medical problems, have been seen as engaging in denial of significant symptoms, or lacking necessary health knowledge, or possessing a poor memory, any of which could lead to the ignoring of serious symptoms and a failure to seek appropriate medical care. At the same time, health pessimists are portrayed as overreporting trivial symptoms and squandering valuable medical resources. The mortality risk information that we have at present contradicts the usefulness of both of these stereotypes, and suggests that we need to look more closely at our "poor" and "excellent" groups.

The results of the studies of self-assessed health and mortality reviewed here also shed some light on the frequent finding that health optimists outnumber health pessimists (LaRue et al., 1979; Maddox & Douglass, 1973; Ferraro, 1980; Linn & Linn, 1980). A pattern of increasing health optimism with older cohorts is exactly what one would expect if health pessimism were a mortality risk. Studies of younger adults might yield quite different results than we have from these studies of elderly survivors.

WHAT CAN WE CONCLUDE NOW?

The conclusion most of the studies reviewed here draw is that convincing evidence of an association between self-assessed health and mortality has obvious implications for clinical practice: "the ease with which such ratings can be obtained suggest that routine ascertainment of self-rated health during the course of medical care contacts is warranted" (Mossey & Shapiro, 1982, p. 805). There is certainly merit in the view that what people say about their health bears listening to; the negative characterizations of those with incongruent health assessments, the denier and the hypochondriac, need to be rethought with these substantial mortality risks in mind. However, this recommendation to clinicians assumes that the self-assessment elicited in the clinical setting will be the same as that given to a survey researcher, an assumption which should be tested before it is made.

The magnitude and also the meaning of the association between self-assessed health and mortality are clear not only in the presence of good measures of objective health status. The excellent, good, fair, poor categorization, standing alone, is of little use in the survey or in the clinical interview, and it cannot be urged as a substitute for more objective health information. Together, however, the two dangle important clues before our eyes about the nature of psychosocial influences on health. The disjunction between the two is a sort of window through which we can look in on complicated processes of perception, cognition, and meaning-giving that have intriguing implications.

REFERENCES

Anderson, K. H. & Burkhauser, R. V. (1985). The retirement-health nexus: A new measure of an old puzzle. *Journal of Human Resources*, 20, 315–330.

Angel, R. & Gronfein, W. (1988). The use of subjective information in statistical models. *American Sociological Review*, 53, 464–473.

Angel, R. & Thoits, P. (1987). The impact of culture on the cognitive structure of illness. *Culture, Medicine and Psychiatry*, 11, 465–494.

Baumann, L. J. & Leventhal, H. (1985). "I can tell when my blood pressure is up, can't I?" *Health Psychology*, **4**, 203–218.

Brook, R. H., Ware, J. E., Davies-Avery, A., Stewart, A. L., Donald, C. A., Rogers, W. H., Williams, K. N. & Johnston, S. A. (1979). Overview of adult health status measures fielded in Rand's Health Insurance Study. *Medical Care*, Supplement, **17**, i–89.

Burtless, G. (1987). Occupational effects on the health and work capacity of older men. In G. Burtless (Ed.), *Work, Health, and Income among the Elderly*. Washington, DC: Brookings, pp. 103–150.

Butler, J. S., Burkhauser, R. V., Mitchell, J. M. & Pincus, T. P. (1987). Measurement error in self-reported health variables. *Review of Economics and Statistics*, **69**, 644–650.

Cockerham, W. C., Sharp, K. & Wilcox, J. A. (1983). Aging and perceived health status. *Journal of Gerontology*, **38**, 349–355.

Costa, P. T. & McCrae, R. R. (1985). Hypochondriasis, neuroticism, and aging: When are somatic complaints unfounded? *American Psychologist*, **40**, 19–28.

Croyle, R. T. & Uretsky, M. B. (1987). Effects of mood on self-appraisal of health status. *Health Psychology*, **6**, 239–253.

DeLongis, A., Folkman, S. & Lazarus, R. S. (1988). The impact of daily stress on health and mood: Psychological and social resources as mediators. *Journal of Personality and Social Psychology*, **54**, 486–495.

Ferraro, K. F. (1980). Self-ratings of health among the old and the old-old. *Journal of Health and Social Behavior*, **21**, 377–383.

Fienberg, S. E., Loftus, E. F. & Tanur, J. M. (1985). Cognitive aspects of health survey methodology: An overview. *Milbank Memorial Fund Quarterly/Health and Society*, **63**, 547–564.

Fillenbaum, G. G. (1979). Social context and self-assessments of health among the elderly. *Journal of Health and Social Behavior*, **20**, 45–51.

Friedsam, H. J. & Martin, H. W. (1963). A comparison of self and physicians' health ratings in an older population. *Journal of Health and Human Behavior*, **4**, 179–183.

Goldstein, M. S., Siegel, J. M. & Boyer, R. (1984). Predicting changes in perceived health status. *American Journal of Public Health*, **74**, 611–614.

Haberman, P. W. (1969). The reliability and validity of the data. In J. Kosa, A. Antonovsky & I. K. Zola (Eds), *Poverty and Health: A Sociological Analysis*. Cambridge: Harvard University Press, pp. 343–383.

Hansell, S. & Mechanic, D. (1991). Body awareness and self-assessed health among older adults. *Journal of Aging and Health*, **3**, 473–492.

Heyman, D. K. & Jeffers, F. C. (1963). Effect of time lapse on consistency of self-health and medical evaluations of elderly persons. *Journal of Gerontology*, **18**, 160–164.

Idler, E. L. & Angel, R. J. (1990a). Age, chronic pain and subjective assessments of health. *Advances in Medical Sociology*, **1**, 127–148.

Idler, E. L. & Angel, R. J. (1990b). Self-rated and mortality in the NHANES-I Epidemiologic Follow-Up Study. *American Journal of Public Health*, **80**, 446–452.

Idler, E. L. & Kasl, S. V. (1991). Health perceptions and survival: Do global evaluations of health status really predict mortality? *Journal of Gerontology: Social Sciences*, **46**, 555–65.

Idler, E. L., Kasl, S. V. & Lemke, J. H. (1990). Self-evaluated health and mortality among the elderly in New Haven, Connecticut, and Iowa and Washington Counties, Iowa, 1982–1986. *American Journal of Epidemiology*, **131**, 91–103.

Jemmott, J. B., Croyle, R. T. & Ditto, Peter H. (1988). Commonsense epidemiology: Self-based judgments from laypersons and physicians. *Health Psychology*, **7**, 55–73.

Kaplan, G., Barell, V. & Lusky, A. (1988). Subjective state of health and survival in elderly adults. *Journal of Gerontology*, **43**, S114–S120.

Kaplan, G. A & Camacho, T. (1983). Perceived health and mortality: A nine-year follow-up of the Human Population Laboratory cohort. *American Journal of Epidemiology*, **117**, 292–304.

Kaplan, G. A., Seeman, T., Cohen, R. D., Knudsen, L. P. & Guralnick, J. (1987). Mortality among the elderly in the Alameda County Study: Behavioral and demographic risk factors. *American Journal of Public Health*, **77**, 307–312.

LaRue, A., Bank, L., Jarvik, L. & Hetland, M. (1979). Health in old age: How do physicians' ratings and self-ratings compare? *Journal of Gerontology*, **34**, 687–691.

Leventhal, H., Nerenz, D. R. & Steele, D. J. (1984). Illness representations and coping with health threats. In A. Baum, S. E. Taylor & J. E. Singer (Eds), *Handbook of Psychology and Health*. Hillsdale, NJ: Lawrence Erlbaum Associates, pp. 219–252.

Leventhal, H., Nerenz, D. R. & Strauss, A. (1980). Self-regulation and the mechanisms for symptom appraisal. In D. Mechanic (Ed.), *Psychosocial Epidemiology*. New York: Neal Watson, pp. 55–86.

Levkoff, S. E., Cleary, P. D. & Wetle, T. (1987). Differences in the appraisal of health between aged and middle-aged adults. *Journal of Gerontology*, **42**, 114–120.

Liang, J. (1986). Self-reported physical health among aged adults. *Journal of Gerontology*, **41**, 248–260.

Linn, B. S. & Linn, M. W. (1980). Objective and self-assessed health in the old and very old. *Social Science and Medicine*, **14A**, 311–315.

Maddox, G. L. (1962). Some correlates of differences in self-assessment of health status among the elderly. *Journal of Gerontology*, **17**, 180–185.

Maddox, G. L. (1964). Self-assessment of health status: A longitudinal study of selected elderly subjects. *Journal of Chronic Disease*, **17**, 449–460.

Maddox, G. L. & Douglass, E. B. (1973). Self-assessment of health: A longitudinal study of elderly subjects. *Journal of Health and Social Behavior*, **14**, 87–93.

Manning, W. G., Newhouse, J. P. & Ware, J. E. (1982). The status of health in demand estimation; or, beyond excellent, good, fair, and poor. In V. R. Fuchs (Ed.), *Economic Aspects of Health*, Chicago: University of Chicago Press, pp. 143–184.

Martini, C. J. & McDowell, I. (1976). Health status: Patient and physician judgments. *Health Services Research*, **11**, 508–515.

Mechanic, D. & Angel, R. J. (1987). Some factors associated with the report and evaluation of back pain. *Journal of Health and Social Behavior*, **28**, 131–139.

Mechanic, D. & Hansell, S. (1987). Adolescent competence, psychological well-being, and self-assessed physical health. *Journal of Health and Social Behavior*, **28**, 364–374.

Meyer, D., Leventhal, H. & Gutmann, M. (1985). Common-sense models of illness: The example of hypertension. *Health Psychology*, **4**, 115–135.

Mossey, J. M. & Shapiro, E. (1982). Self-rated health: A predictor of mortality among the elderly. *American Journal of Public Health*, **72**, 800–808.

Nagi, S. Z. (1969). Congruency in medical and self-assessment of disability. *Industrial Medicine*, **38**, 27–36.

Pennebaker, J. W. (1982). *The Psychology of Physical Symptoms*, New York: Springer-Verlag.

Pennebaker, J. W. & Skelton, J. A. (1978). Psychological parameters of physical symptoms. *Personality and Social Psychology Bulletin*, **4**, 524–530.

Perlmutter, M. & Nyquist, L. (1990). Relationships between self-reported physical and mental health and intelligence performance across adulthood. *Journal of Gerontology*, **45**, P145–P155.

Pfeiffer, E. (1970). Survival in old age: Physical, psychological and social correlates of longevity. *Journal of the American Geriatrics Society*, **18**, 273–285.

Prohaska, T. R., Leventhal, E. A., Leventhal, H. & Keller, M. L. (1985). Health practices and illness cognition in young, middle aged, and elderly adults. *Journal of Gerontology*, **40**, 569-578.

Salovey, P. & Birnbaum, D. (1989). Influence of mood on health-relevant cognitions. *Journal of Personality and Social Psychology*, **57**, 539-551.

Scheier, M. F. & Carver, C. (1985). Optimism, coping, and health: Assessment and implications of generalized outcome expectancies. *Health Psychology*, **4**, 219-247.

Sickles, R. C. & Taubman, P. (1986). An analysis of the health and retirement status of the elderly. *Econometrica*, **54**, 1339-1356.

Singer, E., Garfinkel, R., Cohen, S. M. & Srole, L. (1976). Mortality and mental health: Evidence from the Midtown Manhattan Restudy. *Social Science and Medicine*, **10**, 517-525.

Streib, G., Suchman, E. & Phillips, B. (1958). An analysis of the validity of health questionnaires. *Social Forces*, **36**, 223-232.

Taubman, P. & Rosen, S. (1982). Healthiness, education, and marital status. In V. R. Fuchs (Ed.), *Economic Aspects of Health*. Chicago, IL: University of Chicago Press, pp. 121-140.

Teachman, J. D. (1983). Analyzing social processes: Life tables and proportional hazard models. *Social Science Research*, **12**, 262-301.

Tessler, R. & Mechanic, D. (1978). Psychological distress and perceived health status. *Journal of Health and Social Behavior*, **19**, 254-262.

Tissue, T. (1972). Another look at self-rated health among the elderly. *Journal of Gerontology*, **27**, 91-94.

Vassend, O. (1989). Dimensions of negative affectivity, self-reported somatic symptoms, and health-related behaviors. *Social Science and Medicine*, **28**, 29-36.

Watson, D. & Pennebaker, J. W. (1989). Health complaints, stress, and distress: Exploring the central role of negative affectivity. *Psychological Review*, **96**, 234-254.

Part II

HEALTH BEHAVIOUR AND HEALTH PROMOTION

3 The Management of Stress in the Prevention of Coronary Heart Disease

DEREK W. JOHNSTON
Department of Psychology, University of St Andrews, St Andrews, Fife KY16 9JV, Scotland

INTRODUCTION

Coronary heart disease (CHD) is a major cause of death in most countries in the Western world. It is the main cause of premature death in the United Kingdom and even countries with improving records of CHD incidence, such as the USA, report rates as much as four times higher than the least affected countries, such as Japan (Shaper, 1988; Smith & Jacobsen, 1988). Such a large variation between countries strongly suggests that high rates of CHD are not inevitable. The search for interventions that will reduce this wasteful and tragic toll of death and disability is therefore being pursued vigorously in most Western countries. Stress is one component in the rich mix of factors thought to predispose individuals to CHD. In this chapter I shall evaluate efforts to lower the risk of CHD by teaching individuals to manage stress.

As Kasl (1984) has pointed out, the term "stress" is used in a number of different ways in psychological studies. These include:
(a) an environmental condition
(b) an appraisal of an environmental situation
(c) a response to the environment condition or its appraisal
(d) to describe the interaction between environmental demands and an individual's capacity to meet these demands.
Precise definitions do not appear to capture all the phenomena one wishes to describe under the term "stress" and I shall follow the current convention of including all the processes that common usage and prevailing practice regard as stress related. This includes environments that are either universally regarded as taxing or as taxing for some individuals, the processes of appraising these environments, including individual characteristics that affect these appraisal processes or indeed act to alter the environment in a stress-enhancing manner, and the behavioural and physiological responses to the stressful stimuli. Stress

International Review of Health Psychology. Edited by S. Maes, H. Leventhal and M. Johnston
©1992 John Wiley & Sons Ltd

management is any behavioural or psychological procedure offered or undertaken that deliberately attempts to alter beneficially any aspect of the stress process, including altering the environment, subjective appraisal of that environment and the subjective, behavioural and physiological responses to the stressful experience.

In this chapter I shall briefly describe the pathophysiology of CHD, review the risk factors for CHD, describe the part stress is thought to play in the development of CHD and the mechanisms through which it may operate (a much more complete coverage of these complex and contentious issues can be found in Steptoe (1981) and Herd (1984)). The main methods of managing stress-related processes will be described and evaluated and the likely therapeutic mechanisms discussed.

STRESS AND CORONARY HEART DISEASE

Coronary, or ischaemic, heart disease refers to disease of the heart that results from the altered functioning of the coronary arteries. The most important of such diseases are angina, acute myocardial infarction and sudden cardiac death. All these conditions are thought to be in part the consequence of atherosclerosis, a process in which atheromatous plaques develop on the walls of the arteries and obstruct the flow of blood. Angina, a powerful pain in the chest and, on occasion, down the left arm, develops when blood flow in the coronary arteries is sufficiently compromised to starve the heart muscle (myocardium) of oxygen. An acute myocardial infarction (MI) occurs when blood flow drops below a critical threshold and myocardial ischaemia is severe enough to lead to the destruction of myocardial tissue. It is now thought that this usually occurs when a thrombus, resulting from the rupture of an atheromatous plaque, further restricts blood flow in an artery already compromised by atheroma. Sudden cardiac death, which is normally defined in terms of rapidity of death following collapse, may be due to acute MI or be the result of a fatal arrhythmia in the absence of an infarction. This typically occurs in patients with diseased arteries or a damaged heart following an earlier MI. In addition to atheroma restricting coronary arteries, coronary arteries can constrict, possibly under sympathetic influence, sufficiently to cause angina, or even infarction, in patients with apparently healthy arteries.

If stress has a role to play in the causation of CHD it is most likely to operate through one of the processes described above. That is, stress most probably influences the development of atheroma and thrombi, the constriction of the coronary arteries or the electrical stability of the diseased heart.

The most obvious route for stress to affect the coronary arteries is through the conventional or classic risk factors. Numerous studies have shown that the risk of CHD relates to raised blood pressure, blood cholesterol and cigarette smoking (Pooling Project Research Group, 1978). The evidence linking stress and blood pressure is impressive and well known. Animals, particularly if genetically susceptible to hypertension, show large and moderately persistent elevations in pressure when placed in stressful environments (Lawler et al., 1980) and similar, although necessarily more acute affects, can be seen in genetically predisposed humans (see Sallis, Dimsdale & Caine, 1988). Hypertension is also more likely in individuals in obviously stressful occupations, such as air traffic controllers, compared to workers in less stressed parts of the air traffic system (Cobb & Rose, 1973). Subjects in arguably low-stress occupations, such as nuns in a secluded order, show much less of an increase in blood pressure with age than do control women from a local community (Timio et al., 1988).

The link between stress and cholesterol is less clear; however, there is evidence that both naturalistic and laboratory stressors can affect cholesterol and the various lipid fractions in humans (Dimsdale & Herd, 1982). As well as such effects of stress on risk, there is a probable connection between stress and behaviours that increase the risk of CHD. The most obvious is smoking. Many argue that smokers start to smoke in part because it is stress reducing and even more argue that smoking cessation is stress enhancing. There is experimental evidence that smoking can be stress reducing in experienced smokers and Epstein & Perkins (1988) have argued that this may be particularly harmful since it may increase exposure to stressful situations (although this is an argument that can be advanced against many stress management aids) and that smoking increases the cardiovascular reactions to stress and hence increases the risk of hypertension, atherosclerosis and CHD. A similar argument can be made for the possible effects of stress on alcohol consumption and aspects of diet.

Stress also has effects that are at least partially independent of the classical risk factors. The very important studies of Manuck, Clarkson and Kaplan and colleagues (Kaplan et al., 1983) show that social stress has a profound effect on the development of atheroma in the coronary arteries of monkeys in the absence of differences in cholesterol. Studies with pharmacological blocking agents show that this effect is sympathetic in origin (Kaplan et al., 1987). Related effects may operate in humans. For example, there is a whole class of stress-related behaviours which appear to predispose individuals to CHD independently of the main classical risk factors. By far the best known is Type A behaviour, a pattern of behaviour characterised by extreme time pressure, hostility and aggression (Rosenman et al., 1964). The research on Type A will be discussed more fully in conjunction with the literature on its reduction. In brief, studies have shown that Type A and hostility, one of its components, may increase the risk of CHD. In addition anger, or its inhibition, is one of the few behavioural styles that relate to hypertension (Gold & Johnston, 1990). More generally, Friedman & Booth-Kewley (1987) have argued that there is a general "disease prone personality" characterised by anxiety, anger and depression and prey to a variety of diseases. This provocative view is not entirely convincing, partly because the "disease prone personality" appears to overlap with the concept of negative affectivity or neuroticism which has a stronger relationship with symptom reporting than with objective indices of health (Watson & Pennebaker, 1989). Nevertheless it points to a possible increase in the risk of CHD in the generally stress prone. The role of stress-inducing work environments has been pointed out by Karasek with an influential model postulating two important dimensions, demand and latitude. High demand and low decision latitude or control have been shown to be associated with job strain and CHD (Karasek et al., 1988).

In addition to the effects of stress on the long-term risk of CHD, stress also affects the acute risk. Lown and Verrier (see Verrier, 1987) have shown that, in dogs with experimentally induced ischaemia, stress, such as electric shock or anger, reduces the threshold for the induction of potentially fatal arrythmias. In humans it is hard to demonstrate such effects, although anecdotal accounts of stress-induced cardiac deaths abound (Engel, 1971) and epidemiological studies suggest that social stress plays a significant role in sudden death in those with diseased hearts (Ruberman et al., 1984). Electrophysiological studies have shown that the threshold for serious arrhythmias can be lowered by laboratory stressors (Tavazzi, Zotti & Rondanelli, 1986). With advances in measurement it is now possible to study blood flow in the coronary arteries and it is clear that apparently innocuous laboratory stressors, such as mental arithmetic or simulated public speaking, can induce substantial restrictions in coronary blood flow (Rozanski et al., 1988). Stress also affects platelet aggregation and plasma fibrinogen levels, both likely to be involved in atherogenesis and thrombogenesis (Markowe et al., 1985). The immediate psychological precursors of an acute MI have been studied extensively by Appels and colleagues (Appels & Mulder, 1989) who have shown that a combination of fatigue and depression (which they call "vital exhaustion") is common in the year prior to an MI.

It can be seen that stress may play a role in many aspects of the processes leading to CHD. Stress management is usually directed at only one or two specific aspects of the link, perhaps high blood pressure or Type A behaviour. However, there is little in the literature to suggest that the effects of stress are particularly specific and certainly no reason to believe that the effects of stress management will be restricted to only the risk or behaviour that is the primary focus of the intervention. It should therefore be borne in mind that both the effects of stress and of stress management may be pervasive and that this may be important in determining the effects of stress management on CHD. This point will be elaborated after the effects of stress management on specific risk factors have been evaluated.

CLASSICAL RISK FACTORS

Blood pressure

Stress management has been evaluated more thoroughly in the treatment of high blood pressure than in any other cardiovascular risk factor. Since this

---

Note. The section on the use of stress management in the treatment of high blood pressure is based on a paper given at a conference on "Mental stress as a trigger for cardiovascular events" at Veruno, Italy on 19–21 Ocober 1989 and published as a supplement to *Hypertension*.

literature has been reviewed extensively (Johnston, 1982, 1987; Jacob, Wing & Shapiro, 1987) I shall concentrate on providing an overview of the main findings rather than review individual studies.

The form of stress management most often used in the treatment of hypertension is very simple. This is perhaps fortunate given the high prevalence of mild elevations in blood pressure. While different investigators have developed slightly different packages there appears to be a common core involving live, rather than tape-recorded relaxation (Brauer et al., 1979), regular practice of relaxation outside the therapeutic situation, instruction in the application of relaxation in daily life, including before, during and after exposure to stress, and simple counselling in the avoidance and management of stress. A very representative package has been described and most successfully applied by Patel both individually (Patel & North, 1975) and in groups of 8–10 patients (Patel & Marmot, 1988).

Effectiveness in reducing blood pressure

When the literature was reviewed recently (Johnston, 1987) there were 25 published randomised controlled trials of stress management in mild hypertensive patients most of whom had diastolic blood pressure (DBP) of between 90 and 105 mm Hg. In 12 of these studies stress management was reliably better than various control conditions. Johnston (1991) estimated the effects of stress management by averaging the reduction in pressure obtained in the published studies of the technique (prior to September 1989) that had used randomised control conditions. In the studies identified, 823 patients had received stress management, while 578 had received control procedures. The average reduction following stress management in systolic blood pressure (SBP) was 8.8 mm Hg, compared to 3.15 following control treatments. The corresponding figures for DBP were 6.21 and 3.05 mm Hg. It is clear that blood pressure was reduced considerably more effectively by stress management than the control conditions.

The absolute reductions in pressure are sufficient to ensure that the blood pressure of most of the mildly hypertensive patients treated in these studies fell below 90 mm Hg and made it unlikely that they needed drug treatment, particularly as some now argue that moderate reductions in pressure produce the greatest reductions in CHD risk (Alderman et al., 1989). In addition it has been shown that stress management can almost entirely counteract the rise in pressure that occurs when mildly hypertensive patients are taken off long-term diuretic or beta-blocking medication (Patel & Marmot, 1988) or reduce the number of patients on medication by 30% (Lehnert et al., 1987). The long-term follow up of the effectiveness of stress management appears to be generally good with reductions in pressure being found during follow-up periods of from six months (Brauer et al., 1979) to four years (Patel et al., 1985).

Examination of individual studies shows that stress management is more effective than powerful control conditions such as non-directive psychotherapy (Brauer et al., 1979; Taylor et al., 1977; Bali, 1979) and a carefully designed exercise-based placebo which involved as much structure and practice as stress management (Irvine et al., 1986). Contrary results have been reported, the most important and influential of which are related studies reported by Chesney, Agras and colleagues. They found that, in unmedicated mild hypertensives, a variety of stress reduction procedures were no more effective than a simple control procedure (Chesney et al., 1987), while in medicated, but poorly controlled, hypertensives, stress management had a short-term superiority but this disappeared by the end of a two and a half year follow up, because of a reduction in pressure in the control group (Agras et al., 1987). It may be that with some patient samples, perhaps with less severe or less stable hypertension, stress management acts primarily by accelerating a naturally occurring process of pressure normalisation.

Most of the published studies have relied on conventional clinical blood pressure determination. It is well known that the pressure assessed in the clinical situation is only a weak predictor of pressure at other times and, at least in some individuals, is markedly higher than in the home or work place. This is a problem for all therapeutic trials but may be a particular one for stress management. Relaxation and related procedures could lead to reductions in the clinic pressor response without any, or with a much smaller, drop in pressure at other times if patients chose to practice relaxation only when blood pressure was being measured. If pressure remained high at other times then there might be little reduction in the risk of cardiovascular disease. A few investigators have attempted to deal with this by measuring pressure in a wide range of extra-clinic situations including home measurement by the patient (Irvine et al., 1986) professional measurement at the work place (Chesney et al., 1987) and ambulatory measurement with automatic devices while participating in ordinary activities (Southam et al., 1982). Johnston (1991) showed that the average reductions in pressure measured outside the clinic were, like those in the clinic, approximately twice as large following stress management as control interventions. In addition the best study of this to date (Southam et al., 1982; Agras, Southam & Taylor, 1983) showed that stress management lowered pressure measured semi-automatically every 20 minutes in the workplace, both immediately following a course of treatment and 18 months later. A control group did not show such reductions. Very recently van Montfrans et al. (1990) have described a comparison of stress management or a simple form of self-relaxation in which hypertensives had their pressure measured both in the clinic and for 24 hours in daily life, using invasive methods. Pressure, however it was measured, was little affected by either procedure. While this study raises important doubts about the effectiveness of stress management, the failure to find stress management to be effective in the clinic, when so many have, seriously reduces the value of the real life data.

Mechanism

Most studies of stress management have concentrated on the effectiveness of the procedure rather than the mechanisms involved, although a few have examined whether changes in other behavioural risks for hypertension are implicated. There is as yet no convincing evidence that significant changes in other aspects of lifestyle, such as diet or exercise, regularly accompany stress management (Irvine et al., 1986; Patel, Marmot & Terry, 1981). It is therefore reasonable to consider how stress management may operate to lower pressure directly. Johnston (1986) suggests that, expressed as propositions, they include the following.

Relaxation training lowers blood pressure while the patient is relaxing. The repeated short-term lowering of pressure has a long-term beneficial effect on pressure. This simple hypothesis has received surprisingly little support since relaxation training is no more effective than simply sitting still in lowering blood pressure acutely, either in normotensives (Tasto & Huebner, 1976; Lo & Johnston, 1984) or hypertensives (Christoph et al., 1978). At least one study (Irvine et al., 1986) showed reliable long-term effects of stress management but no immediate effect.

Relaxation training reduces the cardiovascular reaction to stress. Since part of the basis for the use of stress management is to reduce the pressor response to stress then it is reasonable to assume that it operates by reducing the repeated response to day-to-day stressors. This has proved difficult to demonstrate. One early study suggested that the pressor response to mental arithmetic and dynamic exercise was reduced following stress management (Patel, 1975) but more recent studies have not confirmed this (Irvine et al., 1986; Jorgensen, Houston & Zurawski, 1981; Zurawski, Smith & Houston, 1987). It may be that investigators have not taken sufficient steps to ensure that patients actually attempt to control their stress response during the artificial laboratory challenges typically used.

Stress management alters neurogenic or hormonal mechanisms involved in the control of blood pressure. Most research on this topic has concentrated on the "stress hormones" or closely related processes. The findings have been mixed. Catecholamines or their breakdown products have been reduced in some (Stone & Deleo, 1976; Cottier, Shapiro & Julius, 1984) but by no means all studies (Brauer et al., 1979; Irvine et al., 1986; McGrady et al., 1981). Patel (Patel, Marmot & Terry, 1981) has shown that plasma aldosterone and renin levels were reduced immediately after treatment but not six months later, although pressure continued to be lowered. Others have reported very mixed findings (Stone & Deleo, 1976; McGrady et al., 1981; Goldstein et al., 1982).

Stress management produces beneficially psychological changes which lead to a reduction in pressure. Although stress management is a psychological treatment there have been surprisingly few studies of the psychological and behavioural changes associated with it. In part this is a technical problem. Hypertensive patients are defined physiologically and not psychologically and hence have few, if any, psychological characteristics in common. It is therefore very difficult to detect psychological change since it may occur in entirely different domains in different patients; for example, while anxious patients may become less anxious and angry patients less irritable, average levels of anxiety or anger in a mixed group of patients may change little. It is therefore not surprising that stress management has no specific effect on negative affects such as anxiety or depression (Irvine et al., 1986) or that if mood change is found it does not relate to reductions in pressure (Wadden, 1984). Recently it has been shown (Steptoe et al., 1987) that four years after stress management patients describe an improvement in several aspects of interpersonal relationships and in enjoyment of life. Bosley & Allen (1989) report that, following a more complex form of stress management, patients use a variety of cognitive coping strategies more frequently than control patients who had discussed stress in non-directive groups.

It is clear that the mechanisms through which stress management lowers pressure are far from understood. While all the mechanisms identified above could doubtless benefit from more, and better focused studies, it is surprising that there has been so little investigation of the psychological effects of this psychological treatment. We urgently need careful behavioural research on the actual processes operating during stress management so that we know which procedures people use and find helpful, whether patients do actually manage stress better or even if they alter their lifestyle either in stress-related or other areas (Johnston, 1986). In a preliminary study Peveler & Johnston (1986) found that relaxation increased the accessibility of positive cognitions, a possible mechhanism for some of the psychological changes thought to follow stress management. If stress management does produce relevant psychological change then these changes must relate to blood pressure reductions through physical mechanism or mechanisms. It is important to understand such mechanisms, but it may be that this will be easier when the main psychological processes are much more clearly specified than they can be at present.

Prediction

Both because of its possible practical value and because it might throw light on mechanisms there is considerable interest in predicting which patients respond best to stress management. Theoretically one would expect that patients showing the greatest psychological effects of stress or with sympathetic involvement in their hypertension would respond best to stress management. So far the yield from this research has been disappointing. Levels of indicators of distress, such as measures of anxiety and depression, do not reliably or consistently predict outcome (Irvine et al., 1986; Zurawski, Smith & Houston, 1987; Wadden, 1983). While some have found that patients with heightened levels of stress-related hormones, such as plasma noradrenaline (NA) (Cottier, Shapiro & Julius, 1984) do best, others have failed to confirm this (Irvine et al., 1986; Blanchard et al., 1989). Cottier, Shapiro & Julius (1984) found that patients with high heart rates, presumably reflecting sympathetic influence, benefited most from stress management. Two studies of biofeedback-based procedures have suggested that patients with slightly elevated levels of urinary cortisol show the largest blood pressure reductions (McGrady et al., 1986; McGrady & Higgins, 1989). These inconsistent findings may well reflect the vast heterogeneity of patients seen in such studies and more clear-cut results might be obtained if subjects were selected to test specific hypotheses, for example, by contrasting patients high and low on noradrenaline, renin, heart rate, anxiety or, even, recent stressful life events.

There appears to be just one reliable predictor of outcome. Patients with the highest pressures prior to treatment show the greatest reduction in pressure. This was first shown in a review by Jacob and colleagues (Jacob, Kramer & Agras, 1977) and succeeding studies have usually confirmed it (eg Agras et al., 1987).

A related topic to prediction is adherence. The primary measure of adherence has been diary measures of how often patients practise relaxation. In general, patients carry out relaxation regularly, at least early in treatment, but this is a poor predictor of outcome and indeed in one study was negatively related to outcome (Irvine et al., 1986). In the latter case patients were recording their own pressure daily and may have responded to a failure of blood pressure to drop with an ineffectual increase in the amount of time spent relaxing. A study of the long-term effects of stress management (Steptoe et al., 1987) showed that very few patients still practised relaxation four years after training but there was a suggestion that those who did practise, even very infrequently, showed greater reductions in pressure than those who had stopped completely.

Effects on coronary heart disease

Mild elevations in blood pressure are controlled in the hope of reducing the risk of cardiovascular disease. Stress management is advocated, in part, because of the disappointing record of antihypertensive drugs in achieving this end. For stress management to be strongly recommended then it should be at least as good as drugs in this respect and, hopefully, better. Since it has been estimated that 18 000 people need to be studied for five years to determine whether antihypertensive drugs reduced the risk of CHD in mild hypertension (Medical Research Council Working Party, 1985) it is not surprising that few adequate studies of the effects of stress management on cardiovascular disease have been carried out. However, Patel and colleagues have provided some interesting pointers. They treated nearly 100 men who were high on at least two of the three main risk factors, raised blood pressure, raised blood cholesterol or cigarette smoking, and followed them for four years (Patel et al., 1985). Compared to a randomised untreated control group of similar size these men experienced reliably fewer new cardiac events. In a subsequent study with only a one-year follow up a similar finding was reported, although it was not reliable in this case (Patel & Marmot, 1988).

Cholesterol

The effects of stress management on blood cholesterol or the various lipid fractions has not been the subject of extensive study, possibly because they are more obviously linked to diet than stress. Two studies specifically directed at the effects of stress management on lipids appear to show that meditation (Cooper & Aygen, 1979) and relaxation (Carson et al., 1988) reduced cholesterol and low-density lipoprotein (which carries most of the cholesterol in the blood and is considered most damaging). Unfortunately neither study had a randomised control group. Cholesterol has been measured in studies primarily directed at lowering blood pressure. Patel et al. (1985) showed a short-term reduction in patients with elevated cholesterol given dietary advice and stress management compared to dietary advice alone. There were no differences in weight or self-reported diet between the two groups. In a latter study a non-significant tendency for stress management to reduce cholesterol in those with initially high levels (more than 7.2 mmol/l) was noted (Patel & Marmot, 1988). Lehnert et al. (1987) found that a complex form of stress management (which reduced the need for antihypertensive medication) did not enhance the modest decrease in cholesterol associated with an inpatient rehabilitation programme. Blood lipids have also been measured in many of the studies of Type A behaviour modification with very mixed results. Cholesterol, the lipid fractions and triglycerides have variously been unaffected (Friedman et al., 1986), improved, at least in subjects who showed behaviour change (Gill et al., 1985) or even worsened (Levenkron et al., 1983) by procedures that altered Type A behaviour.

There is, therefore, at best rather mixed support for the use of stress management in lowering cholesterol. It may be important that the positive findings were found in the three studies in which cholesterol was either the main or an important secondary focus of the intervention. In such studies other factors such as diet that could also reduce cholesterol may have been more tightly controlled and the study therefore more sensitive to the effects of stress management. Clearly further work is required on this aspect of cholesterol reduction.

Smoking

While most would agree that smoking is stress or affect related there has been little systematic work on stress management in the reduction of smoking or, perhaps more critically, the prevention of relapse. It is unlikely that stress management alone would have a widespread relevance in smoking cessation and other more conventional techniques will remain the mainstay of smoking cessation (Jarvis, 1989). However, Epstein & Perkins (1988) have argued cogently that stress and smoking may be interrelated in the production of CHD and that availability and use of a coping response reduce relapse (Shiffman, 1982). Stress reduction may ease both the stressful effects of smoking cessation and reduce the likelihood of smoking as a response to other stressors. Patel et al. (1985) have claimed that, in men at heightened risk for CHD, stress management reduced the number of cigarettes smoked for at least six months after treatment. However, after four years there was no difference between the treated and untreated subjects, primarily because the control subjects had also reduced their smoking in the intervening period. While only limited weight can be given to a single study, this finding is of interest, particularly as it was associated with a reduction in CHD (see above).

PSYCHOLOGICAL RISK FACTORS

Type A behaviour

Description and status as a risk factor

Type A behaviour, a mixture of intense competitiveness, feelings of being under strong time pressure and readily provoked hostility, has had fluctuating fortunes as a risk factor for CHD. Originally proposed on the basis of acute clinical observation of patients with CHD, first cross-sectional and then longitudinal studies showed it to be an independent risk factor for CHD (see Jenkins, 1978, for a review of early studies). The Western Collaborative Group Study (WCGS), a landmark in the study of Type A, and indeed in the whole field of behavioural epidemiology, showed that healthy middle-aged men who were initially Type A were twice as likely to suffer an MI in the subsequent eight and a half years than were men showing the alternative, Type B, pattern (Rosenman et al., 1975). This remained the case when blood cholesterol, blood pressure and smoking status were controlled. Since then both positive (Haynes, Feinleib & Kannel, 1980) and negative (Shekelle et al., 1985) prospective studies have been published. Recently, even the WCGS has been weakened by the report that Type A respondents in that study who suffered an MI were *less* likely to experience a reinfarction (Ragland & Brand, 1988a) and that a 22-year follow up of the original sample failed to find a reliable relationship between Type A behaviour and death from CHD (Ragland & Brand, 1988b).

Type A behaviour is not captured by any one simple category or dimension, and factor analytic and other studies have shown that it is composed of various factors, the actual combination being very much dependent on the measure of Type A examined (Jenkins, Zyzanski & Rosenman, 1971; Musante et al., 1983).

Measures derived from versions of the original structured interview appear to give a more complete and useful measure of the Type A complex than questionnaires, which are limited to respondent self-report. It is now normal to separate speech style from speech content and to derive measures both of the complete Type A complex and the respondents' proneness to hostility and method of expressing anger (Dembroski & Costa, 1988).

The multifactorial nature of the Type A complex obviously allows the possibility that only a subset of the components are predictive of CHD, either alone or interactively. Dembroski, MacDougall and colleagues have shown, in a commendably coherent research programme on patients undergoing coronary angiography, that, while the complete Type A complex (Global Type A in their terms) is an indifferent correlate of coronary artery disease (CAD), "potential for hostility" is a reliable predictor across many data sets (MacDougall et al., 1985; Dembroski et al., 1985). The relationship between the method of expressing anger ("anger-in" and "anger-out") and CAD is less consistent. Similar methods of scoring the components of the structured interview have also been applied to the two main North American prospective data sets which included the structured interview. The WCGS (Hecker et al., 1988) and the multiple risk factor intervention trial (MRFIT) (Dembroski et al., 1989) study. In both cases it is claimed that potential for hostility predicted CHD independently of both Type A and the biological risk factors. A certain caution about such extensive *post hoc* analyses of pre-existing data sets is in order. Nevertheless these findings and similar, although very variable, findings relating hostility on the MMPI derived Cook–Medley (Cook & Medley, 1954) scale to CHD suggest that hostility is a component of stress-related behaviours that should be included in Type A behaviour modification programmes (Gold & Johnston, 1990).

What should be changed?

The apparent complexity of Type A behaviour poses a rather nice problem for those attempting to reduce CHD by behaviour modification. Interventions can, in a pragmatic, piecemeal fashion, attempt to modify all identiable aspects of the Type A behaviour complex, ie speech style and speed, rate of eating and walking, competitiveness in a variety of situations, aspects of hostility, etc. This might well be as inefficient as it is inelegant and has not found many advocates. Most successful investigators have adopted a more theory-driven approach. Some have focused treatment on the possible underlying assumptions which are thought to produce the diverse range of behaviours seen in Type A (Price, 1982). Others have adopted a helpfully simplified position, such as Roskies' (1987) contention that Type A can be seen as a form of behvioural hyper-reactivity mirroring the physiological reactivity that some believe forms the link between Type A and CHD. In practice the most successful approaches use a combination of behavioural and cognitive approaches to alter clients' responses to stress and their perception of the stressful situation. Some also attempt to alter persistent underlying assumptions. Any approach should at the very least attempt to produce alterations in Global Type A and potential for hostility. It is not clear whether anger-in should be modified.

Interventions

Effects on Type A behaviour.   Many of the earliest studies of Type A change were little more than preliminary demonstration projects and will not be reviewed. A review of the methodology of such studies can be found in Levenkron & Moore (1988) and a meta-analysis of the early studies in Nunes, Frank & Kornfeld (1987). The earliest studies relied primarily on questionnaire measures of Type A behviour. This is inadequate, firstly because questionnaires are poor measures of the most important, coronary prone, aspects of Type A behaviour and, secondly, because they are readily open to falsification by patients seeking to show that they have changed their behaviour. Despite these limitations studies of interest include Jenni & Wollersheim's (1979) demonstration that a version of cognitive therapy had a greater effect on self-reported Type A behaviour than stress management training involving the use of relaxation training to combat the effects of stressful imagery. Thurman (1985) also found cognitive methods more effective in altering self-reported Type A behaviour than simply informing subjects about Type A and the desirability of change. Levenkron et al. (1983) describe a comparison of a combined cognitive, behvioural and relaxation-based treatment in a small number of Type A executives. The combined package was more effective than either a minimal treatment or a non-directive group treatment in which information on the need to change Type A behaviour was given. The latter is a powerful control condition since a group of Type A executives would be likely to produce a number of practical methods of Type A change during focused group discussion.

The most satisfactory study of Type A change in a healthy population is undoubtedly the Montreal study of Type A executives (Roskies et al., 1986). Three treatments were compared in 120 middle-aged executives with marked Type A behaviour and excessive cardiovascular responses to laboratory stressors. These were a comprehensive stress management package, and either aerobic exercise (mainly jogging) or weight training. The stress management package, clearly described in a most useful manual (Roskies, 1987), sought to teach coping skills, including relaxation, and train the client to identify stress and modify inappropriate responses. While both forms of physical training had the expected effects on fitness and strength only the cognitive–behavioural intervention led to substantial reductions in Type A behaviour. Most importantly virtually all aspects of Type A were changed including Global Type A, potential for hostility and the various speech stylistics.

The almost complete ineffectiveness of the aerobic exercise programme in reducing Type A behaviour is significant since aerobic exercise has been used in programmes offered to Type A individuals. It is not always clear whether such programmes are directed at altering the behaviour pattern or alleviating its harmful physiological effects. Blumenthal et al. (1980) and Howard et al. (1986) both found that aerobic exercise reduced Type A behaviour. It is noteworthy that Howard et al. were studying not the usual population of young-middle-age executives but an older group on the verge of retirement. In contrast to their earlier findings, when Blumenthal et al. (1988) compared aerobic exercise with a control condition involving strength and flexibility training, they could find no specific alteration in Type A behaviour. In conjunction with Roskies et al.'s findings, this suggests that aerobic exercise, while it may be beneficial in other ways, does not have a specific effect on Type A behaviour.

The pre-eminent study in this area is undoubtedly the Recurrent Coronary Prevention Project. This extensive study has been described in a series of publications (Friedman et al., 1982, 1984, 1986). It involved almost 1000 patients who had experienced at least one MI and were interested in joining a stress reduction programme. Patients who for one reason or another could not be randomly allocated were placed in a non-treatment group while the remainder were randomly allocated on a 2:1 ratio into either a cognitive–behavioural Type A reduction programme plus cardiological care or high-quality cardiological care alone; 592 received the Type A intervention and 270 the cardiological care. Over the four and a half years of the study patients in both conditions met regularly in groups of approximately 10 members. Patients receiving cardiological care alone met an average of 25 times compared to 38 in the behaviour change condition. In the cardiological care condition the group sessions concentrated on the medical management of CHD although some time was spent on the psychological effects of heart disease, but not its prevention. The behaviour change group, while also concerned with the patients' medical management, was primarily aimed at reducing all aspects of Type A behaviour. The methods used were comprehensive, covering cognitive and behaviour change, responses to stress and core assumptions thought to underlie Type A behaviour.

Behavioural outcome was assessed using a videotaped version of the structured interview and a specially constructed questionnaire completed by the patient, and, in the behaviour change condition, by the patient's spouse and an informant at their work place. Questionnaire assessments were carried out annually and with the structured interview on three occasions. While patients in both conditions showed reductions in Type A this was always reliably greater in the behaviour change group. During the programme 17.5% of the behaviour change group displayed a marked reduction in Type A behaviour compared to only 3.7% of the control group (Friedman et al., 1984). Both Global Type A and hostility were affected by the intervention. Participants' Type A behaviour as assessed by spouse and informant also changed following the intervention. The behaviour change persisted for at least one year after the end of the intervention (Friedman et al., 1987).

In a subsidiary study Friedman et al. (1987) showed that patients in the erstwhile control group showed a substantial reduction in Type A when they received a behavioural change programme lasting one year. In a further controlled study the same team (Gill et al., 1985) showed that these methods could be used with equal success in healthy middle-aged men, senior military officers at staff college. In this sample it was also shown that colleagues perceived greater Type A change in those receiving the behaviour change programme but no reduction in their job competence, countering the fear that Type A behaviour is a necessary part of effectiveness and its alteration might impose an unacceptable cost.

To summarise the findings on the behavioural effects on Type A change: there appears no doubt that comprehensive cognitive–behavioural stress reduction programmes can produce reductions in Type A behaviour as assessed either by questionnaire or the structure interview. All the components so far reliably identified as predictive of CHD can be changed. There is no clear evidence on which component of the complex treatments carries most power or which package is most effective. The short-term programme described by Roskies has much to commend it since it appears to be of the same order of effectiveness as the more prolonged programme used by Friedman and Thorsen and has been much better described (Roskies, 1987).

Many questions remain unanswered, the most pressing concern the measurement of Type A change and its long-term persistence. All the studies to date have relied primarily on questionnaire or interview methods. The difficulties with the questionnaires have already been noted. The structured interview also has severe limitations. It is likely that subjects who are knowledgeable about Type A behaviour, as they would be after most of the interventions, could alter their responses in the interview without these changes generalising to other situations. While information by participants' partners and colleagues are of value they correlate very poorly with the subjects' own perception of their behaviour (Friedman et al., 1984) and should be supplemented with direct measures of Type A behaviour in real life situations. The second pressing problem is the persistence of the changes in behviour produced by these programmes. To date there have been no reports of the long-term follow up of patients once therapy has ceased. This is obviously needed.

Physiological mechanisms

It is important to demonstrate that Type A change programmes modify the biological mechanisms relating Type A and CHD as well as behaviour. This enterprise is hampered by our ignorance of the linking step or steps. Two approaches have been adopted. The first is to measure change in other risk factors for CHD, such as blood cholesterol and blood pressure, despite the epidemiological evidence that they are not related to Type A behaviour, the second to assess reductions in the cardiovascular and hormonal response to laboratory stressors. The latter is more reasonable since such hyper-reactivity is the most popular candidate as the biological mechanism linking Type A and CHD, although the very patchy empirical support for this view suggests that its acceptance owes much to the lack of a vigorously promoted alternative (Myrtek & Greenlee, 1984).

By and large, alteration in Type A behaviour does not produce reliable reductions in cholesterol or the various lipid fractions (see the cholesterol section). The findings on reactivity are equally negative. Levenkron et al. (1983) could show no effect of their Type A intervention on the cardiovascular response to a laboratory stressor, although they did show a specific reduction in free fatty acid, important both as an indicator of sympathetic activity and as a determinant of blood lipids. Roskies et al. (1986) carefully selected their subjects so that they were both Type A and cardiovascularly hyper-reactive. Despite this they failed to find any effect of stress management on reactivity, perhaps because of habituation to the laboratory stressors. These findings are very similar to the effects of stress management on cardiovascular reactions in hypertensives. Blumenthal et al. (1988) have shown that aerobic exercise, which did not alter Type A behaviour, did reduce the cardiovascular response to laboratory stressors. This might offer a method of ameliorating the risks associated with the behaviour pattern.

At present, therefore, there is no convincing direct evidence that Type A change programmes can alter the biological substrate relating Type A to CHD. However, until there is clearer evidence on the physiological correlates of Type A behviour it is not clear whether our current failures are critical or where to look next.

Reduction of CHD

The only adequate study of the effect of Type A change on CHD is the Recurrent Coronary Prevention Program of Friedman et al. (1984, 1986). All the patients in this study had experienced at least one MI and were therefore at high risk of a recurrence. Patients were followed up for four and a half years, whether they remained in treatment or not (ie the "intention to treat principle" was used). Almost from the start of the study there was a reduction in the reinfarction rate in the Type A change condition. Over the complete study (Friedman et al., 1986) the average annual reinfarction rate was 4.97% in the control condition and 2.96% in the behaviour change condition. This effect was seen most clearly for total and non-fatal reinfarctions, although it has been claimed that fatal reinfarctions were also reduced in all but the first year of the study. At the end of the study, treatment and control groups did not differ on a variety of relevant, potentially confounding, measures such as medication, arrhythmias and serum cholesterol. Subsidiary analyses showed that the Type A intervention was effective in reducing the reinfarction rate in patients who were receiving vigorous additional medical treatments, including beta blockade and coronary artery bypass graft surgery, but was ineffective in patients with severe pre-treatment MIs (Powell & Thoresen, 1988). In a subsequent small study a proportion of the control subjects took part in a behavioural change programme and showed an apparent reduction in reinfarction rate.

This study is immensely encouraging for the use of stress reduction measures in the prevention of CHD. An exclusively behavioural intervention directed at a non-biological risk factor reduced reinfarction rate by approximately 50%. Naturally some issues remain problematic or unresolved. The participants may not be representative of post-MI patients. They were self-selected volunteers who were interested in a stress reduction programme and indeed over 95% were reported to be Type A (Friedman et al., 1982). Although there were no important pre-treatment differences between the conditions on factors related to the patients' cardiac state there was a non-significant difference in reinfarction rate favouring the experimental group in the first three months of the study. This may be before substantial Type A change had occurred or could affect CHD and must raise a *slight* doubt about the complete comparability of the groups. It is, however, virtually impossible to believe that a 100% difference in reinfarction rate could occur by chance. Finally this was a very complex intervention which must surely have affected a wider range of stress-related behaviours than Type A. The therapeutic effect may therefore represent the alteration in Type A and other stress-related behaviours. As psychological measurement was confined to Type A, this is purely speculative but is consistent with the rather profound effects on reinfarction rate that appear to result from rather limited reductions in Type A behaviour, a risk factor that may not event predict reinfarction consistently (Ragland & Brand, 1988a).

A stress monitoring programme

Most forms of stress management used in the prevention of CHD are either very general and applicable to a wide range of stressors (such as the relaxation-based methods favoured in the treatment of high blood pressure) or are directed at a specific source of stress thought to be particularly likely to cause or exacerbate CHD (such as Type A behaviour). Of course, individuals have very diverse sources of stress which may well not be covered by the specific interventions or they may fail to see the relevance of the more general interventions to some of their problems. In an important, if methodologically suspect, study Frasure-Smith & Prince (1985, 1987, 1989) have attempted to use simple individualised forms of stress reduction in the management of patients following an MI.

Following discharge from hospital post-MI patients were telephoned monthly for 12 months and an interview form of the general hospital questionnaire (GHQ, a meausre of psychological distress) (Goldberg, 1978) administered. They were also contacted if they were readmitted to hospital. All respondents who were above a modest cut-off on the GHQ were then contacted by a nurse and the specific sources of stress explored. Approximately 230 patients were randomly allocated (but see below) to stress monitoring and a similar number to routine care. Slightly over half the patients were visited by the nurse, usually because of an elevated GHQ score. Almost half of the patients visited were dealt with entirely by the nurse, while other health care professions were involved in the remainder of cases as required. Most of the problems related to the effects of heart disease on the patient's life or associated anxiety and depression.

Psychological outcome was assessed by repeating the GHQ after one year. The effect on readmission and further CHD were variously assessed over periods from one to more than seven years. GHQ scores were reliably reduced by the intervention while there were rather complex effects on the measures of physical health. The intervention did not affect the number or duration of admissions to hospital but over the first two years of the study cardiac deaths, particularly sudden cardiac death, was reliably less common in the stress monitoring condition. The effect peaked at approximately 18 months after the infarction, 6 months after the intervention ceased. The intervention had no apparent immediate effect on acute MIs but differences favouring stress monitoring emerged during the second year of follow up and remained significant until the end of the study.

Before considering the implications of these findings a difficulty with this study must be acknowledged. Contrary to normal practice, patients were randomised to either treatment or control group before informed consent was obtained. Patients were then told the condition assigned and asked to consent. If all patients agree to join the study then this procedure is satisfactory. However, if patients refuse to take part then they can, in effect, choose their treatment. The advantages of random allocation are thus lost. In addition, in Frasure-Smith and Prince's study more patients rejected the stress monitoring programme than normal treatment, perhaps because of the heavier demands it made on them. This may have led to blue-collar workers being under-represented in the stress monitoring condition; 53.1% of the control group were blue-collar workers compared to only 35.4% of the experimental subjects. As socio-economic status is predictive of CHD this could have improved the prognosis of the experimental group quite independently of the effects of the stress monitoring programme.

It is also possible that the findings are the result of a secondary effect of stress management on compliance. Medication use was not closely monitored in this study and it is at least plausible that the group receiving extra attention would be more likely to take their medication. Consistent with this possibility is the finding that the effect of the intervention on cardiac death was greatest in those prescribed beta blocking medication, which reduces mortality after an MI.

I have considered this study in some detail because despite its faults, which its authors acknowledge, it involves an important, innovative and above all practical intervention that could be applied in clinical settings to those patients who needed it. It appears to require little in the way of specialist training for the nurse/counsellors and seldom calls on rare and expensive resources. It is to be hoped that further controlled trials building on Frasure-Smith and Prince's efforts are underway.

Stress reduction and dietary change

Coronary heart disease is the product of many processes which are related to the various independent risk factors described earlier. There are many well-known studies describing attempts to alter several of the biological risk factors, such as the community interventions directed at altering diet, blood pressure and smoking habits (Johnson, 1989a), but few attempts to combine stress management with the alteration of other risks.

Lovibond, Birrell & Langeluddecke (1986) offered a package of stress management, smoking cessation, exercise and weight reduction to high-risk middle-aged men. Substantial reductions in most risk factors were achieved, particularly with the most complex and vigorous of the three treatments compared. Ornish et al. (1983) explored the effects of stress management, a vegan diet and other lifestyle changes on patients with very well-documented CHD. Forty-eight patients were randomly assigned either to continue with their normal routine or to spend 14 days in rural retreat where they ate a vegan diet and received 5 hours of stress management per day. The stress management was based primarily on relaxation and meditation. At the end of this period the experimental group were superior to the control group on a wide range of measures, including performance on a standardised exercise test, frequency of angina, amount of medication, plasma cholesterol and triglyceride and measures of the extent to which the efficiency of the heart has been compromised by disease. In a very recent study Ornish et al. (1990) examined the effects of a similar intervention over a 12-month period. As well as replicating most of the effects previously reported, they found a reversal in the extent of occlusion of the coronary arteries, as determined by coronary angiography. This is a highly important finding since it indicates a reversal of the pathology underlying CHD. Unfortunately there are as yet no studies examining the components of this complex package. The effects could be due to the vegan diet, the relaxation-based stress management or, as Ornish presumably believes, the combined effects of both these interventions. The latter is an attractive possibility.

MECHANISMS OF CORONARY HEART DISEASE PREVENTION THROUGH STRESS MANAGEMENT

In earlier sections I have described a variety of interventions that lead to changes in blood pressure, to a lesser extent smoking and blood cholesterol, in Type A behaviour pattern and its components, and in the diffuse stress responses detected by the GHQ. In some instances these changes were associated with reduction in hard evidence of CHD. What mechanisms are likely to be responsible for these changes? At first sight this might seem a trivial question. Let us take high blood pressure as an example. If stress management directed at lowering blood pressure is successful and if the treated group show a reduction in CHD (as Patel et al., 1985 report) then it appears obvious to ascribe the reduction in CHD to the change in blood pressure. However, this is almost certainly incorrect.

Reductions in blood pressure in this and similar studies are most unlikely to have detectable effects on CHD in the small samples studied. Stress has pervasive effects on a wide range of biological and behavioural systems. In as far as these systems are involved in CHD and if stress management affects a number of them simultaneously, then the effects on CHD will be much greater than can be expected from examining the change in any one risk factor. Risk factors are multiplicative in their effects (Johnston, 1989b; Perkins, 1989) and even quite slight alterations in a number of risk factors may lead to useful reductions in CHD risk. It may be significant that Patel et al. treated patients at heightened risk on a number of factors and showed reliable change on smoking, serum cholesterol, and some psychological measures of stress and coping, as well as blood pressure.

Furthermore it is possible that stress-related processes are more directly involved in the enhancement of CHD risk than the conventional biological risk factors. For example, Kjeldsen et al. (1989) in attempting to explain the ineffectiveness of antihypertensive medication in reducing CHD in the mildly hypertensive, present a well-documented case for the proposition that mild elevations in pressure are not a cause of CHD but are a correlate of a sympathetically mediated platelet over activity which contributes to athero-genesis. It can readily be seen that stress reduction procedures might affect blood pressure *and* other sympathetically mediated processes while a more specific agent, such as some antihypertensive drugs, would affect the correlate, blood pressure, but not the cause.

Stress management might also affect the acute processes shortly before an MI. The extreme rapidity with which the Type A change programme reduced MI and cardiac death (Friedman et al. 1986, 1987) suggests that much of the effect of the intervention must have been on the immediate precursors of the cardiac event, by affecting factors such as platelet aggregation, thrombus formation, the occurrence of fatal arrhythmias or, at the psychological level, vital exhaustion (Appels & Mulder, 1989). A similar explanation can be advanced to explain Frasure-Smith & Prince's (1989) finding of a fast-acting effect of stress reduction on sudden cardiac death rather than acute MI. There is, as yet, little direct evidence that stress mangement can affect these processes, although Gruen (1975), in an isolated study, found that brief psychotherapy during hospitalisation for an MI leads to a reduction in serious arrhythmias.

Cost effectiveness

Stress management has to be cost effective if it is to be recommended for widespread use. As yet there are no formal studies examining its cost effectiveness over a range of cardiovascular conditions or a realistic time span. It is obvious that over the period of delivery many forms of stress management will be more expensive than drug therapy and less expensive than surgery. The critical question is the cost over the period of effectiveness. If the effects persist then stress management becomes highly cost effective (as some argue expensive treatments like cardiac surgery can be, Weinstein & Stason, 1985). The positive reports of long-term effectiveness (eg Patel et al., 1985; Frasure-Smith & Prince, 1989) suggests that stress management may indeed be cost effective.

CONCLUSION

The use of stress management in the reduction of CHD is at an interesting stage. Basic research is increasing, showing that stress-related processes play a part in the genesis of coronary artery and coronary heart disease, including the processes of atherogenesis and thrombogenesis and the production of serious arrhythmias. A variety of forms of stress management, some simple, some complex, have been shown to affect these disease processes and, in a rather small number of studies, lead to a reduction in CHD. Much needs to be done on the effectiveness of different forms of stress management in producing behavioural and cognitive change. Equally critically, the effects of stress management on the processes thought to cause the various manifestations of CHD must be demonstrated. This requires careful controlled clinical and laboratory study of the effects of stress reduction on individual risk factors and their interaction. This should include the process thought to be involved in the final stages of CHD as well as in the prevention of atherosclerosis.

As far as current practice is concerned, it is best to be cautiously innovative. It is most unlikely that stress management will prove harmful, unless it is used in preference to a treatment known to be effective. It is therefore applicable as an adjunct to other interventions, perhaps particularly in those under stress or displaying stress-related behaviour patterns. The available evidence suggests that it is likely to be an appropriate intervention for Type A or hostile individuals with diseased hearts and for the mildy hypertensive, perhaps in conjunction with other behavioural interventions directed at weight reduction and alcohol consumption. The multiplicative nature of risk factors suggests that stress management may also be of most benefit in patients at heightened risk on a number of factors, both biological and psychological.

REFERENCES

Agras, W. S., Southam, M. A. & Taylor, B. C. (1983). Long-term persistence of relaxation-induced blood pressure lowering during the working day. *Journal of Consulting and Clinical Psychology*, **51**, 792–794.

Agras, W. S., Taylor, C. B., Kraemer, H. C., Southam, M. A. & Schneider, J. A. (1987). Relaxation training for essential hypertension at the worksite: II. The poorly controlled hypertensive. *Psychosomatic Medicine*, **49**, 264–273.

Alderman, M. H., Wee, L. O., Madhavan, S. & Cohen, H. (1989). Treatment-induced blood pressure reduction and the risk of myocardial infarction. *Journal of the American Medical Association*, **262**, 920–924.

Appels, A. & Mulder, P. (1989). Fatigue and heart disease. The association between "vital exhaustion" and past, present and future coronary heart disease. *Journal of Psychosomatic Research*, 33, 727–738.

Bali, L. R. (1979). Long term effect of relaxation on blood pressure and anxiety levels in essential hypertensive males: A controlled study. *Psychosomatic Medicine*, 41, 637–646.

Blanchard, E. B., McCoy, G. C., Berger, M., Musso, A., Pallmeyer, T. P., Gerardi, R., Gerardi, M. A. & Pangburn, L. (1989). A controlled comparison of thermal biofeedback and relaxation training in the treatment of essential hypertension. IV: Prediction of short-term clinical outcome. *Behaviour Therapy*, 20, 405–415.

Blumenthal, J. A., Emery, C. F., Walsh, M. A., Cox, D. R., Kuhn, C. M., Williams, R. B. & Williams, R. S. (1988). Exercise training in healthy Type A middle-aged men: Effects on behavioural and cardiovascular responses. *Psychosomatic Medicine*, 50, 418–433.

Blumenthal, J. S., Williams, R. S., Williams, R. B. & Wallace, A. G. (1980). Effects of exercise on the Type A (coronary prone) behaviour pattern. *Psychosomatic Medicine*, 42, 289–296.

Bosley, F. & Allen, T. W. (1989). Stress management training for hypertensives: Cognitive and physiological effects. *Journal of Behavioral Medicine*, 12, 77–89.

Brauer, A., Horlick, L. F., Nelson, B., Farquhar, J. W. & Agras, W. S. (1979). Relaxation therapy for essential hypertension: A veterans administration out patients study. *Journal of Behavioural Medicine*, 2, 21–29.

Carson, M. A., Hathaway, A., Tuohey, J. P. & Mckay, B. M. (1988). The effect of a relaxation technique on coronary risk factors. *Behavioral Medicine*, 14, 71–77.

Chesney, M. A., Black, G. W., Swan, G. E. & Ward, M. M. (1987). Relaxation training for essential hypertension at the worksite: I. The untreated mild hypertensive. *Psychosomatic Medicine*, 49, 250–263.

Christoph, P., Luborsky, L., Kron, R. & Fishman, H. (1978). Blood pressure: Heart rate and respiratory responses to a single session of relaxation: A partial replication. *Journal of Psychosomatic Research*, 22, 493–501.

Cobb, S. & Rose, R. (1973). Hypertension, peptic ulcer, and diabetes in air traffic controllers. *Journal of the American Medical Association*, 224, 489–492.

Cook, W. W. & Medley, D. M. (1954). Proposed hostility and pharisaic virtue scales for the MMPI. *Journal of Applied Psychology*, 38, 414–418.

Cottier, C., Shapiro, K. & Julius, S. (1984). Treatment of mild hypertension with progressive muscle relaxation: Predictive value of indexes of sympathetic tone. *Archives of International Medicine*, 144, 1954–1958.

Dembroski, T. M. & Costa, P. T. (1988). Assessment of coronary prone behaviour: A current overview. *Annals of Behavioral Medicine*, 10, 60–70.

Dembroski, T. M., MacDougall, J. M., Costa, P. T. & Grandts, G. A. (1989). Components of hostility as predictors of sudden death and myocardial infarction in the multiple risk factor intervention trial. *Psychosomatic Medicine*, 51, 514–522.

Dembroski, T. M., MacDougall, J. M., Williams, R. B., Haney, T. L. and Blumenthal, J. A. (1985). Components of Type A, hostility, and anger-in: relationship to angiographic findings. *Psychosomatic Medicine*, 47, 219–233.

Dimsdale, J. E. & Herd, J. A. (1982). Variability of plasma lipids in response to emotional arousal. *Psychosomatic Medicine*, 44, 413–430.

Engel, G. L. (1971). Sudden and rapid death during psychological stress: Folklore or folk wisdom? *Annals of Internal Medicine*, 74, 771–782.

Epstein, L. H. & Perkins, K. A. (1988). Smoking, stress, and coronary heart disease. *Journal of Consulting and Clinical Psychology*, 56, 342–349.

Frasure-Smith, N. & Prince, R. (1985). The Ischemic Heart Disease Life Stress

Monitoring Program: Possible therapeutic mechanisms. *Psychology and Health*, **1**, 273-285.

Frasure-Smith, N. & Prince, R. (1989). Long-term follow up of the Ischemic Heart Disease Life Stress Monitoring Program. *Psychosomatic Medicine*, **51**, 485-513.

Friedman, H. S. & Booth-Kewley, S. (1987). The "disease prone personality": A meta-analytic view of a construct. *American Psychologist*, **42**, 539-555.

Friedman, M., Powell, L. H., Thoresen, C. E., Ulmer, D., Price, V., Gill, J. J., Thompson, L., Rabin, D. D., Brown, B., Breall, W. S., Levy, R. & Bourg, E. (1987). Effect of discontinuance of Type A counselling on Type A behaviour and cardiac recurrence rate of post myocardial infarction patients. *American Heart Journal*, **114**, 483-490.

Friedman, M., Thoresen, C. E., Gill, C. E., Ulmer, D., Thompson, L., Powell, L., Price, V., Elek, S. R., Rabin, D. D., Breall, W. S., Piaget, G., Dixon, T., Bourg, E., Levy, R. A. & Tasto, D. L. (1982) Feasibility of altering Type A behaviour patterns after myocardial infarction: Recurrent coronary prevention project study: Methods, baseline results and preliminary findings. *Circulation*, **66**, 83-92.

Friedman, M., Thoresen, C. E., Gill, J. J., Powell, L. H., Ulmer, D., Thompson, L., Price, V. A., Rabin, D. D., Breall, W. S., Dixon, T., Levy, R. & Bourg, E. (1984). Alteration of Type A behaviour and reduction in cardiac recurrences in postmyocardial infarction patients. *American Heart Journal*, **108**, 237-248.

Friedman, M., Thoresen, C. D., Gill, J. J., Ulmer, D., Powell, L. H., Price, V. A., Brown, B., Thompson, L., Arbin, D. D., Breall, W. S., Bourg, E., Levy, R. & Dixon, T. (1986). Alteration of Type A behaviour and its effect on cardiac recurrences in post myocardial infarction patients: Summary results of the recurrent coronary prevention project. *American Heart Journal*, **112**, 653-665.

Gill, J. J., Price, V. A., Friedman, M., Thoresen, C. E., Powell, L. H., Ulmer, D., Brown, B. & Drews, F. R. (1985). Reduction of Type A behaviour in healthy middle-aged American officers. *American Heart Journal*, **110**, 503-514.

Gold, A. & Johnston, D. W. (1990). Does anger relate to hypertension and heart disease? In P. Bennett, M. Spurgeon & J. Weinman (Eds), *Current Developments in Health Psychology*. London: Harwood, pp. 105-127.

Goldberg, D. (1978). *Manual of the General Health Questionnaire*. Oxford: NFER.

Goldstein, I. B., Shapiro, D., Thananopavarn, C. & Sambhi, M. P. (1982). Comparison of drug and behavioural treatments of essential hypertension. *Health and Psychology*, **1**, 7-26.

Gruen, W. (1975). Effects in brief psychotherapy during the hospitalization period on the recovery process in heart attacks. *Journal of Clinical and Consulting Psychology*, **43**, 223-232.

Haynes, S. G., Feinleib, M. & Kannel, W. (1980). The relationship of psychosocial factors to coronary heart disease in the Framingham study: III. Eight year incidence of coronary heart disease. *American Journal of Epidemiology*, **111**, 37-58.

Hecker, M. H. L., Chesney, M. A., Black, G. W. & Frautschi, N. (1988). Coronary-prone behaviors in the Western Collaborative Group Study. *Psychosomatic Medicine*, **50**, 153-164.

Herd, J. A. (1984). Cardiovascular disease and hypertension. In W. D. Gentry (Ed.), *Handbook of Behavioral Medicine*. New York: Guilford Press, pp. 221-281.

Howard, J. H. Rechnitzer, P. A., Cunningham, D. A. & Donner, A. P. (1986). Change of Type A behaviour a year after retirement. *The Gerontologist*, **26**, 643-649.

Irvine, J., Johnston, D. W., Jenner, D. & Marie, G. V. (1986). Relaxation and stress management in the treatment of essential hypertension. *Journal of Psychosomatic Research*, **30**, 437-450.

Jacob, R. G., Kramer, H. G. & Agras, W. S. (1977). Relaxation therapy in the treatment of hypertension. *Archives of General Psychiatry*, **34**, 1417-1427.

Jacob, R., Wing, R. & Shapiro, A. P. (1987). The behavioral treatment of hypertension: Long term effects. *Behaviour Therapy*, **18**, 325–352.

Jarvis, M. (1989). Helping smokers give up. In S. Pearce & J. Wardle (Eds), *The Practice of Behavioural Medicine*. Oxford: BPS Books, pp. 285–305.

Jenkins, C. D. (1978). Behavioural risk factors in coronary artery disease. *Annual Review Medicine*, **29**, 543–562.

Jenkins, C. D., Zyzanski, S. J. & Rosenman, R. H. (1971). Progress toward validation of a computer-scored test for the Type A coronary-prone behaviour pattern. *Psychosomatic Medicine*, **33**, 193–202.

Jenni, M. A., & Wollersheim, J. P. (1979). Cognitive therapy: Stress management training and the Type A behaviour pattern. *Cognitive Therapy Research*, **3**, 61–73.

Johnston, D. W. (1982). Behavioural treatment in the reduction of coronary risk factors: Type A behaviour and blood pressure. *British Journal of Clinical Psychology*, **21**, 281–294.

Johnston, D. W. (1986). How does relaxation training reduce blood pressure in primary hypertension. In T. D. Dembroski, T. H. Schmidt & C. Blumchen (Eds) *Biological and Psychological Factors in Coronary Heart Disease*. Berlin: Springer-Verlag, pp. 550–567.

Johnston, D. W. (1987). The behavioural control of high blood pressure. *Current Psychological Research and Reviews*, **6**, 99–114.

Johnston, D. W. (1989a). The prevention of cardiovascular disease by psychological methods. *British Journal of Psychiatry*, **154**, 183–194.

Johnston, D. W. (1989b). Will stress management prevent coronary heart disease? *The Psychologist*, **7**, 275–278.

Johnston, D. W. (1991). Stress management in the treatment of mild primary hypertension. *Hypertension*, **17** (Suppl. 111), 111-63–111-68.

Jorgensen, R. S., Houston, B. K. & Zurawski, R. M. (1981). Anxiety management training in the treatment of essential hypertension. *Behaviour Relaxation and Therapy*, **19**, 467–474.

Kaplan, J. R., Manuck, S. B., Adams, M. R., Weingand, K. W. & Clarkson, T. B. (1987). Inhibition of coronary atherosclerosis by propranolol in behaviourally predisposed monkeys fed an atherogenic diet. *Circulation*, **76**, 1364–1372.

Kaplan, J. R., Manuck, S. B., Clarkson, T. B., Lusso, F. M., Taub, D. M. & Miller, E. W. (1983). Social stress and atherosclerosis in normocholesterolemic monkeys. *Science*, **220**, 733–734.

Karasek, R. A., Theorell, T., Schwartz, J. E., Schnall, P. L., Pieper, C. F. & Michela, J. L. (1988). Job characteristics in relation to the prevalence of myocardial infarction in the US health examination survey (HES) and the health and nutrition examination survey (HANES). *American Journal Public Health*, **78**, 910–911.

Kasl, S. V. (1984). Stress and health. *Annual Review of Public Health*, **5**, 319–341.

Kjeldsen, S. E., Neubig, R. R., Weber, A. B. & Zweifler, A. J. (1989). The hypertension-coronary heart disease dilemma: The catecholamine–blood platelet connection. *Journal of Hypertension*, **7**, 851–860.

Lawler, J. M., Barker, G. F., Hubbard, J. W. & Allen, M. T. (1980). The effects of conflict on tonic levels of blood pressure in the genetically borderline hypertension rat. *Psychophysiology*, **17**, 363–370.

Lehnert, H., Kaluza, K., Vetter, H., Losse, H. & Dorst, K. (1987). Long-term effects of complex behavioral treatment of essential hypertension. *Psychosomatic Medicine*, **49**, 422–430.

Levenkron, J. C., Cohen, J. D., Mueller, H. S. & Fisher, E. B. (1983). Modifying the Type A coronary-prone behaviour pattern. *Journal of Consulting and Clinical Psychology*, **51**, 192–204.

Levenkron, J. C. & Moore, L. G. (1988). The Type A behaviour pattern: Issues for intervention research. *Annals of Behavioral Medicine*, 10, 78–83.

Lo, C. R. & Johnston, D. W. (1984). The self-control of the cardiovascular response to exercise using feedback of the product of the interbeat interval and pulse transit time. *Psychosomatic Medicine*, 46, 115–125.

Lovibond, S. H., Birrell, P. C. & Langeluddecke, P. (1986). Changing coronary heart disease risk factor status: The effects of three behavioural programs. *Journal of Behavioral Medicine*, 9, 415–437.

MacDougall, J. M., Dembroski, T. M., Dimsdale, J. E. & Hackett, T. P. (1985). Components of Type A: Hostility and anger-in: Further relationships to angiographic findings. *Health Psychology*, 4, 137–152.

McGrady, A. & Higgins, J. T. (1989). Prediction of response to biofeedback-assisted relaxation in hypertensives: Development of a hypertensive predictor profile (HYPP). *Psychosomatic Medicine*, 51, 277–284.

McGrady, A., Utz, S., Woerner, M., Bernal, G. A. A. & Higgins, J. T. (1986). Predictors of success in hypertensive treatment with biofeedback-assisted relaxation. *Biofeedback and Self-Regulation*, 11, 95–103.

McGrady, A. V., Yonker, R., Tan, S. Y., Fine, T. H. & Woerner, M. (1981). The effect of biofeedback-assisted relaxation on blood pressure and selected biochemical parameters with essential hypertension. *Biofeedback and Self-Regulation*, 6, 343–354.

Markowe, H. L. J., Marmot, M. G., Shipley, M. J., Bulpitt, C. J., Meade, T. W., Stirling, Y., Vickers, M. V. & Semmence, A. (1985). Fibrinogen: A possible link between social class and coronary heart disease. *British Medical Journal*, 291, 1312–1314.

Medical Research Council Working Party (1985). MRC trial of treatment of mild hypertension: Principal results. *British Medical Journal*, 291, 97–104.

Musante, L., MacDougall, J. M., Dembroski, T. M. & Van Horn, A. E. (1983). Component analysis of the Type A coronary-prone behaviour pattern in male and female college students. *Journal of Personality and Social Psychology*, 45, 1104–1117.

Myrtek, M. & Greenlee, M. E. W. (1984). Psychophysiology of Type A behaviour pattern: A critical analysis. *Journal of Psychosomatic Research*, 28, 455–466.

Nunes, E. V., Frank, K. A. & Kornfeld, D. S. (1987). Psychologic treatment for the Type A behaviour pattern and coronary heart disease: A meta-analysis of the literature. *Psychosomatic Medicine*, 48, 159–173.

Ornish, D., Brown, S. E., Scherwitz, L. W., Billings, J. H., Armstrong, W. T., Ports, T. A., McLanahan, S. M., Kirkeeide, R. L., Brand, R. J. & Gould, K. L. (1990). Can lifestyle changes reverse coronary heart disease? *Lancet*, 336, 129–133.

Ornish, D., Scherwitz, L. W., Doody, R. S., Kesten, D., McLanahan, S. M., Brown, S. E., Depuey, G., Sonnemaker, R., Haynes, C., Lester, J., McAllister, G. K., Hall, R. J., Burdine, J. A. & Gotto, A. M. (1983). Effects of stress management training and dietary chance in treating ischemic heart disease. *Journal of American Medical Association*, 249, 54–59.

Patel, C. (1975). Yoga and biofeedback in the management of "stress" in hypertensive patients. *Clinical Science and Molecular Medicine*, Supplement 28, 171–174.

Patel, C. & Marmot, M. G. (1988). Can general practitioners use training in relaxation and management of stress to reduce mild hypertension? *British Medical Journal*, 296, 21–24.

Patel, C., Marmot, M. G. & Terry, D. J. (1981). Controlled trial of biofeedback-aided behavioural methods in reducing mild hypertension. *British Medical Journal*, 282, 2005–2008.

Patel, C., Marmot, M. G., Terry, D. J., Carruthers, M., Hunt, B. and Patel, M. (1985). Trial of relaxation in reducing coronary risk: Four year follow up. *British Medical Journal*, 290, 1103–1106.

Patel, C. & North, W. R. S. (1975). Randomised controlled trial of yoga and biofeedback in the management of hypertension. *Lancet*, **ii**, 93–95.

Perkins, K. A. (1989). Interactions among coronary heart disease risk factors. *Annals of Behavioural Medicine*, **11**, 3–11.

Peveler, R. & Johnston, D. W. (1986). Subjective and cognitive effects of relaxation. *Behaviour Research and Therapy*, **24**, 413–420.

Pooling Project Research Group (1978). Relation of blood pressure, serum cholesterol, smoking habit, relative weight and ECG abnormalities to incidence of major coronary events: Final report of the Pooling Project. *Journal of Chronic Disease*, **31**, 201–306.

Powell, L. H. & Thoresen, C. E. (1988). Effects of Type A behavioral counselling and severity of prior acute myocardial infarction on survival. *The American Journal of Cardiology*, **62**, 1159–1163.

Price, V. A. (1982). *Type A Behaviour Pattern: A Model for Research and Practice*. New York: Academic Press.

Ragland, D. R. & Brand, R. J. (1988a). Type A behaviour and mortality from coronary heart disease. *The New England Journal of Medicine*, **318**, 65–69.

Ragland, D. R. & Brand, R. J. (1988b). Coronary heart disease mortality in the Western Collaborative Group Study: Follow-up experience of 22 years. *American Journal of Epidemiology*, **127**, 462–475.

Rosenman, R. H., Brand, R. J., Jenkins, C. D., Friedman, M., Strauss, R. & Wurm, M. (1975). Coronary heart disease in the Western Collaborative Group Study: Final follow-up experience of 8½ years. *Journal of American Medical Association*, **233**, 872–877.

Rosenman, R. H., Friedman, M., Strauss, R., Wurm, M., Kositchek, R., Hahn, W. & Werthessen, N. T. (1964). A predictive study of coronary heart disease. *Journal of American Medical Association*, **189**, 15–26.

Roskies, E. (1987). *Stress Management for the Healthy Type A*. New York: Guilford.

Roskies, E., Seraganian, P., Oseasohn, R., Hanley, J. A., Collu, R., Martin, N. & Smilga, C. (1986). The Montreal Type A intervention project: Major findings. *Health Psychology*, **5**, 45–69.

Rozanski, A., Bairey, C. N., Krantz, D. S., Friedman, J., Resser, K. J., Morell, M., Hilton-Chalfen, S., Hestrin, L., Bietendorf, J. & Berman, D. S. (1988). Mental stress and the induction of silent myocardial ischemia in patients with coronary artery disease. *The New England Journal of Medicine*, **318**, 1006–1012.

Ruberman, W., Weinblatt, E., Goldberg, J. D. & Chaudhary, B. S. (1984). Psychosocial influences on mortality after myocardial infarction. *New England Journal of Medicine*, **311**, 552–559.

Sallis, J. F., Dimsdale, J. E. & Caine, C. (1988). Blood pressure reactivity in children. *Journal of Psychosomatic Research*, **32**, 1–12.

Shaper, A. G. (1988). *Coronary Heart Disease: Risks and Reasons*. London: Current Medical Literature.

Shekelle, R. B., Hulley, S. B., Neaton, J. D., Billings, J. H., Borhani, N. O., Gerace, T. A., Jacobs, D. R., Lasser, N. L., Mittlemark, M. B. & Stamler, J. (1985). The MRFIT behaviour pattern study: II. Type A behaviour and incidence of coronary heart disease. *American Journal of Epidemiology*, **122**, 559–569.

Shiffman, S. M. (1982). Relapse following smoking cessation: A situational analysis. *Journal of Consulting and Clinical Psychology*, **54**, 809–813.

Smith, A. & Jacobsen, B. (1988). *The Nation's Health: A Strategy for the 90's*. London: King's Fund.

Southam, M. A., Agras, W. S., Taylor, C. B. & Kraemer, H. C. (1982). Relaxation training: Blood pressure during the working day. *Archives of General Psychiatry*, **39**, 715–717.

Steptoe, A. (1981). *Psychological Factors in Cardiovascular Disorders*. London: Academic Press.

Steptoe, A., Patel, C., Marmot, M. & Hunt, B. (1987). Frequency of relaxation practice, blood pressure reduction and the general effects of relaxation following a controlled trial of behaviour modification for reducing coronary risk. *Stress Medicine*, 3, 101–107.

Stone, R. A. & Deleo, J. (1976). Psychotherapeutic control of hypertension. *New England Journal of Medicine*, 294, 80–84.

Tasto, D. L. & Huebner, L. A. (1976). The effects of muscle relaxation and stress on the blood pressure levels of normotensives. *Behaviour Relaxation and Therapy*, 14, 89–91.

Tavazzi, L., Zotti, A. M. & Rondanelli, R. (1986). The role of psychologic stress in the genesis of lethal arrhythmias in patients with coronary artery disease. *European Heart Journal*, 7 (Suppl A), 99–106.

Taylor, C. B., Farquhar, J. W., Nelson, E. & Agras, W. J. (1977). Relaxation therapy and high blood pressure. *Archives of General Psychiatry*, 34, 339–342.

Thurman, C. W. (1985). Effectiveness of cognitive–behavioural treatments in reducing Type A behaviour among university faculty. *Journal of Consulting Psychology*, 32, 74–83.

Timio, M., Verdecchia, P., Venanzi, S., Gentili, S., Ronconi, M., Francucci, B., Montanari, M. & Bichisae, E. (1988). Age and blood pressure changes: A 20-year follow-up study in nuns in a secluded order. *Hypertension*, 12, 457–461.

van Montfrans, G., Karemeker, J., Wieling, W. & Dunning, A. J. (1990). Relaxation therapy and continuous ambulatory blood pressure in mild hypertension: A controlled study. *British Medical Journal*, 300, 1368–1372.

Verrier, R. L. (1987). Mechanisms of behaviorally induced arrhythmias. *Circulation*, 76, (suppl. I), I-48–I-56.

Wadden, T. A. (1983). Predicting treatment response to relaxation therapy for essential hypertension. *Journal of Nervous and Mental Disease*, 171, 681–689.

Wadden, T. A. (1984). Relaxation therapy for essential hypertension: Specific or nonspecific effects? *Journal of Psychosomatic Research*, 28, 53–61.

Watson, D. & Pennebaker, J. W. (1989). Health complaints, stress, and distress: Exploring the central role of negative affectivity. *Psychological Review*, 96, 234–254.

Weinstein, M. C. & Stason, W. B. (1985). Cost effectiveness of interventions to prevent or treat CHD. *Annual Review of Public Health*, 6, 41–63.

Zurawski, R. M., Smith, T. W. & Houston, B. K. (1987). Stress management for essential hypertension: Comparison with a minimally effective treatment, predictors of response to treatment, and effects on reactivity. *Journal of Psychosomatic Research*, 31, 453–462.

4 Conservative Treatment of Childhood and Adolescent Obesity

VERONIKA BREZINKA
Department of Health Psychology, Leiden University, PO Box 9555, 2300 RB Leiden, The Netherlands

INTRODUCTION

Obesity is considered the most prevalent and serious nutritional disease in Western societies (Brownell & Stunkard, 1978; Brownell, Wadden & Foster, 1985; Coates & Thoresen, 1980; Dietz, 1983), affecting 5–25% of children and adolescents (Brownell & Stunkard, 1978; Dietz, 1983; Stark et al., 1981); the prevalence seems to be growing (Gortmaker et al., 1987). It is also the leading cause of elevated blood pressure in children (Fripp et al., 1985; Lauer et al., 1975; Rames et al., 1978; Rocchini, 1984); the share of paediatric hypertension associated with obesity has increased (Gortmaker et al., 1987). Obese children tend to remain obese as adults (Dietz, 1983; Garn & La Velle, 1985; Mossberg, 1989; Straw, 1983); by the age of 17 the children of two obese parents are three times as fat as the children of two lean parents; if one child in a family is obese, there is a 40% chance that a second child in the family is obese (Garn & Clark, 1976). The greater the number of obese persons in the immediate family, including grandparents, the greater the likelihood of the obese child remaining obese (Garn & La Velle, 1985). Several studies have suggested links between childhood obesity and cardiovascular risk (Aristimuno et al., 1984; Smoak et al., 1987). Obese and very obese children show an accelerated trend towards elevated adult levels for risk factors over five years. The health risks associated with obesity are more prevalent among persons with childhood-onset obesity (Blackburn & Kanders, 1987).

Childhood obesity has been treated with conservative methods, such as dietary counselling, physical exercise and behaviour therapy and, in cases of massive obesity, with radical treatments such as very-low-calorie diets, pharmacotherapy and gastric surgery. This review focuses on the effectiveness of conservative treatments of childhood obesity. Conservative treatments are characterized by seven elements (Stunkard, 1987):

1. Self-monitoring
2. Stimulus control

International Review of Health Psychology. Edited by S. Maes, H. Leventhal and M. Johnston
©1992 John Wiley & Sons Ltd

3. Development of techniques to control the act of eating
4. Reinforcement for the prescribed behaviours
5. Cognitive restructuring
6. Nutrition education
7. Increasing physical activity.

We will, however, only be considering experimental studies with a no-treatment control group to evaluate the results as well as their long-term maintenance. In a second part, we will focus on the impact of different components of conservative weight reduction programmes such as parent participation, physical exercise, age at onset of treatment, dietary counselling and duration of the programme. Again, only experimental studies will be considered.

All the cited studies consider a child as obese when the fraction weight for height is greater than 120% of the ideal body weight, controlled for age and sex. As children tend to become heavier as they grow, it has become common practice to describe overweight and weight losses relatively, that is, in percentages. The advantage of this is that weight changes in children and adolescents remain comparable over the years, the disadvantage being that weight losses seem larger than they actually are when described in percentages. This is the reason why, in some studies, the difference between the treatment- and the control group is significant in percentage of overweight, but not in absolute weight (e.g. Mellin, Slinkard & Irwin, 1987; Weiss, 1977)—level of significance is reached faster with percentages.

GLOBAL EFFECTS OF CONSERVATIVE WEIGHT REDUCTION PROGRAMMES

In the 1970s, behavioural scientists began to use their methods to treat childhood obesity; shortly after, the first reviews appeared (Brownell & Stunkard, 1978; Coates & Thoresen, 1980; Israel & Stolmaker, 1980). The early studies focused primarily on changing food habits and eating behaviour and were called "behavioural" treatments in contrast to "traditional" treatments which placed the emphasis on diet, nutrition education and increasing physical activity. In recent years, however, these two directions have moved closer together and, as Stunkard (1987, p. 1145) pointed out, "programs that began as behavioural have increasingly incorporated features of traditional ones while traditional programs have incorporated behavioral measures. Very few purely behavioral or purely nonbehavioral programs exist at the present time." As this is true not only for treatment programmes for obese adults, but also for those for obese children and adolescents, we judged it appropriate to call the intervention programmes that will be discussed in this paper "conservative" rather than "behavioural". In current treatment programmes for obese children and adolescents, the three major components are diet, exercise and behaviour modification. A well-balanced diet should help the obese child to restrict intake and produce weight change; an exercise programme should increase caloric expenditure and physical fitness; behaviour modification techniques are used to help children change their eating and exercise behaviour. Parents participate in many programmes, as it has been shown that parental behaviour can influence children's food intake, physical activity and relative weight (Klesges et al., 1986).

We found 13 studies with a no-treatment control group. The first experimental study on the treatment of childhood obesity using behavioural methods is that of Aragona, Cassady & Drabman (1975). As the number of subjects is very small, however, we will only mention that participants in the two treatment groups lost weight significantly, whereas participants in the control group gained weight. Because of the small number of subjects, this study will not be cited in our tables. Table 4.1 shows nine clinical studies with a no-treatment control group and gives information on the following: duration of the programmes, age of participants, methods, group size, mean weight loss at the end of treatment and after the one-year follow-up, as far as is presented by the authors themselves. The purpose of this table is to give a complete overview of all studies with a no-treatment control group, independently of the completeness of data. With the exception of the study of Israel et al. (1984), where the participating parents themselves decided in which group they wanted to participate, participants were selected at random and assigned to the different treatment groups. In some studies, the no-treatment control group consisted of children and parents who had registered too late for the programme and had been told that the groups were full, but that they could participate in the following programme. With two exceptions (Mellin, Slinkard & Irwin, 1987; Weiss, 1977), the control groups were offered a weight loss programme on completion of the treatment. Unfortunately, therefore, the follow-up data of the treatment groups cannot be compared with those of the original control group. In the nine studies, treatment was associated with significant short-term weight losses, whereas children who had not received treatment mostly gained weight over the same period. Mean short-term weight losses of the treatment groups lie between -0.9 (Weiss, 1977) and -3.6 kg (Senediak & Spence, 1985) or between -4.1 (Wheeler & Hess, 1976) and -19.3% (Epstein et al., 1984a). Only two studies (Mellin, Slinkard & Irwin, 1987; Weiss, 1977) present data on the control group at the one-year follow-up: the mean difference between the treatment and control groups lies between -4.2 and -9.2 kg (Weiss, 1977) or between -4.6 and -16.4% (Weiss, 1977).

Table 4.2 shows three experimental weight loss programmes that were carried out in schools. School programmes have many advantages when compared to clinical programmes: the school represents an important location for both prevention and early intervention. Children can be contacted daily over a period of nearly 10 months a year; more children can be reached than with a clinical programme; the weight loss programme can be provided largely by school personnel or peers (Brownell & Kaye, 1982), which makes school programmes cost-effective. Physical exercise programmes can be integrated in the daily routine, low-calorie school lunches can be served. To maximize social support for

Table 4.1. Clinical studies with a no-treatment control group (the weight losses refer to pretreatment weight)

Author	Duration (weeks)	Age (years)	Groups, methods	Number of subjects	Mean weight loss at end of treatment %	kg	Mean weight loss at 1-year follow-up %	kg
Wheeler & Hess (1976)	28	2–10	1. Mother–child pairs individually treated with food recording, reinforcement, stimulus control, new eating habits	14	−4.1*	—	—	—
			2. Mother–child pairs as control group	14	+6.3	—	—	—
Kingsley & Shapiro (1977)	8	10–11	Nutrition information, reduced intake, food recording, contract management, token economy, reinforcement					
			1. Mother+child together	8	—	−1.8*	—	—
			2. Children only	10	—	−1.7*	—	—
			3. Mothers only	8	—	−1.8*	—	—
			4. Waiting list control group	10	—	+1.0	—	—
Weiss (1977)	12	9–18	1. No-treatment control group	7	+1	+2.1	+7.4	+9.0
			2. Diet–no reward, points could be earned for following the diet, but were not exchanged for reinforcers	9	−3.2	−0.4	+2.8	+4.8
			3. Diet–reward, earned points could be exchanged for self-administered reinforcers	10	−5.2*	−1.4	−0.1	+3.8
			4. Stimulus control, points exchanged for reinforcers	12	−5.5*	−0.9*	−10.5*	−0.2
			5. Stimulus control/diet-reward, a combination of programmes of groups 3 and 4. Parents were asked to refrain from any interference	9	−6.9*	−1.5*	−9.0*	+0.8

Study		Age	Treatment	n				
Kirschenbaum, Harris & Tomarken (1984)	9	9–13	Behavioural weight reduction programme, self-monitoring, exercise, stimulus control, contracting, social support, nutrition education, low-calorie school lunch					
			1. Mother and child together	16	−6.3*	−2.1*	−7.6	−3.2
			2. Children only	15	−7.1*	−2.7*	−6.2	−2.8
			3. Waiting list control group	9	+0.6	+0.2	—	—
Israel et al. (1984)	9	8–12	Behavioural weight reduction with self-monitoring, reinforcement, low-calorie diet, exercise					
			1. After the fourth session parents participate in their own weight loss programme	34	−8.8*	−2.4*	−4.0	+6.4
			2. After the fourth session parents learn skills as a helper to facilitate their child's weight loss	19	−9.2*	−2.7*	−3.8	+6.5
			3. Waiting list control group	10	+0.4	+1.7	—	—
Epstein et al. (1984a, 1989)	24	8–12	Behavioural weight reduction with contract management, point economies, social reinforcers, self-monitoring					
			1. Children and parents receive a diet	18	−16.9*	—	−15	—
			2. Children and parents receive diet plus exercise	18	−19.3*	—	−15	—
			3. Waiting list control group	17	+2.0	—	—	—
Israel, Stolmaker & Andrian (1985)	9	8–12	Behavioural weight reduction, self-monitoring, exercise, stimulus control, reinforcement, low caloric nutrition					
			1. Children and parents participate in the programme	12	−11.6*	−2.5*	−1.3	+8.0

continued overleaf

Table 4.1. (continued)

Author	Duration (weeks)	Age (years)	Groups, methods	Number of subjects	Mean weight loss at end of treatment		Mean weight loss at 1-year follow-up	
					%	kg	%	kg
			2. Parents also receive a short course in general child management skills	12	−7.2*	−2.2*	−10.2	+7.3
			3. Waiting list control group	9	−0.9	+1.2	—	—
Senediak & Spence (1985)		6–13	Behavioural programme with diet, exercise, self-monitoring, contracting, reinforcement, stimulus control, modelling, social support					
	4		1. Rapid procedure, eight sessions	12	−5.3*	−1.7*	—	—
	15		2. Gradual procedure, eight sessions	9	−13.6*	−3.6*	—	—
	4		3. Non-specific control group, eight sessions	11	−1.4	−0.3	—	—
	4		4. Waiting list control group	10	+2.3	+0.8	—	—
Mellin, Slinkard & Irwin (1987)	14	14–18	1. Behavioural programme for adolescents with self-monitoring, social support, exercise, nutrition education, reinforcement, two parent sessions	37	−5.9*	−3.1	−9.9*	−3.9
			2. No-treatment control group	29	−0.3	+0.1	−0.1	+1.3

* = p < 0.05.

Table 4.2. School programmes with a no-treatment control group (the weight losses refer to pretreatment weight)

Author	Duration (weeks)	Age (years)	Groups, methods	Number of subjects	Mean weight loss at end of treatment		Mean weight loss at 1-year follow-up	
					%	kg	%	kg
Brownell & Kaye (1982)	10	5–12	1. Behavioural school programme, low-calorie school lunch, exercise, self-monitoring, stimulus control, contract management, social support, nutrition education	63	−15.4	−4.4	—	—
			2. Control group	14	+2.8	+1.2	—	—
Lansky & Vance (1983)	12	12–13	1. Behavioural school programme, self-monitoring, exercise, diet, problem-solving, stimulus control, reinforcement, four parent sessions	30	−5.7*	—	—	—
			2. Control group	25	+2.4	—	—	—
Foster, Wadden & Brownell (1985)	12	6–9	1. Behavioural school programme carried out by peer counsellors, reinforcement for low-calorie lunch, stimulus control, self-monitoring, exercise	43	−5.3*	−0.2*	—	—
			2. Control group	41	+0.3	+1.3	—	—

* $= p < 0.05$.

overweight children, parents, teachers, physical education teachers and peers can take part in the programme. Although there have been several pilot studies in schools (Ward & Bar-Or, 1986), we have only considered programmes with an experimental design. The mean weight losses associated with school programmes are comparable to the successes reached with clinical programmes in smaller groups.

However, none of the school programmes offer long-term follow-up data, therefore nothing can be said about long-term maintenance of the weight losses obtained. Also, not every clinical study offers long-term follow-up data. As weight loss is not a linear process but must come to a limit sooner or later, it cannot be expected that the weight loss induced by a weight reduction programme should become even greater after the intervention, although this

Table 4.3. Experimental studies with follow-up data over one year (the weight losses refer to pretreatment weight)

Author	Groups	Mean weight loss at end of treatment (%)	Mean weight loss at 1-year follow-up (%)	Stability (<2%)
Weiss (1977)	1. Control group	+1	+7.4	No
	2. Diet–no reward	−3.2	+2.8	No
	3. Diet–reward	−5.2	−0.1	No
	4. Stimulus control	−5.5*	−10.5*	Yes
	5. Diet–reward + stimulus control	−6.9*	−9.0*	Yes
Brownell,	1. Mother–child separately	−17.1*	−20.5*	Yes
Kelman &	2. Mother–child together	−7	−5.5	Yes
Stunkard (1983)	3. Child alone	−6.8	−6	Yes
Kirschenbaum,	1. Child + mother	−6.3*	−7.6	Yes
Harris &	2. Child alone	−7.1*	−6.2	Yes
Tomarken (1984)	3. Control group	+0.6	—	—
Israel et al.	1. Parents' own programme	−8.8*	−4.0	No
(1984)	2. Parents helper	−9.2*	−3.8	No
	3. Control group	+0.4	—	—
Epstein et al.	1. Diet only	−16.9*	−15	Yes
(1984a, 1989)	2. Diet + exercise	−19.3*	−15	No
	3. Control group	+2.0	—	—
Israel,	1. Weight reduction	−11.6*	−1.3	No
Stolmaker &	2. Parent training	−7.2*	−10.2	Yes
Andrian (1985)	3. Control group	−0.9	—	—
Epstein et al.	1. Diet + exercise	−17.3	−25.4	Yes
(1985b)	2. Diet	−11.9	−18.7	Yes
Epstein et al.	1. Diet + aerobic	−10.8	−6.8	No
(1985a)	2. Diet + lifestyle	−12.8	−18.0*	Yes
	3. Diet + Callisthenics	−10.8	−7.2	No
Mellin, Slinkard	1. Weight loss programme	−5.9*	−9.9*	Yes
& Irwin (1987)	2. Control group	−0.3	−0.1	No

* = p < 0.05.

would be desirable in some cases of massive overweight. Therefore, to assess long-term effectivity of a weight reduction programme, we do not use enlargement, but rather stability or maintenance of weight loss as criteria. The mean weight loss of a group will be called stable if the mean weight gain during the follow-up year does not exceed 2%. Table 4.3 shows the nine experimental studies found which offer follow-up data over one year. Although six of these studies—those with a no-treatment control group—have already been shown in Table 4.1, they are shown again here to give a complete overview of those studies which offer follow-up data over one year. The three studies that are new in Table 4.3 (Brownell, Kelman & Stunkard, 1983; Epstein et al., 1985a, 1985b) have an experimental design, but do not include a no-treatment control group. These studies focus on the efficacy of special components of treatment such as parent participation or exercise. They will be discussed later in this chapter, but are shown in Table 4.3 because they also offer long-term follow-up data. As Table 4.3 shows, weight loss was stable in 13 treatment groups and in some cases even enlarged. But weight loss was unstable in eight treatment groups. However, the proposed criterion (weight gain not larger than 2%) is arbitrary and associated with the following problem: the greater the original weight loss, the less relevant a weight gain of 2% seems to be; group 2 in the study of Epstein et al. (1984a) had lost − 19.3% during training and maintained a weight loss of − 15% one year after training. According to the 2% criterion, this group did not succeed in maintaining its mean weight loss, although this weight loss is the highest of all the studies. But if we enlarge the stability criterion to a weight gain of, for example, not more than 4% in one year, groups with lower original weight losses would be assessed as stable, although they almost returned to their pretreatment weight.

SPECIFIC COMPONENTS OF CONSERVATIVE WEIGHT REDUCTION PROGRAMMES

Parent participation

Theoretically, parent participation is to be recommended for several reasons:
1. It is known that obesity runs in families and that many overweight children have overweight parents; weight loss of the child becomes easier if the whole family changes its eating behaviour
2. Klesges et al. (1986) showed that parents significantly influence the eating and exercise behaviour of their children by reinforcing specific behaviours such as activity or eating. Therefore, parent participation makes child weight loss more probable
3. Long-term behaviour changes are reached more easily if parents are instructed in behavioural management strategies to reinforce desired behaviour and to extinguish undesired behaviour (Epstein & Wing, 1987). Do data confirm these assumptions?

Table 4.4. Controlled studies on the impact of parent participation (the weight losses refer to pretreatment weight)

Author	Parent participation	Mean weight loss at end of treatment		Mean weight loss at follow-up		Effect of parent participation
		%	kg	%	kg	
Kingsley & Shapiro (1977)	1. Mother–child	—	−1.8*	—	—	Participants in mother–child group seemed most satisfied
	2. Children only	—	−1.7*	—	—	
	3. Mothers only	—	−1.8*	—	—	
	4. Control group	—	+1.0	—	—	
Coates, Killen & Slinkard (1982)	1. Parent participation	−8.6*	—	−8.4*	—	No difference in long-term effectiveness
	2. Adolescents only	−5.1	—	−8.2*	—	
Brownell, Kelman & Stunkard (1983)	1. Mother–child separately	−17.1*	−8.4*	−20.5*	−7.7*	Group 1 lost significantly more weight than the other two groups
	2. Mother–child together	−7	−5.3	−5.5	+2.9	
	3. Child alone	−6.8	−3.3	−6	+3.2	
Lansky & Vance (1983)	1. Parent participation	−9.5	—	—	—	Parental participation correlated with weight change
	2. No parents	−3.9	—	—	—	
	3. Control group	+2.4	—	—	—	
Kirschenbaum, Harris & Tomarken (1984)	1. Parent + child	−6.3*	−2.1*	−7.6	−3.2	Drop-out rate in group 2 significantly greater
	2. Children only	−7.1*	−2.7*	−6.2	−2.8	
	3. Control group	+0.6	+0.2	—	—	
Israel et al. (1984)	1. Parents' weight reduction programme	−8.8*	−2.4*	−4.0	+6.4	No differential effects
	2. Parents' helper role	−9.2*	−2.7*	−3.8	+6.5	
	3. Control group	+0.4	+1.7	—	—	
Israel, Stolmaker & Andrian (1985)	1. Weight reduction	−11.6*	−2.5*	−1.3	+8.0	Maintenance of weight loss superior in parent-training condition
	2. Parent training	−7.2*	−2.2*	−10.2	+7.3	
	3. Control group	−0.9	+1.2	—	—	
Foster, Wadden &, Brownell (1985)	1. Weight reduction, half of the parents participated randomly	−5.7*	—	—	—	Parent involvement had no effect on weight loss
	2. Control group	+2.4	—	—	—	

Study	Group					Comments
Epstein et al. (1986b, 1987b)	1. Parent control	-12.4	—	-5.7	—	Long-term results favoured parent-managed treatment
	2. Child self-control	-11.7	—	+0.1	—	
Epstein et al. (1981, 1987a)	1. Parent–child target	significant weight loss		-12.7	—	After five years children of parent–child target group showed better maintenance
	2. Child target			+4.3	—	
	3. Non-specific target			+8.3	—	
Graves, Meyers & Clark (1988)	1. Problem-solving child + parent	-13.5*	-4.2*	-24.5*	-4.5*	Children in the problem-solving group lost significantly more weight than the other groups
	2. Behavioural weight loss child + parent	-8.9	-2.4	-10.2	+0.3	
	3. Instruction only child + parent	-4.7	-1.6	-9.5	+1.3	

* = $p < 0.05$.

Table 4.4 summarizes the most important results concerning parent participation. Only the study of Foster, Wadden & Brownell (1985) shows no effect of parent participation on child weight loss. In this study parents of half the children, selected at random, were invited to attend an introductory meeting and another meeting during the tenth week. The other group of parents attended five meetings, scheduled during weeks 1, 3, 5, 7 and 10. Parents in this intensive group were given information on nutrition and physical activity, and were taught principles of positive reinforcement and behaviour modification. Parent participation had no influence on weight loss.

In the study of Coates, Killen & Slinkard (1982), overweight adolescents were randomly assigned to either a parent participation group or a no-parent participation group. The participating parents met in separate classes to learn skills for supporting their children's weight loss. At post-treatment, adolescents in the parent participation group showed a greater weight loss than participants of the no-parent group; they maintained their weight loss at the nine-month follow-up. Adolescents in the no-parent group matched the parent participation group's performance at follow-up. Thus, parent participation enhanced short-term weight changes in adolescents, but both groups showed equivalent changes at follow-up.

Lansky & Vance (1983) report a positive correlation between parent participation and child weight loss; children whose parents participated had a mean weight loss of − 9.5%, children whose parents did not participate had a mean weight loss of − 3.9%. As parent participation in this study was based on self-selection, it can be assumed that the non-participating parents were not really interested in the weight loss programme of their child, in contrast to other studies, where parents wanted to participate, but were not allowed to because of randomization of treatment. In the study of Kirschenbaum, Harris & Tomarken (1984), for example, there were no differences in weight loss between the groups with and without parent participation at post-treatment or after one year's follow-up, but the attrition rate was 33% in the group without, and 0% in the group with, parent participation. Kingsley & Shapiro (1977) also reported no differences in weight loss between the groups, but participants in the child plus parent group were more satisfied with the programme than participants in the other two groups. Parental involvement did not enhance programme effectiveness, but led to differences in expressed satisfaction with the groups.

Other studies show that specific forms of parent participation can also influence a child's weight loss. Brownell, Kelman & Stunkard (1983) compared three ways of parent participation in a weight reduction programme for overweight adolescents; adolescents were assigned randomly to three treatment conditions:
1. Mother–child separately, where mothers and children attended separate groups
2. Mother–child together, where mothers and children attend the same group
3. Child alone, where children attended the group alone and mothers were not involved.

The mother–child separately group lost significantly more weight than the other two groups. At the follow-up, one year later, differences between the groups increased; children in the mother–child separately group could maintain their weight losses significantly better than participants of the other two groups.

Children whose parents not only participated in the weight reduction programme but also received a short course in general child management skills before training maintained their weight loss better than children whose parents only participated in the weight reduction programme (Israel, Stolmaker & Andrian, 1985). In contrast, no significant group differences were found by Israel et al. (1984): after the fourth session, parents had to decide whether they wanted to participate in their own weight reduction programme or whether they wanted to choose a helper role and to improve their skills as a helper to facilitate their child's weight loss. There were no group differences at the end of treatment or at the one-year follow-up; a possible explanation could be that parents were confronted with the problem of childhood obesity in both treatment groups and, therefore, learned similar strategies to deal with it. Epstein et al. (1986b, 1987b) randomly assigned overweight children and one parent to either a group that focused on parent control or a group that focused on child self-control. There were no short-term differences between groups, but the long-term results favoured parent-managed treatment. Epstein et al. (1981) randomly assigned overweight children and one parent to one of three treatment conditions: in the parent/child target group, reinforcement was contingent on either parent and child weight loss; in the child target group reinforcement was contingent on child weight loss and in the non-specific target group on attendance. Children and parents participated in separate groups. Significant changes in overweight percentages were equivalent for children in the three treatment groups at the end of treatment and at the 13-month follow-up. At the five-year follow-up (Epstein et al., 1987a), children in the parent/child target group showed significantly greater reductions in percentage overweight (-12.7%) than children in the child target group ($+4.3\%$) or in the non-specific target group ($+8.2\%$), whose percentage overweight had slightly increased above baseline. A possible explanation for these results is that parental management skills that could be used to support children's behaviour change were provided only in the parent/child target group and could be used even if the parents were unsuccessful in regulating their own behaviour. Similar results are reported by Graves, Meyers & Clark (1988) who evaluated the efficacy of including parental problem-solving training in a behavioural weight reduction programme. Children and their parents were randomly assigned to a problem-solving, behavioural, or instruction-only weight loss group. Children in the problem-solving group lost significantly more weight than those in other groups. These differences were maintained at the six-month follow-up. The ability of problem-solving families to devise situation-specific strategies for managing problematic situations seemed to have served during the follow-up period to aid families to identify potential relapse situations.

In view of the above results, the question whether parent participation is a necessary component of behavioural weight reduction programmes for children can be answered as follows: there seem to be no negative effects of parent participation. In contrast, it can enhance satisfaction with, and motivation for, the training and lower the attrition rate (Kingsley & Shapiro, 1977; Kirschenbaum, Harris & Tomarken, 1984; Lansky & Vance, 1983). Programmes which instruct parents in special skills have positive effects: children whose parents were instructed in principles of behaviour modification showed better long-term maintenance of their weight loss (Israel, Stolmaker & Andrian, 1985); the same is true for children whose parents had learnt problem-solving strategies (Graves, Meyers & Clark, 1988) or parental management skills (Epstein et al., 1987a). The question whether parents should participate in the same group as their children or in a separate one was investigated by Brownell, Kelman & Stunkard (1983): separate participation of mothers and children yielded significantly better results. The age of the children could have played a role in these results: actually they were already adolescents and perhaps reacted in a negative way to too much parental involvement. The mother–child separately group allowed both parties to discuss sensitive issues, whereas mothers and children in the mother–child together group were reluctant to express negative feelings about each other. The age of the participating children could also be a reason why in the study of Coates, Killen & Slinkard (1982) no differential effects appeared in the long term between adolescents whose parents participated and adolescents of the no-parent participation group. Adolescents might already have enough self-control so that parental involvement and support are less important for the success of a weight reduction programme than for children of primary-school age. However, parent participation did not have an effect on weight loss in the programme of Foster, Wadden & Brownell (1985) either, although children were between six and nine years old. As there are no negative effects of parent participation reported, and as the possible advantages may be high, parent participation should be a necessary component of weight reduction programmes especially for younger children. To maximize its effect, parents should learn specific problem-solving or child management skills.

Physical exercise

Table 4.5 shows three studies that explored the impact of physical exercise on weight loss: Epstein et al. (1984a) randomly assigned 53 overweight children and one parent to one of three groups: diet, diet plus exercise and no-treatment control. After six months, parents and children in both treatment groups had equal and significantly better weight change than members of the control group. After one year, parents receiving diet plus exercise showed better weight losses than parents receiving the diet alone. No treatment group differences were found for children at the one-year follow-up. The results clearly demonstrated that the

Table 4.5. Controlled studies on the impact of physical exercise (the weight losses refer to pretreatment weight)

Author	Groups	Mean weight loss at end of treatment		Mean weight loss at follow-up		Effect of physical exercise
		%	kg	%	kg	
Epstein et al. (1984a)	1. Diet	−16.9*	—	−15	—	No treatment group differences
	2. Diet + exercise	−19.3*	—	−15	—	
	3. Control group	+2.0	—			
Epstein et al. (1985b)	1. Diet + exercise	−17.3	−4.5	−25.4	−3.9	Diet + exercise group improved significantly in fitness
	2. Diet	−11.9	−3.2	−18.7	−1.4	
Epstein et al. (1985a)	1. Diet + aerobics	−10.8	−3.7	−6.8	+13.2	At month 24 group 2 maintained relative weight changes, while the other two groups had returned to baseline level
	2. Diet + life-style	−12.8	−4.4	−18.0*	+4.8*	
	3. Diet + callisthenics	−10.9	−4.4	−7.2	+12.4	

$* = p < 0.05$.

addition of exercise to a diet improves the amount of relative weight change at six months and one year in adults. On the other hand, however, exercise did not add to the general effects of dieting for children after six months and one year. Results after five years of follow-up were available for half the participating children (Epstein et al. 1989). Again there were no treatment group differences.

Epstein et al. (1985b) randomly assigned obese girls to one of two groups: diet and diet plus exercise. Identical behavioural methods were used in both groups to promote eating and exercise habit changes, such as self-monitoring, modelling, contracting and reinforcement. Children in the exercise group received an aerobic exercise programme designed to increase caloric expenditure. During the first six weeks children met three mornings a week for exercise sessions that included 10 minutes of stationary aerobic exercise, warm-up games, and a three-mile walk or run. Parents were instructed to model and support the walking programme and, during the maintenance phase, to walk three miles with their children three times a week. After two months, both groups had lost weight significantly without group differences. At the one-year follow-up it was found that both groups had maintained their weight without treatment group differences, but that only children in the diet plus exercise group showed a significant improvement in fitness.

Epstein et al. (1985a) compared life-style exercise, aerobic exercise and callisthenics on weight loss in obese children. Thirty-five obese children and their parents were randomly assigned to one of three groups: diet plus programmed aerobic exercise, diet plus life-style exercise and diet plus callisthenic exercise. Behavioural procedures such as self-monitoring, modelling, contingency contracting and parental management skills were used to influence behaviour change. The aerobic exercise programme consisted of walking, running, cycling or swimming; parents and children were asked to exercise three times per week starting with one mile of walking or running, two miles of bicycling or three-quarters of a mile of swimming. In the life-style exercise programme, subjects were allowed to choose exercises from an exercise menu and were not instructed to exercise at a particular intensity. Participants of the callisthenics programme had to perform 6 of 12 callisthenics three times per week. Significant decreases in overweight percentages were observed for all three groups from 0 to 2, 6, and 12 months. At month 24, the life-style group had maintained relative weight changes, while the other two groups had returned to baseline levels.

Although physical exercise does not seem to enlarge weight losses (Table 4.5), improvement in fitness through exercise is desirable for obese children and adolescents. Dietz & Gortmaker (1985) observed a significant association of the time spent watching television and the prevalence of obesity. In 12- to 17-year-old adolescents, the prevalence of obesity increased by 2% for each additional hour of television viewed. The associations persisted when controlled for prior obesity, region, season, population density, race, socio-economic class, and a variety of other family variables. Waxman & Stunkard (1980) compared caloric intake and expenditure of obese boys and their non-obese brothers. The obese boys consumed more calories and were less active than their non-obese brothers. Fripp et al. (1985) evaluated correlations between aerobic capacity, obesity and atherosclerotic risk factors in adolescents. Subjects with higher levels of fitness had a more favourable atherosclerotic risk profile. Berkowitz et al. (1985) assessed intensity of physical activity using ambulatory microcomputers attached to the child for 24 hours that could register 16 intensity levels. A low amount of high-level physical activities was positively correlated to the child's obesity.

Positive effects of physical exercise include improvement in cardiovascular and muscular fitness, decreasing blood pressure, favourable modification of body composition, possible manipulation of fat cell development and increased probability of weight loss maintenance. Epstein, Masek & Marshall (1978) observed a depression of lunch food consumption by obese children who had exercised prior to the meal. A negative correlation was noted between the amount of exercise and the quantitative change in food intake (see also Dickson-Parnell & Zeichner, 1985; Woo, Garrow & Pi-Sunyer, 1982); Epstein et al. (1984b) showed that resting metabolic rate can increase through regular physical exercise. The study of Epstein et al. (1985a) also indicates that the specific sort of exercise programme can influence the adherence of participants: very low intensity of exercise does not seem to improve fitness, very high intensity seems to have negative effects on subjects' adherence to the programme.

What is the most appropriate age for intervention?

The literature regarding childhood obesity often pleads for early intervention. As a consequence, most of the controlled studies have been designed for children aged 6–12 years. Epstein et al. (1986a) could even show in an uncontrolled study that obesity can be treated successfully in young children (aged one to six) without detrimental effects on growth or nutrient intake. We found four controlled studies with obese adolescents (Brownell, Kelman & Stunkard, 1983; Coates, Killen & Slinkard, 1982; Coates et al., 1982; Mellin, Slinkard & Irwin, 1987). Mean weight losses at the end of treatment lay between − 5.1 and − 17.1%, and at the one-year follow-up, between − 5.1 and − 20.5% (see Tables 4.1 and 4.4). They are, therefore, comparable with the mean weight losses obtained in programmes for younger children. Based on the available data, there is no reason to delay an intervention, as it has been well established that obese children mostly do not lose, but gain weight over time (Aristumuno et al., 1984; Dietz, 1983). There is also no reason for pessimism concerning weight loss programmes for obese adolescents.

Should a weight reduction programme for children contain diet?

In every study described in this review, participants were given nutritional information or a specific diet. The only exception is group 4 in the study of

Weiss (1977), which was only instructed in stimulus control, but lost more weight than groups 2 and 3, which received a conventional diet (see Table 4.1). Participants in the stimulus-control group maintained their weight loss significantly better than those in the other two groups. This result does not argue against the utility of diets, but demonstrates that behaviour changes necessary for adherence to a diet are facilitated through behavioural techniques such as stimulus control. A well-balanced diet poses no recognized hazard for continued growth during weight reduction and seems to be essential to obtain significant weight losses (Dietz, 1983; Hammar, Campbell & Woolley, 1971; objections to these views are raised by Mallick, 1983). Epstein and colleagues, the authors of most of the studies on behavioural weight reduction for obese children, use the so-called traffic light diet, which separates food in the major food groups into three colours, red, yellow and green, which correspond to the colours of a traffic light. Green foods, which signal GO and eat, are those that are less than 20 kcal per average serving. Yellow foods, which you should approach with caution, are within 20 kcal of the average for foods within that food group (ie fruit = 40 kcal, dairy products = 80 kcal), and red foods (STOP, do not eat) are those that are more than 20 kcal greater than the average serving for that group. The goals of the diet are to decrease saturated fat and sugar intake and increase nutrient density per calorie.

More restricted diets should be used only with extreme caution and under medical supervision, as they can be associated with potential life-threatening cardiac arrythmias (Dietz, 1983; Schmidinger et al., 1987).

What is the optimal duration of a weight reduction programme for obese children?

The duration of controlled weight reduction programmes for children and adolescents lies between 4 (Senediak & Spence, 1985) and 28 weeks (Wheeler & Hess, 1976). The lowest mean weight loss obtained was in group 2 in the study of Weiss (1977), which received a conventional diet only; duration of the programme was 12 weeks. The highest mean weight loss obtained was in group 2 in the study of Epstein et al. (1984a), which was treated with behaviour therapy, diet and physical exercise; duration of the programme was 24 weeks. These examples already show the methodological problems of a comparison of weight loss programmes on their duration: the programmes not only differ in their duration, but also in the methods used (behaviour therapy, diet, physical exercise, etc.). The only study comparing the effects of the same programme on a rapid versus a gradual scheduling is that of Senediak & Spence (1985). Subjects were randomly assigned to one of four conditions: a rapid behavioural group, a gradual behavioural group, a non-specific control condition and a waiting list control group. In the rapid behavioural group, the eight sessions were conducted twice weekly for four weeks; in the gradual behavioural group the eight treatment sessions were spaced in a manner so as to gradually fade out therapist contact, with increasingly extended intervals between meetings, over a 15-week period. Sessions 1 to 4 occurred weekly, sessions 5 and 6 fortnightly and sessions 7 and 8 after a three-week interval. No significant differences were found between the rapid and gradual procedures in the long term. Currently, there are not enough data available for special recommendations on the optimal duration of a child weight loss programme. More research is required in this field, because duration of a programme is also linked with its cost. Contacts between the end of treatment and follow-up sessions such as monthly telephone calls or problem-solving sessions were used by Epstein et al. (1981, 1985b, 1985c), Israel et al. (1984) and Israel, Stolmaker & Andrian (1985). Although one could expect beneficial effects from these strategies, the mean weight losses obtained were no higher than in other studies.

Related with the question of the optimal duration of a weight loss programme is the question of the optimal frequency of therapeutic contact. Coates, Killen & Slinkard (1982) report that participants in their training found the daily 'weigh-ins' very helpful; they suggest that initial changes may require strong external support. Similar results are reported by Coates et al. (1982), who investigated the effects of frequency of therapeutic contact and monetary reinforcers. Obese adolescents were assigned randomly to one of four treatment groups in a 2×2 factorial design; the factors were monetary reinforcers (for weight loss versus caloric change) and frequency of therapeutic contact (five times versus once per week). The treatment group receiving rewards for weight loss and coming to the clinic five times per week was the only group to reduce significantly in percentage overweight during the treatment programme. In the very successful school programme of Foster, Wadden & Brownell (1985), children saw their peer counsellor three times a week and their therapist once a week. The few data available to answer the question of optimal frequency of therapeutic contact suggest that short meetings several times a week can lead to better results than one long session per week. It could be argued, however, that in clinical programmes, many meetings can lower compliance, especially if the clinic is so far away from school and home that special activities are required from children and parents (e.g. car trips). This problem can be prevented in school programmes. Again, more research is required in this field before the question of optimal therapeutic frequency can be answered.

How important is self-control in the treatment of overweight children and adolescents?

Some considerations on the role of self-control in the treatment of childhood and adolescent obesity might be useful here: self-regulation techniques such as self-praise for weight control, self-monitoring of food intake and weight change, restricting food intake, increasing energy output to counteract weight gains, and restraining eating in tempting situations have been an integrated element of treatment programmes that make use of the techniques of self-monitoring, stimulus control and self-reinforcement. However, it is interesting to note that their specific effectiveness has been examined very little. The results of Cohen et al. (1980) point to the importance of self-regulation in the maintenance of weight loss in children and adolescents. They showed in a correlational study that children who had lost weight and maintained it differed from regainers with respect to the degree of self-regulation of weight and amount of physical exercise. In contrast to these findings, Epstein et al. (1986b, 1987b) could find no short-term differences between a group that focused on parent control and a group that focused on child self-control. The long-term results, however, favoured parent-managed treatment. Parents in the parent control group determined when goals were met and points awarded, whereas children in the child self-control condition learned to determine this on their own.

Given the intrinsically reinforcing properties of eating it seems logical that self-regulatory practices should be implicated in the maintenance of weight loss. However, little is known about their specific effectiveness and, moreover, apart from Epstein et al. (1986b, 1987b), no controlled studies have investigated possible differential effects of treatments with and without self-control techniques. Neither did we find any controlled studies which make use of the concepts of self-efficacy, body image or self-esteem. One possible reason might be that self-control is not as important an issue for the treatment of obese children as it is for obese adults. As pointed out earlier, most of the controlled weight reduction programmes have been designed for children aged 6–12 years. Apparently, self-control has not been considered as a crucial element for successful treatment of this age group, whereas the influence of parent participation and parent control has received much attention.

CONCLUSION

The main question to be answered in this review is whether conservative treatments can be regarded as effective in childhood weight control. Analysis of experimental studies with no-treatment control groups showed unanimously that significant short-term weight losses can be achieved. The mean weight losses lie between − 1.8 (Kingsley & Shapiro, 1977) and − 3.6 kg (Senediak & Spence, 1985) or between − 4.1 (Wheeler & Hess, 1976) and − 19.3% (Epstein et al., 1984a).

To maximize the effects of a weight reduction programme, further individualization of treatment has frequently been suggested (Epstein & Wing, 1987; Israel & Stolmaker, 1980). For some overweight children and adolescents, training could focus more on physical exercise, for others more on nutritional behaviour change or on instruction of parents in child management skills. Currently, however, not enough data are available to justify selection of obese children and adolescents for treatments with a special focus as described above. As childhood obesity is a prevalent disorder, further individualization of treatment on the client level quickly comes to personal and financial limits. It seems to be more cost-effective not to design *individual* treatment strategies, but to design different *types of programmes* and to compare their efficiency. For example, comparisons could be made between programmes focusing on the modification of eating behaviour, programmes focusing on physical exercise and programmes focusing on child management skills, as well as between different combinations of these programmes. One methodological problem of the more complex, integrated programmes which are based on diet, exercise and behaviour modification is actually that it remains unclear as to which element is responsible for the success of these programmes. In this respect, school programmes seem the most promising, because they are more cost-effective than clinical programmes and more participants can be reached.

In future studies, the presentation of one-year follow-up data should become self-evident, because otherwise the significance and effectiveness of a weight loss programme cannot be judged appropriately. Future research should also focus on the development of specific relapse prevention strategies and successful maintenance of post-treatment weight losses. Partly, strategies that have been used successfully with adults (Brownell et al. 1986) could be efficient with children as well—but more attention should be turned towards the development of child-specific relapse prevention strategies. Emphasis must lie on innovative cognitive–behaviour therapy techniques designed specifically for long-term health behaviour change in obese children and their families (Varni & Banis, 1985).

Parent participation in a weight reduction programme for obese children and adolescents can enhance motivation for and satisfaction with the training and reduce attrition rate; this can have positive effects on weight loss. Maintenance of weight loss at follow-up succeeds better in programmes which instructed parents in specific parent management or problem-solving skills. In future studies, the impact of different forms of parent participation should be investigated systematically, perhaps in combination with the age of the children.

Although physical exercise does not necessarily enhance weight losses, it improves fitness and can reduce cardiovascular risk factors. Problems that must be investigated in future studies are bad compliance and high attrition rates in physical exercise programmes (Martin & Dubbert, 1982). Measurements of adherence must be developed to see whether participants do exercise at home (Israel, Silverman & Solotar, 1988).

At what age treatment of childhood obesity is the most successful cannot be judged by reported data. There are only few studies which focus on the treatment of overweight in babies and small children (Epstein et al., 1986a; Pisacano et al., 1978); specific treatment strategies for these age groups should be developed urgently. On the other hand, there seems to be no reason not to treat obese adolescents or not to design weight reduction programmes for this age group.

The development of large-scale school programmes, the systematic comparison of different types of programmes and their effectiveness and focus on child-specific maintenance strategies could maximize the effects and minimize the costs of conservative weight reduction programmes for children and adolescents.

REFERENCES

Aragona, J., Cassady, J. & Drabman, R. (1975). Treating overweight children through parental training and contingency contracting. *Journal of Applied Behavior Analysis*, 8, 269–278.

Aristimuno, G., Foster, T., Voors, A., Srinivasan, S. & Berenson, G. (1984). Influence of persistent obesity in children on cardiovascular risk factors: The Bogalusa Heart Study. *Circulation*, 69, 895–904.

Berkowitz, R., Agras, S., Korner, A., Kraemer, H. & Zeanah, C. (1985). Physical activity and adiposity: a longitudinal study from birth to childhood. *Journal of Pediatrics*, 106, 734–738.

Blackburn, G. & Kanders, B. (1987). Medical evaluation and treatment of the obese patient with cadiovascular disease. *American Journal of Cardiology*, 60, 55G–58G.

Brownell, K. & Kaye, F. (1982). A school-based behavior modification, nutrition education and physical activity program for obese children. *American Journal of Clinical Nutrition*, 35, 277–283.

Brownell, K., Kelman, J. & Stunkard, A. (1983). Treatment of obese children with and without their mothers. Changes in weight and blood pressure. *Pediatrics*, 71, 515–523.

Brownell, K., Marlatt, G., Lichtenstein, E. & Wilson, G. (1986). Understanding and preventing relapse. *American Psychologist*, 41, 765–782.

Brownell, K., & Stunkard, A. (1978). Behavioral treatment of obesity in children. *American Journal of Diseases in Childhood*, 132, 403–412.

Brownell, K., Wadden, T. & Foster, G. (1985). A comprehensive treatment plan for obese children and adolescents: Principles and practice. *Pediatrician*, 12, 89–96.

Coates, T., Jeffery, R., Slinkard, L., Killen, J. & Danaher, B. (1982). Frequency of contact and monetary reward in weight loss, lipid change and blood pressure reduction with adolescents. *Behavior Therapy*, 13, 175–185.

Coates, T., Killen, J. & Slinkard, L. (1982). Parent participation in a treatment program for overweight adolescents. *International Journal of Eating Disorders*, 1, 37–48.

Coates, T. & Thoresen, C. (1980). Obesity among children and adolescents: The problem belongs to everyone. In B. Lahey & A. Kazdin (Eds), *Advances in child clinical psychology*, Vol. 3. New York: Plenum, pp. 215–264.

Cohen, E., Gelfland, D., Dodd, D., Jensen, J. & Turner, C. (1980). Self-control practices associated with weight loss maintenance in children and adolescents. *Behavior Therapy*, 11, 26–37.

Dickson-Parnell, B. & Zeichner, A. (1985). Effects of a short-term exercise program on caloric consumption. *Health Psychology*, 4, 437–448.

Dietz, W. (1983). Childhood obesity: Susceptibility, cause and management. *Journal of Pediatrics*, 103, 676–686.

Dietz, W. & Gortmaker, S. (1985). Do we fatten our children at the television set? Obesity and television viewing in children and adolescents. *Pediatrics*, 75, 807–812.

Epstein, L., Kuller, L., Wing, R., Valoski, A. & McCurley, J. (1989). The effect of weight control on lipid changes in obese children. *American Journal of Diseases in Children*, 143, 454–457.

Epstein, L., Masek, B. & Marshall, W. (1978). Prelunch exercise and lunch time caloric intake. *Behavior Therapy*, 1, 15.

Epstein, L., Valoski, A., Koeske, R., & Wing, R. (1986a). Family-based behavioral weight control in obese young children. *Journal of the American Dietetic Association*, 86, 481–484.

Epstein, L. & Wing, R. (1987). Behavioral treatment of childhood obesity. *Psychological Bulletin*, 101, 331–342.

Epstein, L., Wing, R., Koeske, R., Andrasik, F. & Ossip, D. (1981). Child and parent weight loss in a family-based behavior modification program. *Journal of Consulting and Clinical Psychology*, **49**, 674–685.

Epstein, L., Wing, R., Koeske, R. & Valoski, A. (1984a). Effects of diet plus exercise on weight change in parents and children. *Journal of Consulting and Clinical Psychology*, **52**, 429–437.

Epstein, L., Wing, R., Koeske, R. & Valoski, A. (1985a). A comparison of lifestyle exercise, aerobic exercise and calisthenics on weight loss in obese children. *Behavior Therapy*, **16**, 345–356.

Epstein, L., Wing, R., Koeske, R. & Valoski, A. (1986b). Effects of parent weight on weight loss in obese children. *Journal of Consulting and Clinical Psychology*, **54**, 400–401.

Epstein, L., Wing, R., Koeske, R. & Valoski, A. (1987a). Longterm effects of family-based treatment of childhood obesity. *Journal of Consulting and Clinical Psychology*, **55**, 91–95.

Epstein, L., Wing, R., Penner, B. & Kress, M. (1985b). Effect of diet and controlled exercise on weight loss in obese children. *Journal of Pediatrics*, **107**, 358–361.

Epstein, L., Wing, R., Valoski, A. & Gooding, W. (1987b). Long-term effects of parent weight on child weight loss. *Behavior Therapy*, **18**, 219–226.

Epstein, L., Wing, R., Woodall, K., Penner, B., Kress, M. & Koeske, R. (1985b). Effects of family-based behavioral treatment on obese 5 to 8 year old children. *Behavior Therapy*, **16**, 205–212.

Epstein, L., Woodall, K., Goreczny, A., Wing, R. & Robertson, R. (1984b). The modification of activity patterns and energy expenditure in obese young girls. *Behavior Therapy*, **15**, 101–108.

Foster, G., Wadden, T. & Brownell, K. (1985). Peer-led program for the treatment and prevention of obesity in the schools. *Journal of Consulting and Clinical Psychology*, **53**, 538–540.

Fripp, R., Hodgson, J., Kwiterovick, P., Werner, J., Schuler, H. & Whitman, V. (1985). Aerobic capacity, obesity, and atherosclerotic risk factors in male adolescents. *Pediatrics*, **75**, 813–818.

Garn, S. & Clark, D. (1976). Trends in fatness and the origins of obesity. *Pediatrics*, **57**, 443–456.

Garn, S. & LaVelle, M. (1985). Two-decade follow-up of fatness in early childhood. *American Journal of Diseases in Children*, **139**, 181–185.

Gortmaker, S., Dietz, W., Sobol, A. & Wehler, C. (1987). Increasing pediatric obesity in the United States. *American Journal of Diseases in Children*, **141**, 535–540.

Graves, T., Meyers, A. & Clark, L. (1988). An evaluation of parental problem-solving training in the behavioral treatment of childhood obesity. *Journal of Consulting and Clinical Psychology*, **56**, 246–250.

Hammar, S., Campbell, V. & Woolley, J. (1971). Treating adolescent obesity: Long-range evaluation of previous therapy. *Clinical Pediatrics*, **10**, 46–52.

Israel, A., Silverman, W. & Solotar, L. (1988). The relationship between adherence and weight loss in a behavioral treatment program for overweight children. *Behavior Therapy*, **19**, 25–33.

Israel, A. & Stolmaker, L. (1980). Behavioral treatment of obesity in children and adolescents. In M. Hersen, R. Eisler & P. Miller (Eds), *Progress in Behavior Modification*, Vol. 10. New York: Academic Press, pp. 81–109.

Israel, A., Stolmaker, L. & Andrian, C. (1985). The effects of training parents in general child management skills on a behavioral weight loss program for children. *Behavior Therapy*, **16**, 169–180.

Israel, A., Stolmaker, L., Sharp, J., Silverman, W. & Simon, L. (1984). An evaluation of two methods of parental involvement in treating obese children. *Behavior Therapy*, 15, 266–272.

Kingsley, R. & Shapiro, J. (1977). A comparison of three behavioral programs for the control of obesity in children. *Behavior Therapy*, 8, 30–36.

Kirschenbaum, D., Harris, E. & Tomarken, A. (1984). Effects of parental involvement in behavioral weight loss therapy for preadolescents. *Behavior Therapy*, 15, 485–500.

Klesges, R., Malott, J., Boschee, P. & Weber, J. (1986). Parental influences on children's food intake, physical activity and relative weight: An extension and replication. *International Journal of Eating Disorders*, 5, 335–346.

Lansky, D. & Vance, M. (1983). School-based intervention for adolescent obesity: Analysis of treatment, randomly selected control and self-selected subjects. *Journal of Consulting and Clinical Psychology*, 51, 147–148.

Lauer, R., Connor, W., Leaverton, P., Reiter, M. & Clarke, W. (1975). Coronary heart disease risk factors in school children: The Muscatine Study. *Journal of Pediatrics*, 86, 697–706.

Mallick, M. (1983). Health hazards of obesity and weight control in children: A review of the literature. *American Journal of Public Health*, 73, 78–82.

Martin, J. & Dubbert, P. (1982). Exercise applications and promotion in behavioral medicine: current status and future directions. *Journal of Consulting and Clinical Psychology*, 50, 1004–1017.

Mellin, L., Slinkard, L. & Irwin, C. (1987). Adolescent obesity intervention: Validation of the Shapedown program. *Journal of the American Dietetic Association*, 87, 333–338.

Mossberg, H. (1989). Forty-year follow-up of overweight children. *Lancet*, **August 26**, 491–493.

Pisacano, J., Lichter, H., Ritter, J. & Siegal, A. (1978). An attempt at prevention of obesity in infancy. *Pediatrics*, 61, 360–364.

Rames, L., Clark, W., Connor, W., Reiter, M. & Lauer, R. (1978). Normal blood pressures and the evaluation of sustained blood pressure elevation in childhood: The Muscatine Study. *Pediatrics*, 61, 245–251.

Rocchini, A. (1984). Childhood hypertension: Etiology, diagnosis and treatment. *Pediatric Clinics of North America*, 31, 1259–1273.

Schmidinger, H., Weber, H., Zwiauer, K., Weidinger, F. & Widhalm, K. (1987). Potential life-threatening cardiac arrhythmias associated with a conventional hypocaloric diet. *International Journal of Cardiology*, 14, 55–63.

Senediak, C. & Spence, S. (1985). Rapid versus gradual scheduling of therapeutic contact in a family based behavioural weight control programme for children. *Behavioural Psychotherapy*, 13, 265–287.

Smoak, C., Burke, G., Webber, L., Harsha, D., Srinivasan, S. & Berenson, G. (1987). Relation of obesity to clustering of cardiovascular disease risk factors in children and young adults: The Bogalusa Heart Study. *American Journal of Epidemiology*, 125, 364–372.

Stark, O., Atkins, E., Wolff, O. & Douglas, J. (1981). Longitudinal study of obesity in the National Survey of Health and Development. *British Journal of Medicine*, 283, 13–17.

Straw, M. (1983). Coping with obesity. In G. Burish & L. Bradley (Eds), *Coping with Chronic Disease. Research and Applications*. New York: Academic Press, pp. 219–258.

Stunkard, A. (1987). Conservative treatments for obesity. *American Journal of Clinical Nutrition*, 45, 1142–1154.

Varni, J. & Banis, H. (1985). Behavior therapy techniques applied to eating, exercise and diet modification in childhood obesity. *Journal of Developmental and Behavioral Pediatrics*, 6, 367–372.

Ward, D. & Bar-Or, D. (1986). Role of the physician and physical education teacher in the treatment of obesity at school. *Pediatrician*, **13**, 44–51.

Waxman, M. & Stunkard, A. (1980). Caloric intake and expenditure of boys. *Journal of Pediatrics*, **96**, 187–193.

Weiss, A. (1977). A behavioral approach to the treatment of adolescent obesity. *Behavior Therapy*, **8**, 720–726.

Wheeler, M. & Hess, K. (1976). Treatment of juvenile obesity by successive approximation control of eating. *Journal of Behavior Therapy and Experimental Psychiatry*, **7**, 235–241.

Woo, R., Garrow, J. & Pi-Sunyer, F. (1982). Effect of exercise on spontaneous calorie intake in obesity. *American Journal of Clinical Nutrition*, **36**, 470–477.

5 Health Promotion at the Worksite

STANISLAV V. KASL
Department of Epidemiology and Public Health, Yale University School of Medicine, 60 College Street, PO Box 3333, New Haven, CT 06510, USA

SETH SERXNER
University of Hawaii at Manoa Cancer Research Center of Hawaii, 1236 Lauhala Street, Honolulu, Hawaii 96813, USA

A CHOICE OF PERSPECTIVES

In approaching the literature on health promotion at the worksite (HPWS), it is important to realize that a variety of frameworks and perspectives can be applied to studies dealing with HPWS. Thus, for example, from a traditional scholarly perspective, the HPWS literature is somewhat of a methodological and theoretical wasteland: a diligent search would reveal only relatively few methodologically sound studies that also make an important theoretical–scientific contribution. However, such a scholarly perspective is likely to be inappropriately too narrow. The great majority of the HPWS studies appear to be demonstration studies: they are pragmatic and atheoretical, they describe a program and, generally, some aspect of its impact, or presumed impact. But "what you see is what you get"; it is difficult to go beyond the concrete and immediate information provided and derive generalizable principles or conclusions.

Thus the reviewer of the HPWS literature faces a dilemma regarding what framework or perspective to apply to these generally atheoretical demonstration studies. Any one framework will always be more a reflection of the reviewer's own predilections than a faithful and plausible way of characterizing the majority of such studies. Any such framework will be a Procrustean bed that fits but a few of the very diverse studies. But without imposing some framework and perspective on the HPWS studies, the reader will be left bewildered, wondering: what does it all mean? What does it add up to? What can I make of it?

It is useful to offer a number of concrete examples of what is implied by choosing a perspective or framework and imposing it on the HPWS studies.
1. One perspective could be a *comparative* approach to understanding the dynamics of successful HP: we look only at studies which compare two (or more) contrasting settings, one of which is the worksite (WS). However, this would leave us with very few studies to review. The HPWS literature

International Review of Health Psychology. Edited by S. Maes, H. Leventhal and M. Johnston
©1992 John Wiley & Sons Ltd

simply does not allow comparative inferences; at best, one only learns what is the difference between offering and not offering a program in the WS, but one does not usually know how the picture would be different in other settings, and why.

2. Another perspective could be that of *clinical* (biomedical) medicine. From this perspective, information on changes in risk factors by the end of the HPWS program would be viewed as insufficient evidence without additional information on long-term adherence and long-term changes. Once again, we would end up ignoring the vast majority of the HPWS studies. Furthermore, such outcomes as doctor's visits and work absences would be viewed, from this perspective, with bemused puzzlement since they are such poor indicators of health status.

3. A comprehensive *public health* perspective represents another highly relevant framework. In this approach, one would examine the contribution of HPWS to the reduction of a particular public health problem, such as cigarette smoking, in the total community; the target of the program are individuals in the community (including those at the WS) who have the problem. Thus data on participation rates in a program would leave us unimpressed unless we specifically know the participation of those with the target problem. Similarly, programs which seek to recruit only the motivated client who is ready to change, clearly violate this public health framework, since the bulk of those with the problem may be unmotivated and their readiness for change needs to be promoted first. The public health perspective represents a community-level approach in which different institutions and different settings, including WS, are seen as offering alternative, or supplementary, or complementary, or synergistic approaches to a public health problem. Clearly then, the vast majority of HPWS studies cannot be fitted into this public health perspective. It should be noted, incidentally, that since many risk factors have a continuous distribution, a risk reduction intervention need not just target those defined as "high risk"; lowering the mean level in the total population may, in fact, be the preferred strategy.

4. Another appropriate framework could focus on the work role and the work environment; here HP would be seen as an effort to enhance the health benefits of work. In this approach, the work environment is seen as etiologically salient for selected risk factors and health outcomes and some form of the "person–environment fit" formulation (eg French, Caplan & Van Harrison, 1982) would be appropriate for guiding HP efforts. Once again, the vast majority of HPWS studies ignore the environmental strategy and focus on the workers, their behavior and their risk factors.

The above four perspectives have been stated as separate and distinct alternatives when, in fact, they are at least complementary and overlapping, if not also hierarchically interrelated. We consider them all as *appropriate* formulations for the topic of HPWS. However, as already indicated, the problem is that the vast majority of actual HPWS studies are at best but a very fragmentary representation of one or another of these perspectives. Thus they cannot be used as a means of organizing and evaluating the HPWS studies. Alas, these perspectives can only be used as a background, as a way of reminding the reader of ways of thinking about the cumulative HPWS evidence, and a way of exhorting future HPWS investigators to pay more attention to the value of these perspectives.

There is one perspective which we find *inappropriate* to our purposes: the cost–benefit approach. By saying this, we do not wish to deny in any way two obvious points:

(a) Considerations of costs of programs are inescapable: since currently corporations and businesses in North America, where the vast majority of the HPWS programs are offered (Conrad, 1988a), pay for the costs, it is reasonable that they also wish to quantify the benefits in economic terms.

(b) A comprehensive evaluation of costs–benefits of HPWS programs leads inevitably and centrally to a close scrutiny of the evidence on effectiveness of programs and of methodological limitations (eg DeMuth et al., 1986; Warner et al., 1988).

Effectiveness and limitations are certainly of concern in this review as well. However, we do not wish to concern ourselves with studies and reports which deal with cost containment rather than HP, and/or which primarily focus on health care costs or such outcomes as absences and outpatient visits, wherein the health benefits (improved health status, reduced risk factors) are not easily detected (eg Baun, Bernacki & Tsai, 1986; Bernacki et al. 1986; Blair et al., 1986b; Bly, Jones & Richardson, 1986; Lorig et al., 1985; Vickery et al., 1986). In any case, precise and comprehensive estimates of costs and benefits are difficult (Warner et al., 1988) and the temptation to overstate the economic benefits of HP (eg Cumming, 1986) has led to an atmosphere of "selling health promotion" (Warner, 1987).

SOME THEORETICAL COMMENTS ON SETTINGS FOR HEALTH PROMOTION

While control of a particular public health problem can be approached from a variety of perspectives, including public policy, medical, psychological, and social (Benfari & Ockene, 1982; Breslow, 1982; Kuller et al., 1982; Syme & Alcalay, 1982), the most common distinction which has been made for settings for HP with adults has been between the community (eg Farquhar, 1978) versus the clinic (eg Syme, 1978). The community, of course, includes such specific settings as the family (eg Baranowski et al., 1982), the church (eg Lasater et al., 1986), and elderly housing (eg Pickard & Collins, 1982). The WS is presumably part of the community, but since clinic-based interventions can certainly be set up at the WS, the distinction becomes blurred.

The general HP and disease prevention literature pays little attention to the setting (and its dynamics) in which the intervention is carried out (Kirscht, 1983), though occasionally one can find rather elaborate classificatory schemas dealing not only with types of settings but also using the life-cycle perspective (Green, 1984). Comparative conceptual analyses of advantages and disadvantages of different settings for HP are rare, and comparative evaluative research is even rarer.

Investigators dealing with HPWS generally do not address the issue of the special dynamics of the WS pertinent to HP. Those who do address it tend to make several points (eg Conrad, 1987a; Glasgow & Terborg, 1988):

(a) the convenient and cost-efficient access to large numbers of target adults
(b) the availability of staff committed to HP
(c) organizational structures backing and enabling the program
(d) the potential for utilizing indigenous peer social support, both for participation and, later, for compliance.

The social support theme is a particularly prominent one. This is not only because of the presumed importance of social support in the etiological dynamics of work-related health problems (eg House & Cottington, 1986; Kasl & Wells, 1985), but also because social support in the WS can be enhanced through other mechanisms than peers, including supervisors and organizational change processes (Williams & House, 1985). In addition, the recent attention being paid to the promise of competition in HPWS (eg Brownell & Felix, 1987) is also linked closely to social support dynamics.

Overviews of HPWS work tend to summarize findings and issues in a non-specific way, that is, the setting in which the HP activity took place is pretty much ignored (eg Ivancevich & Matteson, 1988). For example, the prevention of relapse is clearly a major issue in the whole HP literature (eg Brownell et al., 1986), but there is very little theoretical discussion available which might pinpoint the special advantages and disadvantages of the WS for dealing with this problem. Recidivism appears to be much less of a problem among those who have changed on their own, such as in smoking behavior or obesity (Schachter, 1982), but it remains unclear if the WS has special advantages for precipitating or facilitating "self-change", or for helping the individual through the stages of change which have been identified (DeClemente & Prochaska, 1982).

Blueprints for setting up HPWS programs tend to be pragmatic and atheoretical (eg Felix et al., 1985). The chapter by Abrams and his colleagues (Abrams et al., 1986) represents perhaps the most explicit effort to apply social learning theory to the WS setting. In this approach, a good deal of emphasis is placed on the entire culture of the organization and on creating "a new social climate and physical environment for a permanent pro-health oriented philosophy in the majority of members of the organization" (p. 32). Proximal and distal sources of influence are discussed, and various strategies uniquely applicable at the group level and organizational levels are offered. The individual level concept of stages of readiness for change leads to a social level concept, a diffusion of change process in which individuals with high readiness to change are seen as early adopters who can serve as role models. While this chapter contains a number of useful ideas, based on relevant theory, it is somewhat unfortunate that the proposed strategy emphasizes organizational change. Such a change is difficult to achieve; one would presume that an HPWS program would first wish to exploit fully the organizational climate and structures which exist before going on to tackling organizational change. In this connection, it is interesting to notice that the authors of the chapter are conducting a community-wide effort to reduce cardiovascular risk (Elder et al., 1986). In this major effort, the approach through organizations alone proved to be slow and labor intensive, and the investigators switched to community activities as the major focus. A mixing of strategies, such as the early use of mass media to influence organizations, appears to be a promising strategy (Flora, Maibach & Maccoby, 1989) when one is trying to influence all segments of a community.

There are potentially a number of interesting issues which have received relatively little conceptual analysis. One such issue is the interplay between when and where the target (desired) behavior takes place and the optimal way of setting up the HPWS. For example, certain target behaviors, such as regular exercise, need not take place in more than one setting, such as the WS, and when this is accomplished, the goal has been achieved. But other target behaviors, such as smoking cessation or weight control, need to take place in a variety of settings and it is not clear how the HPWS programs should differ, depending on how much one is trying to generalize the behavior change beyond the work setting itself. In fact, for certain areas of behavior, such as nutrition, the optimal setting for effective behavior change may be the home and the family, and the easier direction of generalization of behavior is from the family setting to the work setting rather than the reverse. In general the interplay between community interventions and parallel WS efforts has not been exploited. Important issues are complementarity, consistency of message, and opportunities to practice new behaviors.

Another interesting issue is that the HPWS programs tend to be set up with relatively little regard for individual differences in organizational settings or in target participants. It is possible that taking into consideration such variables as gender (Spilman, 1988), blue-collar versus white-collar (King et al., 1988), or the unique fit between a particular program and a particular organizational setting (Orlandi, 1986) will enhance considerably the effectiveness of such program. The participants' perspective, such as their emphasis on fitness rather than health *per se* (Conrad, 1988b), would also seem to be an important issue. Finally, participants' preferences for specific program content or program activities appear to be another neglected consideration. An old study by Schwartz & Dubitsky (1968) was one of the few efforts where participants' views about different program approaches (in this case, smoking cessation) were solicited. Participants preferred most a method which would provide them with instructions about how to quit on their own; the least preferred method involved lectures and individual or group counselling. Lower-class participants were particularly strong in their pre-existing preferences. From these results one has a sense that those who set up the programs may be using approaches which are less preferred by the participants. In general, then, while planning for WS programs often does take into consideration organizational issues such as work schedules, the possible intrusiveness of programs, and corporate willingness to give time off for participation, it remains true that individual differences among target participants and the organization–program fit have received little systematic attention.

OVERVIEW OF THE HPWS PICTURE IN THE USA

A number of surveys, including nation-wide efforts, have suggested that around two-thirds (or more) of companies surveyed report having some form of an HPWS or wellness program (eg Chen, 1988; Christenson & Kiefhaber, 1988; Davis et al., 1984; Fielding & Breslow, 1983; Fielding & Piserchia, 1989; Hollander & Lengermann, 1988; Windom, McGinnis & Fielding, 1987). Since in these surveys it is left to the responding companies to define what it means to have a program, and what kinds of programs fall within the purview of the survey, then the apparently high prevalence of such programs may not mean much more than the fact that the corporate culture accepts such programs as legitimate, desirable, and, very likely, image-enhancing.

The HPWS programs clearly represent a change from the earlier narrower emphasis on health protection, on occupational safety and health issues; they focus on health and well-being, not just work-related disease (Conrad, 1988a; House & Cottington, 1986). By broadening these concerns, the emphasis has shifted from the occupational environment to the individual: the work setting is etiologically less salient and environmental modification becomes a much less frequent strategy.

Traditional older programs, such as accident prevention, pre-employment medical examination, and employee assistance programs (EAPs) for alcohol or drug abuse problems, are included in the general label of HP (Davis et al., 1984; Fielding & Breslow, 1983; Roman & Blum, 1988). The newer programs include health risk assessment, smoking cessation, blood pressure control and treatment, weight control, exercise and fitness, nutrition, back problem prevention and care, and stress management. Other activities are likely to be added to these programs in the future, such as specific types of cancer screening services (eg Davis et al., 1984), parenting classes, how to care for elder family members, and dealing with menopause.

It has been suggested (Conrad, 1988a) that the growth and popularity of HPWS programs are a uniquely American phenomenon, while in Europe (particularly in the Scandinavian countries) the concern has remained with "humanizing" the workplace. To the extent that HPWS programs are also common in Canada (eg O'Laughlin, Boivin & Suissa, 1988), one needs to recognize this phenomenon as "North American" rather than as purely of the

USA. In addition, it appears that many European countries are following the North American models of HPWS programs, but that the development is too recent to be already reflected in publications.

An analysis of the reasons for the growth of HPWS programs (Alexander, 1988; Conrad, 1988a; Mullen, 1988) suggests three important issues:
1. The absence of a national health insurance (USA but not Canada)
2. Cost containment and corporate perceptions about excessive employee demands and/or utilization
3. The growing emphasis within the public health and medical community (both academic and governmental) on life-style factors as salient, person-based risk factors in disease etiology which, in turn, has tended to influence broad cultural values about "wellness".

The growth of HPWS programs and their ready embrace by so many corporations has led to some disquietude among observers of the scene (eg Allegrante & Sloan, 1986; Becker, 1986; Conrad, 1987a; McLeroy, Gottlieb & Burdine, 1987; Roman & Blum, 1987). Many of these concerns are labelled as *ethical* issues, but, in fact, scientific concerns and efficacy issues are present as well. The salient concerns can be grouped as follows:
1. The ambiguous or less than benign role of the employer or corporation:
    (a) expansion of corporate jurisdiction and increase in social control over the lives of the employees
    (b) threats to employees' privacy
    (c) conflicting loyalties of service providers: they may give appearance of providing services in the usual provider–client role setting which targets the client's health and well-being, but their primary loyalty may in fact be to the corporation which may have targeted cost containment, absenteeism, or performance
2. The marketing of the HPWS programs:
    (a) service providers are usually selling a "product" to the corporation
    (b) efficacy of programs may be exaggerated, while program evaluation may be opposed or undermined
    (c) existing scientific evidence may not be responsibly or properly translated into program characteristics
    (d) promises of health benefits, if unfulfilled, may create adverse consequences
3. The blaming of the victim:
    (a) HPWS programs tend to place responsibility for health on the shoulders of individual employees
    (b) health issues may become coercive and moralized
    (c) employees with risk factors or health problems may be blamed and/or stigmatized
    (d) limitations of the efficacy of personal life-style changes may be underestimated or ignored (eg Kaplan, 1984)
    (e) possible harmful effects of work role and work settings may be neglected.

AN OVERVIEW OF METHODOLOGICAL ISSUES

Certainly, this is not the place to embark on a general discussion of methodological issues which arise in the course of conducting HPWS intervention studies; excellent textbooks are well known and easily available (eg Cook & Campbell, 1979; Cronbach, 1982). Instead, what we will do is to enumerate some of the typical and common problems and issues which apply to the HPWS studies. The intent is not to criticize the various studies, since many of them never aspired to be rigorous program evaluations; rather the intent is to remind the reader of some of the issues which need to be considered when one is attempting to arrive at rigorous conclusions about the impact (particularly health impact) of the HPWS programs. Later sections of this review, which deal with specific types of programs, will come back to additional, more specific methodological issues. A number of points listed below have been analyzed and discussed in other reviews (eg Breslow et al., 1990; Fielding, 1982; Warner et al., 1988).

One set of issues arises when the HPWS program is intended as a primary or secondary prevention which targets physical health, but the outcomes which are monitored are not themselves health outcomes, such as myocardial infarction or stroke; this is, of course, the typical situation since only a tiny fraction of HPWS studies deal with such health events. The primary concern then becomes the tightness of the link between the monitored dependent variable and the unmonitored health outcome(s) of interest. For example, cessation of cigarette smoking has well-established health benefits (and fairly prompt ones in the case of cardiovascular disease) (Ockene et al., 1990), and thus it is a very defensible outcome to monitor. Of course, long-term adherence or reliance purely on self-reports may be additional, but separate issues. Similarly, reduction in high blood pressure is another appropriate outcome to monitor because of its solid linkage to health benefits; and again, long-term control is a crucial component of this outcome. On the other hand, moderate weight loss among moderately overweight subjects, and in the absence of a change in lipid profiles or of an increase in cardiovascular fitness, may have no physical health benefits. In general, it has to be remembered that when the risk factor evidence comes only from prospective observational (non-experimental) studies, then the benefits of risk reduction are better viewed as presumptive rather than established. There are two primary reasons for this:

(a) the cumulative effect of prior exposure to the risk factor may have precipitated irreversible (pre-clinical) structural changes and the intervention comes "too late"

(b) the risk factor identified may only be an indicator for the true etiological variable and is not causally linked to it.

When the monitored dependent variable represents an index of psychological well-being or distress (life or job satisfaction, symptoms of dysphoria), then the link to physical health outcomes must be considered tenuous and dubious.

Major prospective epidemiological studies do not reveal psychological distress to be an important etiological variable in physical health outcomes (angina comes to mind as a possible exception) (eg Kasl, 1984a,b). And even cross-sectional data relating distress to biological risk factors, such as blood pressure or total cholesterol, fail to show meaningfully strong associations (eg Caplan et al., 1975). Finally, it must be noted that certain monitored outcome variables, such as illness absences or doctor's visits, are likely to have close linkages to economic variables, but their links to specific health status indicators may be more difficult to establish. Nevertheless, they are likely to have a broad association with mental health and social health status and are worth monitoring.

The issue of how good is the scientific evidence which underpins a particular HP activity goes beyond the question of closeness of linkage between monitored outcome and eventual health status benefit. It also relates to various aspects of the "technology" utilized in the HP activities. One good example is the use of health risk assessment (HRA): about 30% of private sector WSs specifically list HRA as one of their activities (Fielding & Piserchia, 1989). The HRA approach has three components: an assessment of health habits and risk factors based on self-reports, a quantitative (or sometimes only qualitative) estimation of future risk (for death or a specific health event), and a provision of an educational message. Yet there are major questions about the scientific validity and accuracy of this approach (eg DeFriese & Fielding, 1990; Schoenbach, 1987), such as:

(a) the quality of the epidemiological evidence which supports the etiological linkage between HRA items and health status outcomes, with stress and social support items being particularly questionable when included in the total instrument
(b) the adequacy of self-reports for measuring risk status, particularly for variables which are not self-observable habits, such as blood pressure level
(c) the complexity of quantifying risk based on disparate items of information in a single formula
(d) the possibility of misinterpreting the HRA, such as seeing it as an adequate substitute for a physical, or assuming that if a risk factor is not on the instrument then it must be unimportant (rather than simply unsuitable for self-reports).

It can be seen that if an HP activity has embedded in it an unproven technology, then adequate program evaluation may not only have to monitor the proximal and distal outcomes of interest but also directly address the issue of the efficacy of the technology in question.

There are two other methodological issues worth noting: self-selection and length of follow-up. The first refers to a combination of concerns:

(a) the all-too-frequent unavailability of pre-program baseline data
(b) the inability to design a proper evaluation in the form of a fully randomized clinical trial
(c) the frequent self-selection of individuals into HP programs who are healthy, health-conscious, and with fewer risk factors

(d) the inappropriate analysis of program impact on only those who showed a certain level of participation rather than the appropriate analysis of data on all those to whom the program was offered, irrespective of their level of participation.

(It is noteworthy that one of the best-known programs, Johnson and Johnson's LIVE FOR LIFE, does evaluate the impact on the entire workforce, regardless of active participation; see Wilbur, Hartwell & Piserchia, 1986.)

The second methodological issue concerns a multifaceted dilemma:

(a) HPWS programs target for change many behaviors and risk factors which must show enduring change if they are to lead to health status benefits
(b) recidivism for many life-style changes tends to be very high
(c) program evaluations with long follow-up periods are difficult and costly.

Conceptually, it is possible to think of three temporal components of program impact:

(a) the impact of the program on a monitored outcome while the programe is still going on (or immediately at the end of the program)
(b) the maintenance of change in the monitored outcome after the program ends
(c) the period when distal health status benefits may begin to appear and can be detected.

The length of the period of observation needed for the maintenance phase is obviously difficult to determine a priori; generally, some three data points would seem to be needed in order to document that the group has reached a steady state.

Reviewers of the methodology of HPWS programs (eg Beehr & O'Hara, 1987; Komaki & Jensen, 1986; Warner et al., 1988) have pointed out many other methodological problems which are very common to this area of research. Many of the problems are generic to evaluation research and are so fundamental (eg small numbers, inadequate comparison groups, objectives which are not clearly specified, program content which is inadequately described, etc.) that no didactic benefit can be derived from dwelling on them here. However, to the extent that they delimit our conclusions about what we can learn from the HPWs literature, we shall return to them selectively in reviewing specific content areas.

EMPLOYEE PARTICIPATION

Employee participation in HPWS programs is presumably the essential first step in the successful realization of the intervention goals of disease prevention, health promotion, and cost containment. (An exception to this would be the case where the mere availability of a new HPWS program initiates or precipitates beneficial changes in life style among non-participating employees.) At the same time, participation rates alone tell us very little about program impact and cannot substitute for information on changes in risk factors or health status.

There appears to be a large degree of variation in reported levels of participation in HPWS programs (Fielding, 1984), including among well-established and highly publicized programs (eg Anderson & Jose, 1987; Bly, Jones & Richardson, 1986). Participation is not a straightforward concept: it includes both participation in baseline health screening, or specific disease screening, as well as diverse behaviors over time reflecting adherence to a particular health promotion regimen.

Participation is seen as being a function of characteristics of both the program and of individuals (Sloan, 1987; Sloan & Gruman, 1988). Characteristics of the program, such as its content, quality, and continuity of care, as well as program location, time offered, and number of sessions, have been found to be general determinants of participation (eg Parkinson & Associates, 1982).

With respect to characteristics of individuals, the available evidence (eg Baun, Bernacki & Tsai, 1986; Bernacki & Baun, 1984; Breslow et al., 1990; Conrad, 1987b; Davis et al., 1987; Eakin et al., 1988; Lynch et al., 1990) suggests that participants are systematically different from non-participants. The participants are more likely to:
(a) value health, be interested in health issues, be concerned about risk of disease, be committed to health promotion/disease prevention
(b) have fewer adverse health habits, especially smoking
(c) be in good health, evaluate their health positively, and have fewer past hospitalizations
(d) be "better" employees, such as in terms of better job performance ratings and fewer illness absences.

Participants are also more likely to perceive their supervisors as supportive of their participation. It is important not to overstate the magnitude or the consistency of these differences between participants and non-participants. For example, differences on indicators of health status tend to be small and the important ones are on life-style habits (Breslow et al., 1990). Furthermore, comparing characteristics of those who have decided to participate with characteristics of those who chose not to do so, is not the same design as trying to predict future participation. Davis et al. (1987) used the latter, more rigorous design: they found job stress and trait anxiety to be important predictors, while intent to change a particular behavior, or degree of satisfaction with a health area, were not predictors, though one would have expected them to be on the basis of many other cross-sectional comparisons.

Participation in HP activities which represent only short-term time commitment, such as a physical examination or specific disease screening, have not yielded remarkable findings. For example, in one study of participation in a baseline health screen (Settergen et al., 1983), non-participants had more of some adverse life-style habits (smoking) and fewer of others (lack of regular exercise) and presented with more positive health attitudes. This would suggest that health-conscious employees may be attracted to long-term fitness programs but not necessarily to short-term screening efforts. Studies of screening for cancer reveal rather low participation rates (eg Goodspeed et al., 1988; Laville, 1989) in the work setting. Furthermore, absence of symptoms or of positive findings from an earlier examination tend to be major reasons for non-participation (Goodspeed et al., 1988; Vernon et al., 1990). This is a typical finding for screening in general and, of course, represents the "wrong" reason from a prevention perspective. Overall, one has the impression that the WS offers no special advantages for cancer screening.

Attrition from an ongoing long-term WS program represents another aspect of participation. In a study of characteristics of drop-outs from a weight loss program (Fowler et al., 1985), the discriminating characteristics of drop-outs included: more previous weight loss attempts in formal treatment programs, more optimistic expectations about amount of weight loss and about maintenance, and later onset of obesity. Attempts at reducing attrition have included the introduction of various incentives, including financial ones, and competition between groups (eg Follick, Fowler & Brown, 1984; Forster et al., 1985; Schumaker et al., 1979; Seidman, Sevelius & Ewald, 1984).

This brief review of participation leads to two additional comments. First, the data suggest that if one were to target HPWS programs to subsets of employees, one would target those who currently are more likely to be non-participants. That is, from a public health perspective, the wrong segment of the employee population are self-selecting themselves into the HPWS programs. The suggestion that one should initially screen out unmotivated employees in order to improve program effectiveness (Brownell, 1986a), is exactly the wrong solution, from this public health perspective. Rather, the HPWS programs need to include more outreach efforts and need to pay more attention to motivational variables underlying initial and continued participation. Second, given the potential for self-selection biases to operate, proper program evaluation becomes more difficult. Thus, for example, program participants may have fewer illness absences and lower turnover (Baun, Bernacki & Tsai, 1986; Tsai, Baun & Bernacki, 1987), but these associations need to be interpreted as pre-existing characteristics, not program impact, unless one has pre-program baseline data and a longitudinal design. Furthermore, program impact needs also to be examined among all those who were offered access to a program, not just those who self-selected themselves into the program. This becomes another way of trying to deal with potential self-selection biases.

The next five sections of this chapter deal with five specific targets of interventions. Some of the evidence in each section is based on single-outcome interventions, but much other evidence derives from multi-component interventions. Thus, it is necessary to offer a strong caution here: to the extent that program components may interact (particularly as the presence of one may enhance the efficacy of another, such as physical fitness and weight loss), the summary of evidence below must be viewed as somewhat incomplete. However, a detailed exploration of interactive effects would be most difficult and would take us beyond the scope of this chapter.

CONTROL OF HIGH BLOOD PRESSURE

Hypertension control is seen as the "gold standard" for the evaluation of HPWS programs (Warner et al., 1988) and general reviews of the literature leave no doubt about the fact that successful programs of screening and hypertension control can be set up in the workplace (eg Fielding, 1982, 1984; Glasgow & Terborg, 1988; Leviton, 1987; Spilman et al., 1986; Taylor, Agras & Sevelius, 1986). Specific studies conducted since 1983 (eg Alderman & Melcher, 1983; Breslow et al., 1990; Brown et al., 1989; Foote & Erfurt, 1983) would seem to suggest some straightforward conclusions:
(a) screening for blood pressure is seen as acceptable by employees and yields relatively high participation rates (Leviton, 1987)
(b) initiating treatment is no longer a problem after years of health education efforts (in the USA) publicizing the control of high blood pressure
(c) maintaining patients in treatment and with adequate compliance seems to be mostly a matter of how much effort and how many resources go into aggressive monitoring and follow-up.
   Several comments are in order regarding the above conclusions:
(a) The picture of success refers to pharmacologic control of hypertension and a similar conclusion does not apply if one attempts to control high blood pressure with stress management and relaxation techniques (eg Agras et al., 1987; Charlesworth, Williams & Baer, 1984; Chesney, 1987; Chesney et al., 1987).
(b) Monitoring activities during follow-up do not seem to succeed as health education efforts and must be maintained indefinitely if return to pre-intervention low levels of compliance and control is to be avoided (eg McKenney et al., 1973: Wilber & Barrow, 1969).
(c) "Yield" from high blood pressure screening is often described in terms of percent of previously unaware hypertensives who can be started on treatment. Thus yield from more recent screening activities, whether at work or in the community, will have come down considerably from a decade earlier because the overall US picture is one of greater awareness and better control (National Center for Health Statistics, 1986). Increasingly, the remaining uncontrolled hypertensives will be more difficult to control.
   The work on high blood pressure screening at the WS has led to an interesting debate on the possible iatrogenic effects of detecting a previously unknown condition, ie the possible effect of labelling. An early Canadian study (Haynes et al., 1978) showed an increase in illness days after identification at screening; only those who entered treatment and were compliant failed to go up in illness days. However, other studies (eg Alerman & Melcher, 1983; Rudd et al., 1987) have not supported the original observation. It appears that the phenomenon may be rather complicated, restricted to those who were unaware (but not those who were merely untreated) and who were offered only "usual" care (Polk et al., 1984).

There are only a few studies in which antihypertensive treatment at the WS was compared with that in the community. A couple of studies (Logan et al., 1982; Ruchlin, Melcher & Alerman, 1984) appear to suggest the superiority of the WS setting; however, it is not clear that a meaningful comparison can be made, since the WS represented "stepped up" care, while the community represented "usual" care. A third study (Sexton, Yuhas & Guyther, 1985) also favored the WS, but the two groups in the study design were not equivalent through randomization; rather, a small group of employees—those who made little use of community physicians—opted for WS-based treatment.

Attempts at high blood pressure control at the WS through some manipulation of the work environment (defined either objectively and/or subjectively) have apparently not been carried out. This is quite characteristic of the whole field of HPWS (eg Conrad, 1987a; Sloan, 1987). However, in this instance, it is not clear that it should even be attempted, given the uncertainty of the evidence linking the work environment and high blood pressure. For example, bus drivers appear to be at greater risk for hypertension (Ragland et al., 1987), but unexpectedly it was the subroup of bus drivers reporting fewer stressors and fewer job demands who had higher blood pressure levels (Albright et al., in press; Winkleby, Ragland & Syme, 1988). Cross-sectional studies of job stress and blood pressure levels only occasionally yield significant associations (eg Matthews et al., 1987); in fact, the evidence even for such "established" environmental risk factors as work noise appears to be somewhat unclear (eg Talbott et al., 1985). And reasonably well-researched psychosocial hypotheses, such as regarding job control and cardiovascular health, still do not provide sufficiently convergent evidence to design a work environment intervention with confidence (Kasl, 1989).

From the perspective of health psychology and behavioral medicine, a fair amount of evidence has accumulated regarding community control of high blood pressure (Kasl, 1978). Studies of HPWS dealing with hypertension show that a successful program can be set up, given sufficient commitment and resources (Fielding, 1984), and that it will be cost-effective (Warner et al., 1988). However, such studies are demonstration studies: they utilize available social–psychological knowledge but do not add to it.

SMOKING CESSATION

The smoking cessation literature is examined in the general reviews of HPWS (eg Fielding, 1982, 1984; Glasgow & Terborg, 1988; Leviton, 1987), as well as in recent reviews devoted solely to this topic (Glasgow, 1987; Hallett, 1986; Klesges & Glasgow, 1986). An excellent overview of the issues in modifying smoking behavior in general is given by Pechacek & McAlister (1980).

Smoking programs at the WS represent several strategies: prohibition, incentives, some form of educational intervention or treatment, and a combination of two or more strategies. Intervention and/or treatment programs include a variety of approaches, including self-help, public service programs, physician advice and counseling, and various behavior modification strategies including aversion therapy. More effective programs represent a combination of strategies, particularly skills training (self-help) and motivation (Glasgow, 1987; Hallett, 1986).

In general, relatively small variations in programs tend to produce only minor differences in outcome (eg Davis, Faust & Ordentlich, 1984; Glasgow et al., 1984), and small additions to programs show only small increments in success (eg Sutton & Hallett, 1988). There is some tendency for the more costly programs to be more effective and for self-help groups to be more *cost*-effective (though not most effective if cost is ignored) (Altman et al., 1987). Very inexpensive programs, such as advice from a physician or a health care provider to quit, plus handing out some educational pamphlets, are not very effective but might, in fact, cost the least in terms of costs per quitter. Such cost-effective programs may not make much of a total reduction in the smoking rates, but they look good to the accountant if not to the public health professional.

Because maintenance of cessation is such an important problem (eg Brownell et al., 1986; Ockene, 1984), quit rates at the end of a program are hardly indicative of cessation rates one or two years later; similarly, initially differential program effectiveness may vanish during follow-up. It is difficult to know what the appropriate length of follow-up is; in most studies it is one year or less (Hallett, 1986) which would seem to be insufficient. Reported quit rates vary so much that a summary estimate is not really meaningful (Hallett, 1986; Klesges & Glasgow, 1986; Leviton, 1987). Such variation may reflect a number of issues, such as:

(a) small numbers in many of the studies
(b) variation in requirement that self-reports be verified with a biological indicator, such as serum thiocyanate
(c) whether a program is attracting those who are ready to quit versus those who are difficult cases because of higher levels of addiction and many previous failed attempts to quit.

The two-year quit rates from the Johnson and Johnson program (Shipley et al., 1988) may be viewed as representative results: 22.6% of smokers in the LIVE FOR LIFE program quit, compared to 17.4% of smokers who participated in the health screen only. The differences were more striking among smokers at high risk for coronary heart disease (32% versus 13%). The superiority of smoking cessation programs for high-risk smokers has been reported in other studies (Hallett, 1986). In fact, even such minimal efforts as physician advice to quit tend to be effective in the face of the likelihood of severe health consequences (Pederson, 1982).

Given that cigarette smoking as a life-style habit is likely to have its onset during adolescence, it may be inferred that aspects of the work environment do not play an important role in the etiology of this relatively stable habit.

Variables measuring job satisfaction and various job strains do not show meaningfully large correlations with cigarette smoking (eg Caplan et al., 1975; French, Caplan & Van Harrison, 1982). Thus neither onset nor maintenance of the habit appear linked to work conditions.

However, with respect to setting up smoking cessation programs at the WS, various aspects of the organization and organizational setting may play an important role. The following are some illustrative results:

1. We know very little about why organizations that do not have a program might be reluctant to adopt one. For example, in a community-wide intervention to reduce cardiovascular risk, after nine months of effort only one organization had elected to begin a stop-smoking program (Elder et al., 1987).

2. In a study of workers' atttitudes about smoking cessation and of occupational norms about smoking, ten suburban WSs were found to be different in average attitudes and norms (Sorensen, Pechacek & Pallonen, 1986); furthermore, smokers receiving discouragement from co-workers had less confidence in their ability to quit.

3. Participation in a WS smoking cessation program may be substantial (around 70%) if the company provides release time, but minuscule (under 5%) if it does not (McCarthy & Brown, 1987).

4. A company policy of restricting WS smoking may not, by itself, be very effective: consumption at work may go down without total daily consumption showing a change (Gottlieb et al., 1990). The primary benefit seemed to be the lower annoyance of non-smoking co-workers; the observed decline in interaction between smokers and non-smokers may possibly be a negative effect (see Venters et al., 1987).

5. Setting up a formal competition at the WS may improve both the recruitment into the program as well as the eventual quit rates (Klesges, Vasey & Glasgow, 1986).

It is fair to conclude that researchers have thus far failed to exploit the unique characteristics of the workplace (Hallett, 1986). The use of competition is one exception to this conclusion, while the reliance on no more than restricting smoking places is a good example of it. Ready-made programs, such as aversion therapy or use of nicotine chewing gum, are unlikely to prove superior in the work setting if they are simply transferred there without embedding them in supportive organizational and co-worker dynamics. The WS has the potential for tailoring programs for subgroups of workers, such as older smokers who appear more motivated but also have a harder time quitting (Glasgow et al., 1988). Above all, we need to pay attention to the fact that over 90% of those who have quit smoking have done it on their own (Ockene, 1984). A better understanding of this "spontaneous" process might help us to design better WS programs, since work life is part of the ordinary everyday dynamics (unlike the clinic) to which, presumably, the "spontaneous" process is anchored.

WEIGHT REDUCTION

Weight reduction programs at the WS can be part of more comprehensive health promotion efforts which may also include nutrition and/or exercise components, or they can be specific programs devoted solely to weight control. This section will discuss only the latter type of program.

Estimating the health benefits of weight loss is a bit more complicated than for control of hypertension or for smoking cessation. While the relationship of obesity to higher risk of mortality is well documented (Bray, 1987; Manson et al., 1987), there is a fairly broad range of values (eg percent overweight or body mass index) within which the risk rises very slowly. Furthermore, in many of the studies, the role of associated biomedical and behavioral risk factors, and co-morbidity, has not been controlled. However, follow-up data from the Framingham study did show obesity to be a risk factor for cardiovascular disease independent of the contribution of the other, standard risk factors (Hubert et al., 1983). Furthermore, weight gain after young adulthood was also associated with increased cardiovascular risk, independently of initial weight and of levels of other risk factors after the weight gain. Another complication in trying to estimate the health benefits of weight loss is the recent evidence that the distribution of body fat (specifically, upper-body obesity or the waist to hip ratio) may be the primary factor in the health risks due to obesity (Lapidus et al., 1984; Larsson et al., 1984). Data on changes in waist to hip ratio following weight loss are only now beginning to come in (Wadden et al., 1988) and the health implications are not yet clear. Sex differences in upper-body obesity would suggest differential benefits of weight reduction for men and women; thus the disproportionate participation of women (white women, that is, primarily of middle and upper social class origins) in general weight reduction programs (Stunkard, 1984) represents inappropriate self-selection, from a public health perspective.

Reviews of the WS weight control literature (eg Brownell, 1986a,b; Brownell, Stunkard & McKeon, 1985; Fielding, 1984; Glasgow & Terborg, 1988) suggest that high rates of dropping out remain a problem. While it may be true that the easy availability of WS weight reduction programs attracts some inadequately motivated clients, the solution is not to screen out the unmotivated (Brownell, 1986a) but to target the appropriate subgroups through outreach efforts and to increase their motivation. Monetary incentives appear effective in reducing attrition rates (Follick, Fowler & Brown, 1984; Jeffery, Forster & Snell, 1985). Setting up competition appears to be another way of reducing attrition (Abrams & Follick, 1983; Brownell et al., 1984; Stunkard, Cohen & Felix, 1989), particularly if it is team competition (Cohen, Stunkard & Felix, 1987) which does not involve group meetings (Schumaker et al., 1979; Seidman, Sevelius & Ewald, 1984).

Recidivism, or failure to maintain weight loss achieved at the end of treatment, is a major problem (Fielding, 1984; Forster, Jeffery & Snell, 1988; Follick,

Fowler & Brown, 1984; Stunkard, Cohen & Felix, 1989). Competition is claimed to improve retention of weight loss (Brownell, 1986a) but a recent major study failed to support this claim (Stunkard, Cohen & Felix, 1989).

It has been argued that effective weight reduction programs are those in which individuals change by their own efforts and where the interventions are least intrusive (Loro, Fisher & Levenkron, 1979). Furthermore, it would appear that exercise plays an important role in weight loss during treatment and in maintenance of weight loss (Foreyt, 1987; Perri et al., 1986), thus leading to the recommendation that WS weight loss programs not accompanied by an exercise program may not be worth setting up. Very likely, nutrition education/intervention should also be part of such a multi-component program (Glanz & Seewald-Klein, 1986).

In short, the WS may not have special advantages over clinic settings in promoting weight loss maintenance (Forster, Jeffery & Snell, 1988). Special dynamics at the WS, such as competition and financial incentives, may promote participation but not necessarily maintenance. Other dynamics remain unexplored, though it is interesting to note that one report (Fisher et al., 1982) concluded that having friends and supervisors aware of and involved in weight control efforts of participants was actually counterproductive.

PHYSICAL FITNESS

A recent report (Blair et al., 1989) represents a particularly good documentation of the benefits of physical fitness, as measured by a maximal treadmill exercise test, on lowering all-cause mortality in men and women. The analysis of results included statistical adjustments for age, smoking status, cholesterol levels, systolic blood pressure, and blood glucose. The benefits of physical fitness are particularly strong for cardiovascular indicators of health (eg Kannell & Sorlie, 1979; Powell et al., 1987). There is little question that participation in fitness programs is associated with improvements on various indicators of energy expenditure and fitness, such as recovery pulse and performance on standardized graded exercise tests (eg Barnard & Anthony, 1980; Blair et al., 1986a; Breslow et al., 1990; Fielding, 1982; King et al., 1988). Fitness should be measured by standardized tests, not self-reports (Gionet & Godin, 1989). Specific indicators of cardiovascular risk, such as blood pressure and total cholesterol, also show changes but somewhat less consistently. And specific clinical health status benefits (eg reduced rates of future heart attacks) of exercise and fitness intervention programs have not yet been demonstrated.

A fair amount of attention has been focused on the impact of participating in fitness programs on absenteeism. On balance, the evidence (eg Baun, Bernacki & Herd, 1987; Baun, Bernacki & Tsai, 1986; Cox, Shephard & Corey, 1987; Fielding, 1982; Jones, Bly & Richardson, 1990; Warner et al., 1988) suggests the following:

(a) there is a self-selection effect in that those who participate are more likely to have lower prior rates of absenteeism

(b) aside from self-selection, there does seem to be a small effect in reducing absenteeism

(c) the effect may not be uniform across subgroups, such as males versus females or blue-collar versus white-collar.

Lower employee turnover and better job performance are also associated with better participation (Baun, Bernacki & Herd, 1987; Tsai, Baun & Bernacki, 1987), but these appear to be self-selection effects. Health care costs appear to be reduced only slightly (Baun, Bernacki & Tsai, 1986; Bowne et al., 1984; Breslow et al., 1990) and there appears to be no increased cost due to injuries (Tsai, Bernacki & Baun, 1988). Effects of fitness programs on job satisfaction and mood are likely to be, at best, small and not long lasting (Baun, Bernacki & Herd, 1987; Cox, Shephard & Corey, 1987; Roth & Holmes, 1987).

Overall, it would seem that exercise/fitness programs are ideally suited for the WS. The programs appear to be popular both with corporations and with employees. Major barriers to regular exercising are reported to be lack of time and inconvenience (Glasgow & Terborg, 1988); these can be overcome at the WS by setting up convenient facilities and by allowing employees time off from work to participate. The exercise behavior does not have to generalize to other settings, as is the case for smoking cessation or nutritional habits: WS participation (if adequate) is a sufficient goal in itself. Nevertheless, fitness programs at work have failed to reach their potential in two ways: the recruits are the healthier, more fit employees and long-term adherence continues to be a problem (eg Fielding, 1982).

STRESS MANAGEMENT

While stress management is a component of HPWS in about 27% of WSs (Fielding, 1989), as reported in surveys of companies, reviews of the effectiveness of HPWS activities (eg Fielding, 1982; Glasgow & Terborg, 1988) tend to omit stress management from their consideration. A major review of the economic aspects of HPWS (Warner et al., 1988) reports finding no economic analyses of stress management programs.

If hypertension control is seen as the "gold standard" for the evaluation of HPWS programs, then stress management is likely to be the farthest away from this gold standard. There are a number of reasons for this:

1. Stress continues to be a confusing concept for researchers and practitioners alike, with relatively little agreement on conceptual definitions and operationalizations (Kasl, 1984a,b).

2. Given the possible great variety of stressors linked to the work environment (eg Kasl, 1990), it appears particularly inappropriate that stress management programs target employees' responses and neglect the strategy of modifying the work environment.

3. Indicators of distress, such as dysphoric mood or job dissatisfaction, which are commonly the target outcomes in these programs, have at best a dubious linkage to future physical health status benefits.

4. Stress management programs are particularly difficult to evaluate, given such issues as non-specific effects (expectations) and reactivity of measures (Beehr & O'Hara, 1987).

5. The record of program effectiveness, particularly in the long run, is poor.

Singer et al. (1986) have pointed out that labor organizations and corporations have widely disparate perspectives on stress reduction in the WS. The former emphasize the biological and physical environment (eg heat, ventilation), and the psychological and interpersonal (eg pace, workload, shiftwork, automatic supervision), while the latter put emphasis on maladaptive personal styles and focus on personal responsibility. Of course, it is the corporate perspective which prevails when stress management programs are designed. It is also interesting to note that 81% of the companies which report that they have a stress management program claim that they also use organizational change strategies to reduce employee stress (Fielding, 1989). It is difficult to evaluate such a claim, or the efficacy of such strategies.

Several recent reviews (eg McLeroy et al., 1984; Murphy, 1984, 1988) make the stress management literature easily accessible. The programs generally include one or more of the following components: biofeedback, meditation, progressive muscle relaxation, breathing exercises, and cognitive/behavioral techniques. Many programs have add-on components which can be broadly characterized as health education efforts. The reviews as well as additional specific studies (Brunning & Frew, 1986; Charlesworth, Williams & Baer, 1984; Cole, Tucker & Friedman, 1987; Fiedler, Vivona-Vaughan & Gochfeld, 1989; Sallis et al., 1987) allow for the following conclusions:

1. Most programs target the "stress reaction" (however ill defined) for modification. They do not deal with sources of the "stress reaction" (ie with work stressors) or with presumed consequences of the reaction, such as absenteeism or alcohol consumption.

2. Comparison of effectiveness of different techniques is not yet possible. Nor can one say anything definite about the needed duration of the stress management program so that it may be effective in the long run.

3. Program evaluations generally have a follow-up period no longer than 6–12 months. This is not adequate for detecting physical health status changes, such as reducing risk of clinical events. For other outcomes, such as psychophysiological symptoms or dysphoric mood, any changes in the short follow-up period need not be indicative of the long-term stable benefits of the program. Research on how to maintain long-term benefits is not yet being pursued very vigorously.

4. The documented benefits of stress management (given the limited length of follow-up) are somewhat variable. Measures of anxiety–tension tend to show the largest decline (but how enduring?), less so for depression, and even less

so for somatic complaints. Data on blood pressure permit no single, simple conclusion. Other outcomes, such as job satisfaction and absenteeism, also show variable effects, presumably, partly because they are complex variables sensitive to complex processes.

5. It has been difficult to identify effective program components since the evaluation designs are generally not set up to isolate the effectiveness of separate parts of an intervention. It has also been difficult to distinguish between specific and non-specific program effects.

6. We do not have data on acceptability of various components of stress management programs to intended (prospective) consumers, nor do we understand the dynamics of compliance with individual program components. The fact that most programs involve white-collar workers raises the question of applicability of the existing programs to blue-collar workers.

Overall, three points stand out:

1. The programs do not modify the work stressors (environmental exposures, stimulus conditions)

2. They are not set up to reveal any cause effect dynamics, any work stressor–health outcome connections

3. They are not set up to reveal the dynamics of successful stress management for that particular setting, ie the interplay of program characteristics and WS dynamics.

CONCLUDING REMARKS

This review has been somewhat selective and certain types of WS programs were not examined, such as those dealing with nutrition (Cumming, 1986; Glanz & Seewald-Klein, 1986), dental health (Ayer et al., 1986), and cancer control (Levy et al., 1986). Also unexamined was the large literature on alcoholism, partly because of limitations of space. Most of the alcoholism programs are treatment oriented, not prevention oriented, and have their firm locus within the employee assistance programs (EAPs) (Kurtz, Googins & Howard, 1984; Sonnenstuhl & Trice, 1986; Trice & Beyer, 1984). However, the preventive orientation is likely to become more important and there may be some convergence of EAPs and HPWS programs (Moskowitz, 1989; Nathan, 1983; Sonnenstuhl, 1988; Trice & Sonnenstuhl, 1988).

An overwhelming majority of HPWS studies are atheoretical demonstration studies; they utilize existing theoretical and empirical knowledge in epidemiology/public health, behavioral medicine, and health psychology, but do not attempt to add to it. The knowledge they provide is generally specific and practical, such as "Will competition reduce attrition rates?"

If one ignores such (serious) issues as self-selection, attrition, and recidivism, then one can conclude that generally HPWS programs do have some effects, when compared to those not exposed to the program, but that seldom is a specific program clearly superior to other programs. Putting more effort and resources into a program seems to increase the impact of a program. However, such effort should *not* go into program intensity (eg more meetings or more highly trained professionals involved), but into program support and facilitation, into outreach efforts intended to recruit and motivate, and into provision of follow-up activities.

To a limited extent, HPWS studies have exploited the (presumptive) unique aspects of the WS, such as with financial incentives, competition, provision of on-site facilities, and time off from work. But in a major way, the HPWS studies represent a missed opportunity to add to our scientific and theoretical knowledge about HP, about the work setting, and about designing more effective HP programs in the WS. Thus the near-total neglect of the strategy of manipulating or modifying the work environment (alone, or in conjunction with specific HP activities) represents one such missed opportunity. Similarly, the failure to explicitly and systematically address, in the WS, such specific problems as improving long-term maintenance or designing programs which mimic the "spontaneous" process of self-change, is another missed opportunity. And the failure to conduct comparative studies of different sites (eg work versus the family) in order to identify and compare optimal strategies uniquely linked to the dynamics of each site, is a third missed opportunity.

The HPWS area of research is in a desperate need of an explicit perspective to guide and organize HPWS research. The economic perspective of cost containment, coming as it does from the corporations, pays for the programs but cannot guide them. In any case, it contains its own seeds of destruction: as corporations succeed in legitimizing more direct ways of reducing health care costs—by cutting employee benefits—their enthusiasm for HPWS activities may wither away.

It might be argued that the perspective on HPWS which most effectively addresses the ethical concerns raised earlier, is the perspective which originates in the concept of "meaning of work", the meaning of work in our society. A number of years ago, Locke (1976) reviewed the job satisfaction literature and on that basis went on to extrapolate creatively from the evidence in order to characterize desirable conditions at work. They are:

1. Work represents mental challenge (with which the worker can cope successfully) and leads to involvement and personal interest
2. Work is not physically too tiring
3. Rewards for performance are just, informative, and in line with aspirations
4. Working conditions are compatible with physical needs and they facilitate work goals
5. Work leads to high self-esteem
6. Agents in the workplace help with the attainment of job values.

Thus, HPWS activities should be linked to creating such desirable work conditions and, falling short of that, they should seek to promote health and well-being by minimizing the adverse impact of inadequacies in the work setting.

ACKNOWLEDGMENT

The authors gratefully acknowledge the many helpful comments provided by Jonathan E. Fielding.

REFERENCES

Abrams, D. B., Elder, J. P., Carleton, R. A., Lasater, T. M. & Artz, L. M. (1986). Social learning principles for organizational health promotion: An integrated approach. In M. F. Cataldo & T. J. Coates (Eds), *Health and Industry: A Behavioral Medicine Perspective*. New York: Wiley, pp. 28–51.

Abrams, D. B. & Follick, M. J. (1983). Behavioral weight-loss intervention at the worksite: Feasibility and maintenance. *Journal of Consulting and Clinical Psychology*, 51, 226–233.

Agras, W. S., Taylor, B. C., Kraemer, H. C., Southam, M. A. & Schneider, J. A. (1987). Relaxation training for essential hypertension at the worksite: II. The poorly controlled hypertensive. *Psychosomatic Medicine*, 49, 264–273.

Albright, C. L., Winkleby, M. A., Ragland, D. R., Fisher, J. & Syme, S. L. (in press). Job strain and prevalence of hypertension in a biracial population of urban bus drivers. *International Journal of Epidemiology*.

Alderman, M. H. & Melcher, L. A. (1983). Occupationally-sponsored, community-provided hypertension control. *Journal of Occupational Medicine*, 25, 465–470.

Alexander, J. (1988). The ideological construction of risk: An analysis of corporate health promotion programs in the 1980s. *Social Science and Medicine*, 26, 559–567.

Allegrante, J. P. & Sloan, R. P. (1986). Ethical dilemmas in workplace health promotion. *Preventive Medicine*, 15, 313–320.

Altman, D. G., Flora, J. A., Fortmann, S. P. & Farquhar, J. W. (1987). The cost-effectiveness of three smoking cessation programs. *American Journal of Public Health*, 77, 162–165.

Anderson, D. R. & Jose, W. S. (1987). Employee lifestyle and the bottom line: Results of the Stay Well Evaluation. *Fitness in Business*, Dec, 86–91.

Ayer, W. A., Seffrin, S., Wirthman, G., Deatrick, D. & Davis, D. (1986). Dental health promotion in the workplace. In M. F. Cataldo & T. J. Coates (Eds), *Health and Industry: A Behavioral Medicine Perspective*. New York: Wiley, pp. 255–269.

Baranowski, T., Nader, P. R., Dunn, K. & Vanderpool, N. A. (1982). Family self-help: Promoting changes in health behavior. *Journal of Communication*, 32, 161–172.

Barnard, R. J. & Anthony, D. F. (1980). Effect of health maintenance programs in Los Angeles City firefighters. *Journal of Occupational Medicine*, 22, 667–669.

Baun, W. B., Bernacki, E. J. & Herd, J. A. (1987). Corporate health and fitness programs and the prevention of work stress. In J. C. Quick, R. S. Bhagat, J. E. Dalton & J. D. Quick (Eds), *Work Stress: Health Care Systems in the Workplace*. New York: Praeger, pp. 217–234.

Baun, W. B., Bernacki, E. J. & Tsai, S. P. (1986). A preliminary investigation: Effect of a corporate fitness program on absenteeism and health care cost. *Journal of Occupational Medicine*, 28, 18–22.

Becker, M. H. (1986). The tyranny of health promotion. *Public Health Review*, 14, 15–25.

Beehr, T. A. & O'Hara, K. (1987). Methodological designs for the evaluation of occupational stress interventions. In S. V. Kasl & C. L. Cooper (Eds), *Stress and Health: Issues in Research Methodology*. Chichester: Wiley, pp. 79–112.

Benfari, R. C. & Ockene, J. K. (1982). Control of cigarette smoking from a psychological perspective. *Annual Review of Public Health*, 3, 101–128.

Bernacki, E. J. & Baun, W. B. (1984). The relationship of job performance to exercise adherence in a corporate fitness program. *Journal of Occupational Medicine*, **26**, 529–531.

Bernacki, E. J., Tsai, S., Shan, R., Miller, S. (1986). Analysis of a corporation's health care experience: Implications for cost containment and disease prevention. *Journal of Occupational Medicine*, **28**, 502–508.

Blair, S. N., Kohl, H. W., III, Paffenbarger, R. S., Jr., Clark, D. G., Cooper, K. H. & Gibbons, L. W. (1989). Physical fitness and all-cause mortality: A prospective study of healthy men and women. *Journal of the American Medical Association*, **262**, 2395–2401.

Blair, S. N., Piserchia, P. V., Wilbur, C. S. & Crowder, J. H. (1986a). A public health intervention model for work-site health promotion. *Journal of the American Medical Association*, **255**, 921–926.

Blair, S. N., Smith, M., Collingwood, T. R., Reynolds, R., Prentice, M. C. & Sterling, C. L. (1986b). Health promotion for educators. Impact on absenteeism. *Preventive Medicine*, **15**, 166–175.

Bly, J. L., Jones, R. C. & Richardson, J. E. (1986). Impact of worksite health promotion on health care costs and utilization: Evaluation of Johnson & Johnson Live For Life program. *Journal of the American Medical Association*, **256**, 3235–3240.

Bowne, D. W., Russell, M. L., Morgan, J. L., Optenberg, S. A. & Clark, A. E. (1984). Reduced disability and health care costs in an industrial fitness program. *Journal of Occupational Medicine*, **26**, 809–816.

Bray, G. A. (1987). Overweight is risking fate: Definition, classification, prevalence, and risks. *Annals of the New York Academy of Sciences*, **499**, 14–28.

Breslow, L. (1982). Control of cigarette smoking from a public policy perspective. *Annual Review of Public Health*, **3**, 129–151.

Breslow, L., Fielding, J., Herrman, A. A. & Wilbur, C. S. (1990). Worksite health promotion: Its evolution and the Johnson & Johnson experience. *Preventive Medicine*, **19**, 13–21.

Brown, H. R., Carozza, N. B., Lloyd, R. & Thater, C. F. (1989). Worksite blood pressure control: The evolution of a program. *Journal of Occupational Medicine*, **31**, 354–357.

Brownell, K. D. (1986a). Public health approaches to obesity and its management. *Annual Review of Public Health*, **7**, 521–533.

Brownell, K. D. (1986b). Weight control at the workplace: The power of social and behhavioral factors. In M. F. Cataldo & T. J. Coates (Eds), *Health and Industry: A Behavioral Medicine Perspective*. New York: Wiley, pp. 143–161.

Brownell, K. D., Cohen, R. Y., Stunkard, A. J., Felix, M. R. J. & Cooley, N. B. (1984). Weight loss competitions at the work site: Impact on weight, morale, and cost-effectiveness. *American Journal of Public Health*, **74**, 1283–1285.

Brownell, K. D. & Felix, M. R. J. (1987). Competitions to facilitate health promotion: Review and conceptual analysis. *American Journal of Health Promotion*, **2**, 28–36.

Brownell, K. D., Marlatt, G. A., Lichtenstein, E. & Wilson, J. T. (1986). Understanding and preventing relapse. *American Psychologist*, **41**, 765–782.

Brownell, K. D., Stunkard, A. J. & McKeon, P. E. (1985). Weight reduction at the work site: A promise partially fulfilled. *American Journal of Psychiatry*, **142**, 47–52.

Brunning, N. S. & Frew, D. R. (1986). Can stress intervention strategies improve self-esteem, manifest anxiety, and job satisfaction? A longitudinal field experiment. *Journal of Health and Human Resource Administration*, **9**, 110–124.

Caplan, R. D., Cobb, S., French, J. R. P., Jr., Harrison, R. V. & Pinneau, S. R., Jr. (1975). *Job Demands and Worker Health*. Washington, DC: US Government Printing Office, HEW Publication No. (NIOSH) 75–160.

Charlesworth, E. A., Williams, B. J. & Baer, P. E. (1984). Stress management at the worksite for hypertension: Compliance, cost–benefit, health care, and hypertension-related variables. *Psychosomatic Medicine*, **46**, 387–397.

Chen, M. S., Jr. (1988). Wellness in the workplace: Beyond the point of no return. *Health Values: Achieving High Level Wellness*, **12**, 16–22.

Chesney, M. A. (1987). Behavioral factors in hypertension: Lessons from the work setting. In J. C. Quick, R. S. Bhagat, J. E. Dalton & J. E. Quick (Eds), *Work Stress: Health Care Systems in the Workplace*. New York: Praeger, pp. 111–129.

Chesney, M. A., Black, G. W., Swan, G. E. & Ward, M. M. (1987). Relaxation training for essential hypertension and the worksite: I. The untreated mild hypertensive. *Psychosomatic Medicine*, **49**, 250–263.

Christenson, G. M. & Kiefhaber, A. (1988). Highlights from the National Survey of Worksite Health Promotion Activities. *Health Values: Achieving High Level Wellness*, **12**, 29–33.

Cohen, R. Y., Stunkard, A. J. & Felix, M. R. J. (1987). Comparison of three worksite weight-loss competitions. *Journal of Behavioral Medicine*, **10**, 467–479.

Cole, G. E., Tucker, L. A. & Friedman, G. M. (1987). Absenteeism data as a measure of cost effectiveness of stress management programs. *American Journal of Health Promotion*, **1**, 12–15.

Conrad, P. (1987a). Wellness in the work place: Potentials and pitfalls of work-site health promotion. *The Milbank Quarterly*, **65**, 255–275.

Conrad, P. (1987b). Who comes to worksite wellness programs? A preliminary review. *Journal of Occupational Medicine*, **29**, 317–320.

Conrad, P. (1988a). Worksite health promotion: The social context. *Social Science and Medicine*, **26**, 485–489.

Conrad, P. (1988b). Health and fitness at work: A participants' perspective. *Social Science and Medicine*, **26**, 545–550.

Cook, T. D. & Campbell, D. T. (1979). *Quasi-Experimentation: Design and Analysis Issues for Field Settings*. Chicago: Rand McNally.

Cox, M. H., Shephard, R. J. & Corey, P. (1987). Physical activity and alienation in the work-place. *Journal of Sports Medicine*, **27**, 429–436.

Cronbach, L. (1982). *Designing Evaluations of Educational and Social Programs*. San Francisco: Jossey-Bass.

Cumming, C. (1986). A review of the impact of nutrition on health and profits and a discussion of successful program elements. *American Journal of Health Promotion*, **1**, 14–22.

Davis, A. L., Faust, R. & Ordentlich, M. (1984). Self-help smoking cessation and maintenance programs: A comparative study with 12 months follow-up by the American Lung Association. *American Journal of Public Health*, **74**, 1212–1217.

Davis, K. E., Jackson, K. L., Kronenfeld, J. J. & Blair, S. N. (1987). Determinants of participation in worksite health promotion activities. *Health Education Quarterly*, **14**, 195–205.

Davis, M. F., Rosenberg, K., Iverson, D. C., Vernon, T. M. & Bauer, J. (1984). Worksite health promotion in Colorado. *Public Health Reports*, **99**, 538–543.

DeClemente, C. D. & Prochaska, J. O. (1982). Self-change and therapy change of smoking behaviors: A comparison of processes of change in cessation and maintenance. *Addictive Behaviors*, **7**, 133–142.

DeFriese, G. H. & Fielding, J. E. (1990). Health risk appraisal in the 1990s: Opportunities, challenges, and expectations. *Annual Review of Public Health*, **11**, 401–418.

DeMuth, N. M., Fielding, J. E., Stunkard, A. J. & Hollander, R. B. (1986). Evaluation of industrial health promotion programs: Return-on-investment and survival of the fittest. In M. F. Cataldo & T. J. Coates (Eds), *Health and Industry: A Behavioral Medicine Perspective*. New York: Wiley, pp. 433–452.

Eakin, J. M., Gotay, C. C., Rademaker, A. W. & Cowell, J. W. F. (1988). Factors associated with enrollment in an employee fitness center. *Journal of Occupational Medicine*, 30, 633–637.

Elder, J. P., McGraw, S. A., Abrams, D. B., Ferreira, A., Lasater, T. M., Longpre, H., Peterson, G. S., Schwertfeger, R. & Carleton, R. A. (1986). Organizational and community approaches to community-wide prevention of heart disease: The first two years of the Pawtucket Heart Health Program. *Preventive Medicine*, 15, 107–117.

Elder, J. P., McGraw, S. A., Rodrigues, A., Lasater, T. M., Ferreira, A., Kendall, L., Peterson, G. & Carleton, R. A. (1987). Evaluation of two community-wide smoking cessation contests. *Preventive Medicine*, 16, 221–234.

Farquhar, J. W. (1978). The community-based model of life style intervention trials. *American Journal of Epidemiology*, 108, 103–111.

Felix, M. R. J., Stunkard, A. J., Cohen, R. & Cooley, N. B. (1985). Health promotion at the worksite. I. A process for establishing programs. *Preventive Medicine*, 14, 99–108.

Fielder, N., Vivona-Vaughan, E. & Gochfeld, M. (1989). Evaluation of a work site relaxation training program using ambulatory blood pressure monitoring. *Journal of Occupational Medicine*, 31, 595–602.

Fielding, J. E. (1982). Effectiveness of employee health improvement programs. *Journal of Occupational Medicine*, 24, 907–916.

Fielding, J. E. (1984). Health promotion and disease prevention at the worksite. *Annual Review of Public Health*, 5, 237–265.

Fielding, J. E. (1989). Worksite stress management: National survey results. *Journal of Occupational Medicine*, 31, 990–995.

Fielding, J. E. & Breslow, L. (1983). Health promotion programs sponsored by California employers. *American Journal of Public Health*, 73, 538–542.

Fielding, J. E. & Piserchia, P. V. (1989). Frequency of worksite health promotion activities. *American Journal of Public Health*, 79, 16–20.

Fisher, E. B., Jr., Lowe, M. R., Levenkron, J. C. & Newman, A. (1982). Reinforcement and structural support of maintained risk reduction. In R. B. Stuart (Ed.), *Adherence, Compliance and Generalization in Behavioral Medicine*. New York: Brunner/Mazel, pp. 145–168.

Flora, J. A., Maibach, E. W. & Maccoby, N. (1989). The role of media across four levels of health promotion intervention. *Annual Review of Public Health*, 10, 181–201.

Follick, M. J., Fowler, J. L. & Brown, R. A. (1984). Attrition in worksite weight-loss interventions: The effects of an incentive procedure. *Journal of Consulting and Clinical Psychology*, 52, 139–140.

Foote, A. & Erfurt, J. C. (1983). Hypertension control at the worksite. *New England Journal of Medicine*, 308, 809–813.

Foreyt, J. P. (1987). Issues in the assessment and treatment of obesity. *Journal of Consulting and Clinical Psychology*, 55, 677–684.

Forster, J. L., Jeffry, R. W. & Snell, M. K. (1988). One-year follow-up study to a worksite weight control program. *Preventive Medicine*, 17, 129–133.

Forster, J. L., Jeffrey, R. W., Sullivan, S. & Snell, M. K. (1985). A work-site weight control program using financial incentives collected through payroll deduction. *Journal of Occupational Medicine*, 27, 804–808.

Fowler, J. L., Follick, M. J., Abrams, D. B. & Rickard-Figueroa, K. (1985). Participant characteristics as predictors of attrition in worksite weight loss. *Addictive Behaviors*, 10, 445–448.

French, J. R. P., Jr., Caplan, R. D. & Van Harrison, R. (1982). *The Mechanisms of Job Stress and Strain.* Chichester: Wiley.

Gionet, N. J. & Godin, G. (1989). Self-reported exercise behavior of employees: A validity study. *Journal of Occupational Medicine*, 31, 969–973.

Glanz, K. & Seewald-Klein, T. (1986). Nutrition at the worksite: An overview. *Journal of Nutrition Education*, 18 (Suppl.), S1–S12.

Glasgow, R. E. (1987). Worksite smoking cessation: Current progress and future directions. *Canadian Journal of Public Health*, 78, 521–527.

Glasgow, R. E., Klesges, R. C., Godding, P. R., Vasey, M. W. & O'Neill, H. K. (1984). Evaluation of a worksite-controlled smoking program. *Journal of Consulting and Clinical Psychology*, 52, 137–138.

Glasgow, R. E., Klesges, R. C., Klesges, L. M. & Somes, G. R. (1988). Variables associated with participation and outcome in a worksite smoking control program. *Journal of Consulting and Clinical Psychology*, 56, 617–620.

Glasgow, R. E. & Terborg, J. R. (1988). Occupational health promotion programs to reduce cardiovascular risk. *Journal of Consulting and Clinical Psychology*, 56, 365–373.

Goodspeed, R. B., DeLucia, A. G., Parravano, J. & Goldfield, N. (1988). Compliance with mammography recommendations at the work site. *Journal of Occupational Medicine*, 30, 40–42.

Gottlieb, N. H., Eriksen, M. P., Lovato, C. Y., Weinstein, R. P. & Green, L. W. (1990). Impact of a restrictive work site smoking policy on smoking behavior, attitudes and norms. *Journal of Occupational Medicine*, 32, 16–23.

Green, L. W. (1984). Modifying and developing health behavior. *Annual Review of Public Health*, 5, 215–236.

Hallett, R. (1986). Smoking intervention in the workplace: Review and recommendations. *Preventive Medicine*, 15, 213–231.

Haynes, R. B., Sackett, D. L., Taylor, D. W., Gibson, E. S. & Johnson A. L. (1978). Increased absenteeism from work after detection and labelling of hypertensive patients. *New England Journal of Medicine*, 299, 741–744.

Hollander, R. B. & Lengermann, J. J. (1988). Corporate characteristics and worksite health promotion programs: Survey findings from Fortune 500 companies. *Social Science and Medicine*, 26, 491–501.

House, J. S. & Cottington, E. M. (1986). Health and the workplace. In L. H. Aiken & D. Mechanic (Eds), *Applications of Social Science to Clinical Medicine and Health Policy*. New Brunswick, N. J.: Rutgers University Press, pp. 392–416.

Hubert, H. B., Feinleib, M., McNamara, P. M. & Castelli, W. P. (1983). Obesity as an independent risk factor for cardiovascular disease: A 26-year follow-up of participants in the Framingham Heart Study. *Circulation*, 67, 968–977.

Ivancevich, J. M. & Matteson, M. T. (1988). Promoting the individual's health and well-being. In C. L. Cooper & R. Payne (Eds), *Causes, Coping and Consequences of Stress at Work*. Chichester: Wiley, pp. 267–299.

Jeffrey, R. W., Forster, J. L. & Snell, M. K. (1985). Promoting weight control at the worksite: A pilot program of self-motivation using payroll-based incentives. *Preventive Medicine*, 14, 187–194.

Jones, R. C., Bly, J. L. & Richardson, J. E. (1990). A study of worksite health promotion program and absenteeism. *Journal of Occupational Medicine*, 32, 95–99.

Kannell, W. B. & Sorlie, P. (1979). Some health benefits of physical activity: The Framingham Study. *Archives of Internal Medicine*, 139, 857–862.

Kaplan, R. M. (1984). The connection between clinical health promotion and health status. *American Psychologist*, 39, 755–765.

Kasl, S. V. (1978). A social–psychological perspective on successful community control of high blood pressure: A review. *Journal of Behavioral Medicine*, 1, 347–381.

Kasl, S. V. (1984a). Chronic life stress and health. In A. Steptoe & A. Mathews (Eds), *Health Care and Human Behaviour*. London: Academic Press, pp. 41–75.

Kasl, S. V. (1984b). Stress and health. *Annual Review of Public Health*, 5, 318–341.

Kasl, S. V. (1989). An epidemiological perspective on the role of control in health. In S. L. Sauter, J. J. Hurrell, Jr. & C. L. Cooper (Eds), *Job Control and Worker Health*. Chichester: Wiley, pp. 161–189.

Kasl, S. V. (1990). Assessing health risks in the work setting. In S. Hobfoll (Ed.), *New Directions in Health Psychology Assessment*. Washington, DC: Hemisphere Publishing Corporation, pp. 95–125.

Kasl, S. V. & Wells, J. A. (1985). Social support and health in the middle years: Work and the family. In S. Cohen, & S. L. Syme (Eds), *Social Support and Health*. Orlando: Academic Press, pp. 175–198.

King, A. C., Carl, F., Birkel, L. & Haskell, W. L. (1988). Increasing exercise among blue-collar employees: The tailoring of worksite programs to meet specific needs. *Preventive Medicine*, 17, 357–365.

Kirscht, J. P. (1983). Preventive health behavior: A review of research and issues. *Health Psychology*, 2, 277–301.

Klesges, R. C. & Glasgow, R. E. (1986). Smoking modification in the worksite. In M. F. Cataldo & T. J. Coates (Eds), *Health and Industry: A Behavioral Medicine Approach*. New York: Wiley, pp. 231–254.

Klesges, R. C., Vasey, M. M. & Glasgow, R. E. (1986). A worksite smoking modification competition: Potential for public health impact. *American Journal of Public Health*, 76, 198–200.

Komaki, J. L. & Jensen, M. (1986). Within-group designs: An alternative to traditional control-group designs. In M. F. Cataldo & T. J. Coates (Eds), *Health and Industry: A Behavioral Medicine Perspective*. New York: Wiley, pp. 86–139.

Kuller, L., Meilahn, E., Townsend, M. & Weinberg, G. (1982). Control of cigarette smoking from a medical perspective. *Annual Review of Public Health*, 3, 153–178.

Kurtz, N. R., Googins, B. & Howard, W. C. (1984). Measuring the success of occupational alcoholism programs. *Journal of Studies on Alcohol*, 45, 33–45.

Lapidus, L., Bengtsson, C., Larsson, B., Pennert, K., Rybo, E. & Sjorstrom, L. (1984). Distribution of adipose tissue and risk of cardiovascular disease and death: A 12 year follow up of participants in the population study of women in Gothenburg, Sweden. *British Medical Journal*, 289, 1257–1261.

Larsson, B., Svarsudd, K., Welin, L., Wilhelmsen, L., Bjorntorp, P. & Tibblin, G. (1984). Abdominal adipose tissue distribution, obesity, and risk of cardiovascular disease and death: 13 year follow up of participants in the study of men born in 1913. *British Medical Journal*, 288, 1401–1404.

Lasater, T. M., Wells, B. L., Carleton, R. A. & Elder, J. P. (1986). The role of churches in disease prevention research. *Public Health Reports*, 101, 125–131.

Laville, E. A., Vernon, S. W., Jackson, G. L. & Hughes, J. I. (1989). Comparison of participants and nonparticipants in a work site cancer awareness and screening program. *Journal of Occupational Medicine*, 31, 221–232.

Leviton, L. C. (1987). The yield from work-site cardiovascular risk reduction. *Journal of Occupational Medicine*, 29, 931–936.

Levy, S. M., Hopkins, B., Chesney, M., Ringen, K., Nathan, P. & MacDougal, V. (1986). Cancer control at the community level: The modification of workers' behaviors associated with carcinogens. In M. F. Cataldo & T. J. Coates (Eds), *Health and Industry: A Behavioral Medicine Perspective*. New York: Wiley, pp. 285–300.

Locke, E. A. (1976). The nature and causes of job satisfaction. In M. D. Dunnette (Ed.), *Handbook of Industrial and Organizational Psychology*. Chicago: Rand McNally, pp. 1297–1349.

Logan, A. G., Milne, B. J., Achber, C., Campbell, W. A. & Haynes, R. B. (1982). A comparison of community and occupationally provided antihypertensive care. *Journal of Occupational Medicine*, **24**, 901–906.

Lorig, K., Kraines, R. G., Brown, B. W., Jr. & Richardson, N. (1985). A workplace health education program that reduces outpatient visits. *Medical Care*, **23**, 1044–1054.

Loro, A. D., Fisher, E. B. & Levenkron, J. E. (1979). Comparison of established and innovative weight reduction treatment procedures. *Journal of Applied Behavior Analysis*, **12**, 141–155.

Lynch, W. D., Golaszewski, T. J., Clearie, A. F., Snow, D. & Vickery, D. M. (1990). Impact of a facility-based corporate fitness program on the number of absences from work due to illness. *Journal of Occupational medicine*, **32**, 9–12.

McCarthy, W. & Brown, R. E. (1987). Correlates of recruitment in a smoking cessation program. Paper presented at the Annual Meeting of the American Public Health Association, New Orleans.

McKenney, J. M., Slining, J. M., Henderson, H. R., Devins, D. & Barr, M. (1973). The effect of clinical pharmacy services on patients with essential hypertension. *Circulation*, **48**, 1104–1111.

McLeroy, K. R., Gottlieb, N. H. & Burdine, J. N. (1987). The business of health promotion: Ethical issues and professional responsibilities. *Health Education Quarterly*, **14**, 91–109.

McLeroy, K. R., Green, L. W., Mullen, K. D. & Foshee, V. (1984). Assessing the effects of health promotion in worksites: A review of the stress program evaluations. *Health Education Quarterly*, **11**, 379–401.

Manson, J. E., Stampfer, M. J., Hennekens, C. H. & Willett, W. C. (1987). Body weight and longevity: A reassessment. *Journal of the American Medical Association*, **257**, 353–358.

Matthews, K. A., Cottington, E. M., Talbott, E., Kuller, L. H. & Siegel, J. M. (1987). Stressful work conditions and diastolic blood pressure among blue collar factory workers. *American Journal of Epidemiology*, **126**, 280–291.

Moskowitz, J. M. (1989). The primary prevention of alcohol problems: A critical review of the research literature. *Journal of Studies on Alcohol*, **50**, 54–88.

Mullen, P. D. (1988). Health promotion and patient education benefits for employees. *Annual Review of Public Health*, **9**, 305–332.

Murphy, L. R. (1984). Occupational stress management: A review and appraisal. *Journal of Occupational Psychology*, **57**, 1–15.

Murphy, L. R. (1988). Workplace interventions for stress reduction and prevention. In C. L. Cooper & R. Payne (Eds), *Causes, Coping and Consequences of Stress at Work*. Chichester: Wiley, pp. 301–339.

Nathan, P. (1983). Failure in prevention: Why we can't prevent the devastating effect of alcoholism and drug abuse. *American Psychologist*, **38**, 459–467.

National Center for Health Statistics (1986). *Blood Pressure Levels in Persons 18–74 Years of Age in 1976–80, and Trends in Blood Pressure from 1960 to 1980 in the U. S.* Washington, DC: US Government Printing Office, Vital and Health Statistics, Series 11, No. 234.

Ockene, J. K. (1984). Toward a smoke-free society (editorial). *American Journal of Public Health*, **74**, 1198–1200.

Ockene, J. K., Kuller, L. H., Svendsen, K. H. & Meilahn, E. (1990). The relationship of smoking cessation to coronary heart disease and lung cancer in MRFIT. *American Journal of Public Health*, **80**, 954–958.

O'Loughlin, J., Boivin, J.-F. & Suissa, S. (1988). A survey of worksite health promotion in Montreal. *Canadian Journal of Public Health*, **79** (Suppl. 1), 5–10.

Orlandi, M. A. (1986). The diffusion and adaption of worksite health promotion innovations: An analysis of barriers. *Preventive Medicine*, 15, 522–536.

Parkinson, R. S. & Associates (Eds) (1982). *Managing Health Promotion in the Worksite: Guidelines for Implementation and Evaluation*. Palo Alto, CA: Mayfield Publishing Co.

Pechacek, T. F. & McAlister, A. L. (1980). Strategies for the modification of smoking behavior. Treatment and prevention. In J. M. Ferguson & C. B. Taylor (Eds), *The Comprehensive Handbook of Behavioral Medicine*, Vol. 3, *Extended Applications and Issues*. New York: Spectrum Publications.

Pederson, L. L. (1982). Compliance with physician advice to quit smoking: A review of the literature. *Preventive Medicine*, 11, 71–84.

Perri, M. G., McAdoo, W. G., McAllister, D. A., Lauer, J. B. & Yancey, D. Z. (1986). Enhancing the efficacy of behavior therapy for obesity: Effects of aerobic exercise and a multicomponent maintenance program. *Journal of Consulting and Clinical Psychology*, 52, 480–481.

Pickard, L. & Collins, J. B. (1982). Health education techniques for dense residential settings. *Educational Gerontology*, 8, 381–393.

Polk, B. F., Harlan, L. C., Cooper, S. P., Stromer, M., Ignatius, J., Mull, H. & Blazkowski, T. P. (1984). Disability days associated with detection and treatment in a hypertension control program. *American Journal of Epidemiology*, 119, 44–53.

Powell, K. E., Thompson, P. D., Casperson, C. J. & Kendrick, J. S. (1987). Physical activity and the incidence of coronary heart disease. *Annual Review of Public Health*, 8, 253–287.

Ragland, D. R., Winkleby, M. A., Schwalbe, J., Holman, B. L., Morse, L., Syme, S. L. & Fisher, J. M. (1987). Prevalence of hypertension in bus drivers. *International Journal of Epidemiology*, 16, 208–214.

Roman, P. M. & Blum, T. C. (1987). Ethics in worksite health programming: Who is served? *Health Education Quarterly*, 14, 57–70.

Roman, P. M. & Blum, T. C. (1988) Formal intervention in employee health: Comparisons of the nature and structure of employee assistance programs and health promotion programs. *Social Science and Medicine*, 26, 503–514.

Roth, D. L. & Holmes, D. S. (1987). Influence of aerobic exercise training and relaxation training on physical and psychological health following stressful life events. *Psychosomatic Medicine*, 49, 355–365.

Ruchlin, H. S., Melcher, L. A. & Alderman, M. H. (1984). A comparative economic analysis of work-related hypertension care programs. *Journal of Occupational Medicine*, 26, 45–49.

Rudd, P., Price, G. M., Graham, L. E., Beilstein, B. A., Tarbell, S. J. H., Bacchetti, P. & Fortmann, S. P. (1987). Consequences of worksite hypertension screening: changes in absenteeism. *Hypertension*, 10, 425–436.

Sallis, J. F., Trevorrow, T. R., Johnson, C. C. Hovell, M. F. & Kaplan, R. M. (1987). Worksite stress management: A comparison of programs. *Psychology and Health*, 1, 237–255.

Schachter, S. (1982). Recidivism and self-care of smoking and obesity. *American Psychologist*, 37, 436–444.

Schoenbach, V. J. (1987). Appraising health risk appraisal. *American Journal of Public Health*, 77, 409–411.

Schumaker, N., Groth, B., Kleinsek, J. & Seay, N. (1979). Successful weight control program for employees. *Journal of the American Dietetic Association*, 74, 466–467.

Schwartz, J. L. & Dubitzky, M. (1968). *Psychosocial Factors Involved in Cigarette Smoking and Cessation*, Berkeley, CA: The Institute for Health Research.

Seidman, L. S., Sevelius, G. G. & Ewald, P. (1984). A cost-effective weight loss program at the worksite. *Journal of Occupational Medicine*, 26, 725–730.

Settergen, S. K., Wilbur, C. S., Hartwell, T. D. & Rassweiler, J. H. (1983). Comparison of respondents and nonrespondents to a worksite health screen. *Journal of Occupational Medicine*, 25, 475–480.

Sexton, M., Yuhas, M. K. & Guyther, J. R. (1985). A hypertension treatment program at the workplace to complement community care. *Preventive Medicine*, 14, 15–23.

Shipley, R. H., Orleans, C. T., Wilbur, C. S., Piserchia, P. V. & McFadden, D. W. (1988). Effect of the Johnson & Johnson LIVE FOR LIFE program on employee smoking. *Preventive Medicine*, 17, 25–34.

Singer, J. A., Neale, M. S., Schwartz, G. E. & Schwartz, J. (1986). Conflicting perspectives on stress reduction in occupational settings: A systems approach to their resolution. In M. F. Cataldo & T. J. Coates (Eds), *Health and Industry: A Behavioral Medicine Perspective*. New York: Wiley, pp. 162–192.

Sloan, R. P. (1987). Workplace health promotion: A commentary on the evolution of a paradigm. *Health Education Quarterly*, 14, 181–194.

Sloan, R. P. & Gruman, J. C. (1988). Participation in workplace health promotion programs: The contribution of health and organizational factors. *Health Education Quarterly*, 15, 269–288.

Sonnenstuhl, W. J. (1988). Contrasting employee assistance, health promotion, and quality of work life programs and their effect on alcohol abuse and dependence. *The Journal of Applied Behavioral Science*, 24, 347–363.

Sonnenstuhl, W. J. & Trice, H. M. (1986). *Strategies for Employee Assistance Programs: The Crucial Balance*. Ithaca, NY: ILR Press.

Sorensen, G., Pechacek, T. & Pallonen, V. (1986). Occupational and worksite norms and attitudes about smoking cessation. *American Journal of Public Health*, 76, 544–549.

Spilman, M. A. (1988). Gender differences in worksite health promotion activities. *Social Science and Medicine*, 26, 525–535.

Spilman, M. A., Goetz, A., Schulz, J., Bellingham, R. & Johnson, D. (1986). Effects of a corporate health promotion program. *Journal of Occupational Medicine*, 28, 285–289.

Stunkard, A. J. (1984). The current status of treatment of obesity in adults. In A. J. Stunkard & E. Stellar (Eds), *Eating and Its Disorders*. New York: Raven Press, pp. 157–174.

Stunkard, A. J., Cohen, R. Y. & Felix, M. R. J. (1989). Weight loss competitions at the work site: How they work and how well. *Preventive Medicine*, 18, 460–474.

Sutton, S. & Hallett, R. (1988). Smoking intervention in the workplace using videotapes and nicotine chewing gum. *Preventive Medicine*, 17, 48–59.

Syme, S. L. (1978). Life style intervention in clinic-based trials. *American Journal of Epidemiology*, 108, 87–91.

Syme, S. L. & Alcalay, R. (1982). Control of cigarette smoking from a social perspective. *Annual Review of Public Health*, 3, 179–199.

Talbott, E., Helmkamp, J., Matthews, K., Kuller, L., Cottington, E. & Redmond, G. (1985). Occupational noise exposure, noise-induced hearing loss, and the epidemiology of high blood pressure. *American Journal of Epidemiology*, 121, 501–514.

Taylor, C. B., Agras, W. S. & Sevelius, G. (1986). Managing hypertension in the workplace. In M. F. Cataldo & T. J. Coates (Eds), *Health and Industry: A Behavior Medicine Perspective*. New York: Wiley, pp. 193–209.

Trice, H. M. & Beyer, J. M. (1984). Work-related outcomes of the constructive-confrontation strategy in a job-based alcoholism program. *Journal of Studies on Alcohol*, 45, 393–404.

Trice, H. M. & Sonnenstuhl, W. J. (1988). Drinking behavior and risk factors related to the work place: Implications for research and prevention. *The Journal of Applied Behavioral Science*, 24, 327–346.

Tsai, S. P., Baun, W. B. & Bernacki, E. J. (1987). Relationship of employee turnover to exercise adherence in a corporate fitness program. *Journal of Occupational Medicine*, **29**, 572–575.

Tsai, S. P., Bernacki, E. J. & Baun, W. B. (1988). Injury prevalence and associated costs among participants of an employee fitness program. *Preventive Medicine*, **17**, 475–482.

Venters, M. H., Solberg, L. I., Kottke, T. E., Brekke, M., Pechacek, T. F. & Grimm, R. H., Jr. (1987). Smoking patterns among social contacts of smokers, ex-smokers, and never smokers. *Preventive Medicine*, **16**, 626–635.

Vernon, S. W., Acquavella, J. F., Yarborough, C. M., Hughes, J. J. & Thar, W. E. (1990). Reasons for participation and nonparticipation in a colorectal cancer screening program for a cohort of high risk polypropylene workers. *Journal of Occupational Medicine*, **32**, 46–51.

Vickery, D. M., Golaszewski, T., Wright, E. & McPhee, L. E. (1986). Life-style and organizational health insurance costs. *Journal of Occupational Medicine*, **28**, 1165–1168.

Wadden, T. A., Stunkard, A. J., Johnston, F. E., Wang, J., Pierson, R. N., Van Itallie, T. B., Costello, E. & Pena, M. (1988). Body fat deposition in adult obese women. II. Changes in fat distribution accompanying weight reduction. *American Journal of Clinical Nutrition*, **47**, 229–234.

Warner, K. E. (1987). Selling health promotion to corporate America: Uses and abuses of the economic argument. *Health Education Quarterly*, **14**, 39–55.

Warner, K. E., Wickizer, T. M., Wolfe, R. A., Schildroth, J. E. & Samuelson, M. H. (1988). Economic implications of workplace health promotion programs: Review of the literature. *Journal of Occupational Medicine*, **30**, 106–112.

Wilber, J. A. & Barrow, J. G. (1969). Reducing elevated blood pressure. *Minnesota Medicine*, **52**, 1303–1305.

Wilbur, C. S., Hartwell, T. D. & Piserchia, P. V. (1986). The Johnson & Johnson LIVE FOR LIFE program: Its organization and evaluation plan. In M. F. Cataldo & T. T. Coates (Eds), *Health and Industry: A Behavioral Medicine Perspective*. New York: Wiley, pp. 338–350.

Williams, D. R. & House, J. S. (1985). Social support and stress reduction. In C. L. Cooper & M. J. Smith (Eds), *Job Stress and Blue Collar Work*. Chichester: Wiley, pp. 207–224.

Windom, R. E., McGinnis, M. J. & Fielding, J. E. (1987). Examining worksite health promotion. *Business and Health*, **4**, 36–37.

Winkleby, M. A., Ragland, D. R. & Syme, S. L. (1988). Self-reported stressors and hypertension: Evidence of an inverse association. *American Journal of Epidemiology*, **127**, 124–134.

Part III

ILLNESS BEHAVIOUR AND HEALTH CARE

6 Psychological Consequences of Chronic Disease in Children

CHRISTINE EISER,
Department of Psychology, University of Exeter, Perry Road, Exeter EX4 4QG, UK

While there may be many hazards involved in parenting healthy children, the difficulties are compounded when dealing with the chronically sick or handicapped. Chronic disease affects some 10% of the school-aged population (Hobbs & Perrin, 1985; Cadman et al., 1987; Gortmaker et al., 1990). Figures from the 1981 National Health Interview Survey (shown in table 6.1) indicate the prevalence of specific conditions. In all cases, there is no currently available cure, but children face a lifetime of medical treatment and daily reminders of their potential vulnerability and dependence on medical staff. Regular visits to hospital and out-patient clinic are the norm, schooling may be interrupted, social life restricted, and increased family tension and distress occur. It is also necessary that children or their families take considerable responsibility for many aspects of the treatment. Children with diabetes, for example, must be especially vigilant about their diets, check their blood-sugar regularly and have daily (or more frequent) insulin injections. Those with cystic fibrosis undergo daily physiotherapy to help clear the lungs, and children with asthma must themselves be prepared to self-administer drugs to reduce the risk of an asthma attack, or to lessen the impact of an attack should it occur.

The extent to which children cooperate with treatments is dependent on many factors, including their understanding of the disease and its prognosis, age, gender, temperament, and relationship with medical staff. Friends and schoolteachers can be important, especially during adolescence. However, the role of the family has received greatest research attention. In the case of the child with diabetes, the family can help by being prepared to make changes in their diet and not openly eating forbidden foods in front of the sick child. Alternatively, the family can be an enormous hindrance, by isolating the child from family meals, eating at irregular intervals and not providing an atmosphere conducive to treatment adherence.

The author is supported by a research grant from the ESRC, UK and the Northcott Devon Medical Foundation.

International Review of Health Psychology. Edited by S. Maes, H. Leventhal and M. Johnston
©1992 John Wiley & Sons Ltd

Table 6.1. Estimated prevalence of chronic conditions
among children and adolescents aged 4 to 17 years:
(National Health Interview Survey 1981).

Condition	Estimated prevalence per 1000
Arthritis	3.4
Asthma	29.3
Blindness	3.3
Cancer	0.6
Cardiac, rheumatic fever, rheumatic or congenital heart disease	0.7
Cerebral palsy	0.9
Cystic fibrosis	0.3
Deafness	5.4
Deformed body part	19.4
Diabetes	1.0
Ear, nose, throat, cleft palate	0.4
Epilepsy	3.0
Gastrointestinal	1.6
Hearing	6.1
Missing body part	2.1
Orthopaedic	9.6
Paralysis	0.3
Sickle-cell anaemia	0.9
Vision	8.4
Any of 19 chronic conditions	89.0

Although it is increasingly recognized that the family plays a critical role in helping the child adjust to the demands of chronic disease and accept any related restrictions, most research has focused rather narrowly on the way in which *either* families or children respond to the situation. Both methodological and theoretical limitations have resulted in a failure to acknowledge the interdependence between child and family responses.

THEORETICAL APPROACHES

Early theoretical work consisted largely of identifying variables which might be expected to be associated with functioning and assumed a unidirectional effect. Lipowski (1971) for example, identified:

1. *Disease-related* factors (severity, chronicity and imposed restrictions on activities)
2. *Intrapersonal* factors (personality, intelligence or social background)
3. *Environmental* factors (attitudes of parents and others to the condition).

Subsequent models have stressed the dynamic nature of coping in that responses change throughout the illness and that child and family functioning is reciprocal and interdependent (Pless & Pinkerton, 1975).

Varni & Wallander (1988) have developed earlier models, emphasizing the role of competence in child and family adjustment. Again, they identify three sets of critical variables:

1. *Intrapersonal* (severity and functional dependence associated with the disease, temperament and coping style)
2. *Interpersonal* (temperament and coping style of the mother)
3. *Social–ecological factors* (marital and family functioning, socio-economic status, family size and service utilization).

Varni & Wallander (1988) stress the reciprocal nature of this set of relationships. They further assume that families with a chronically sick or handicapped child are confronted by an increased number of potentially stressful situations, where "stress" is viewed "as the occurrence of problematic situations requiring a solution or some decision-making process for appropriate action" (Varni & Wallander, 1988, p. 215). This focus on stress in terms of a response to problematic situations implies that individual or family adjustment is determined by personal competence. This is defined as "the effectiveness of the coping responses emitted when an individual is confronted with problematic situations". Effective coping results in change so that the situation is no longer problematic, and at the same time produces additional positive consequences. This model does not make the assumption that the presence of a chronically sick child is necessarily disastrous for a family, but instead implies that active efforts to cope with the situation can be productive. The role of interventions is to foster the development of appropriate responses and awareness of potential resources.

Recognition that many families function "well", allowing as little intrusion of the illness into their everyday lives as possible, has led to a new emphasis in research and theory. Perrin & MacLean (1988) argue that such families should not be considered "deviant" or maladjusted, but as ordinary people coping with very special circumstances. This view has also been taken up by Kazak (1989). She develops a systems and social–ecological approach, emphasizing from systems theory (von Bertalanffy, 1968) the principles of organization and relatedness. The basic assumption is that chronic disease in a child has many implications for the whole family. These changes can result in discomfort and elicit homeostatic processes which provide the family with a greater sense of stability. Reactions that may be interpreted by others as maladaptive (such as over-protectiveness) may in fact function to maintain a protective homeostasis for the family. Systems perspectives also emphasize changes in these processes over time. The demands of chronic disease change throughout the course of treatment, and with developmental changes in the child and family.

> Caring for an infant with a motor delay is different from parenting an adolescent who is confined to a wheel-chair. The additions of other children to the family, divorces, deaths of grandparents, financial problems, relocations, and inclusions of other non-blood kin in the family system are all "normal" events families experience that will affect the way in which the child's illness is perceived and handled over time (Kazak 1989, p. 26).

In order to overcome the criticism that systems theory takes too little account of individual characteristics and experiences, Kazak argues that the approach needs to be linked with theories of developmental psychology. In particular, she uses concepts from social–ecological theory (Bronfrenbrenner, 1979), in order to define the developing child and the contexts in which the individual is involved.

THEORETICAL AND METHODOLOGICAL CRITICISMS

The proliferation of theoretical approaches has not put as much order into the field as might be hoped. For one reason, no approach lends itself easily to empirical testing. Arguing that the size of most clinical populations precludes an evaluation of a complete model, Wallander and his colleagues confine themselves to evaluations of specific components of the model (Wallander et al., 1989). It is clear, too, that the work is daunted by considerable methodological difficulties. Many researchers have relied on semi-structured interviews as a means of collecting data, with scant regard for the reliabilities of their instruments. A variety of more standardized instruments are coming into vogue, although these are not always selected with due care for specific characteristics of the populations under study. It is common to add or delete items from standardized instruments, without acknowledging the substantial changes that can then occur in statistical properties. Finally, the choice of standardized questionnaires can often be inappropriate, or at least, measure different behaviours from those intended. For example, measures of child behaviour invariably rely on mothers' reports, and until recently it was not acknowledged that mothers' own mental health was a source of bias in how she assessed the child's behaviour. Lancaster, Prior & Adler (1989) found that maternal mental health, marital adjustment and confidence in wife–mother roles predicted ratings of child behaviour. Panaccione & Wahler (1986) found that depressed mothers had more negative perceptions of their children and engaged in more aversive parenting. Given the established incidence of depression and other mental health problems in mothers of chronically sick children, these associations need careful examination.

The reliance on paper-and-pencil assessments of marital functioning or parent–child relationships needs to be seen as a very initial step in assessing the impact of chronic disease. Holden & Edwards (1989) succinctly summarize the inadequacies of many questionnaires purported to measure parent–child relationships, emphasizing the ambiguities in wording of many items and the range of alternative interpretations that parents can make. Research needs to move towards more situation-specific assessments of parent–child behaviours and relationships in order to reduce misunderstanding and describe more fully the processes whereby parents evaluate information and make decisions about their children.

There have been a number of previous reviews concerned specifically with the impact of chronic disease on children alone, and separate articles concerned with the impact on families (eg Anderson, 1990; Eiser, 1990; Hobbs & Perrin, 1985; Johnson, 1988; Lavigne & Burns, 1981). Others have reviewed specific effects on marital functioning (Sabbeth & Leventhal, 1984) and healthy siblings (Lobato, Faust & Spirito, 1988; Dyson, 1989). Yet the emphasis is very much on the impact of the disease on specific groups, and reflecting the bias in empirical work, much less on the interdependence between family members. Children, parents and siblings do not function in isolation, but the way in which any member of the family responds is intimately connected with the responses of others. Neither should it be assumed that coping with any illness follows a defined pattern. Many chronic conditions of childhood are characterized by their unpredictability and this is reflected in the diverse responses that families subsequently make.

The present review is far from exhaustive but differs from previous articles in emphasizing family resilience and coping resources, and the interdependence between patients, their families and wider support networks, especially school and medical services.

MOTHERS' ATTITUDES AND BEHAVIOURS

Additional care-giving demands associated with chronic diseases appear to fall more heavily on mothers than fathers. Much of the care in diabetes management, including helping the child self-inject insulin or testing blood-sugar levels, is the responsibility of mothers more often than fathers (Zrebiec, 1987). In a study of 32 families with a child with leukaemia, 19 (59%) agreed that mothers alone were responsible for monitoring the child's medical care; in 2 families (6%) fathers alone were responsible, and in 11 families (34%) both parents shared responsibility (Barbarin, Hughes & Chesler, 1985). Mothers are more likely to communicate with medical staff and bring the child for hospital appointments. In traditional families, this responsibility may fall naturally on mothers especially if she is at home while the father is engaged in full-time outside employment. Yet the combination of increased responsibility for child-care and restricted social life that can accompany the traditional housewife role appears to take its toll on maternal mental health. Compared with mothers of healthy children, mothers of chronically sick children are more likely to be anxious (Daniels et al., 1986) or depressed, and report more mental and physical health complaints (Wallander et al., 1989). Yet there is considerable variability in the extent of health problems that mothers report, and very few indications of severe clinical maladjustment. This variability suggests that mothers' psychological experiences may be aggravated, or buffered by, a number of other variables. Many of these have already been described in the model delineated by Varni & Wallander (1988).

There are few real indications that characteristics of the disease are particularly associated with maternal mental health. Wallander et al. (1989) studied 50 mothers of children aged between 6 and 11 years who were suffering from spina bifida or cerebral palsy. Although as a whole these mothers reported more physical and mental health complaints than mothers of healthy children, these were not related to the degree of the child's disability or amount of practical care mothers were required to give. However, comparative studies of this type are notoriously difficult to conduct, in that it is difficult to quantify the demands or limitations of one disease in relation to another. Even for a single condition, there is not always agreement among medical staff about definitions of severity or limitations. Renne & Creer (1985), for example, have pointed out that asthma can be very mild, affecting children rarely and requiring medication only as the situation arises. At the other extreme, children can suffer very frequent attacks, be routinely hospitalized, and need daily invasive treatments. Across diseases, it is even more difficult to assume that restrictions that characterize some conditions are more stressful than those that characterize others. In any case, it seems that a mother's estimates of her own or the child's difficulties are based much more on her subjective estimates of the severity of the condition, rather than any more objective or medically based estimates (Perrin, MacLean & Perrin, 1989; Ungerer et al., 1988; Walker, Ford & Donald, 1986). In childhood epilepsy, individual family members' perceptions of the degree of disruption caused by a seizure are more important than actual disruption in predicting family adjustment (Appalone-Ford, Gibson & Driefuss, 1983).

If there is no simple relationship between maternal adjustment and characteristics of the disease, it follows that aspects of the social environment may be more critical. In the study previously cited by Wallander et al. (1989), social environment factors were predictive of maternal mental, but not physical, health. Increased mental ill health was associated with less family support. Other factors which appear to reduce the impact of childhood disease on mothers include relationships outside the immediate family circle. Walker, Ortiz-Valdes & Newbrough (1989) studied 95 mothers of children with one of three conditions: cystic fibrosis, diabetes and mental retardation, and compared them with mothers of well children. Irrespective of the condition or socio-economic status, mothers not employed outside the home were more depressed than those involved in outside employment. It is suggested that the social contacts made at work, and opportunities to be involved in issues outside the immediate family context act as a buffer in alleviating stresses associated with caring for a chronically sick child. Before recommending that all mothers should take on outside employment, however, it is important to realize that the demands involved in caring for a chronically sick child can be very much compounded by the demands of outside employment during times of crisis.

Two variables that have been consistently identified as buffers against maternal ill health are (a) social support and (b) paternal attitudes and behaviours.

SOCIAL SUPPORT

It was initially assumed that social support had positive advantages for families of chronically sick children, in that earliest studies suggested that families were often socially isolated (McAlister, Butler & Lei, 1973; Waisbren, 1980). Social support can be measured in a variety of ways. *Structural* aspects refer to the size and density of social groups, with some indications that larger size is associated with better adjustment (Hirsch, 1980). *Density* refers to the extent to which individual members of the network know each other, independently of the focal person (Mitchell & Trickett, 1980). In a study of families of children with spina bifida, Kazak & Wilcox (1984) found smaller and more dense social networks compared with healthy families.

In addition to these structural aspects of social support networks, more qualitative dimensions can be identified. What may be critical is not the size or make-up of a family's support system, but the extent to which they perceive themselves to be able to elicit support, should it be necessary. In subsequent work, Kazak, Reber & Carter (1988) attempted to determine the kind of help associated with different members of the support network, in addition to the structural aspects. Families of children with phenylketonuria (PKU), did not differ substantially from healthy controls either in structural aspects or in perceived helpfulness of the networks. Parents of children with PKU were less likely than parents of healthy controls to identify their spouse as a source of support, and reported extended family members to be less helpful. For all families, it was noted that large, less dense networks were associated with less reported stress, suggesting perhaps that this kind of network system is particularly appropriate for families with pre-school children. There is some suggestion that the size of support networks declines over time. Kazak & Meadows (1989) found that reported social support networks declined over time among 35 adolescents with cancer and their families. This may be part of a natural decline in the size of family support group as children grow up. However, it is also likely that, although others are very prepared to be helpful in the initial stages of a disease, their concern or ability to help declines with the length of time over which the disease extends.

Future work needs to clarify the perceived purpose of different support networks, and in particular to identify both the rewards and costs involved. While there is evidence that social support can be critical in determining adjustment to chronic disease, it is important to recognize the different functions of social support at different times across the course of a disease. It is also unlikely that social support serves the same function regardless of the child's particular condition. Families of a child with spina bifida may be dependent on others for very practical help with transport, for example. At the same time, the very stable nature of the condition may enable then to make arrangements with formal care networks for much of the help that they require. In contrast, families of children with less predictable and less stable conditions, such as cancer, may come to rely on others far more for emotional rather than any practical help. Finally, much more consideration needs to be given to developmental changes in support networks that occur for all families, in order to interpret both structural and more emotional consequences for those with a child with a chronic condition.

FATHERS' ATTITUDES AND BEHAVIOUR

Although there is ample evidence that mothers of chronically sick children suffer from more mental and physical health problems compared with mothers of healthy children, there are essentially no comparable data available concerning fathers. Very little is known systematically about how men adjust to the diagnosis, or the kind of coping strategies they employ to deal with specific crises. It is well documented that they play a lesser role in everyday care (see above), and they tend to be less informed about various aspects of the disease (Johnson et al., 1982; Nolan et al., 1986). Perhaps reflecting this lack of involvement in care and lack of relevant knowledge, fathers are sometimes more optimistic about the child's prognosis compared with mothers. Mulhern, Crisco & Camitta (1981) found that fathers underestimated the severity of the prognosis for children with leukaemia compared with mothers. Banion, Miles & Carter (1983) reported that mothers were more concerned about the possibility of long-term complications in diabetes than fathers. The lack of information about fathers has to be attributed primarily to difficulties involved in recruiting them for research given daily work commitments. Where data are available, it is apparent that fathers may play a major role, particularly in supporting mothers behind the scenes. Walker, Ford & Donald (1986) found that mothers' estimates of the severity of her child's condition were mediated by the amount of paternal support, with more support being associated with less perceived severity.

The focus of much work in this area has been based on estimates of time involved by fathers in many of the routine demands of caring. For all fathers, simple measures of time given may be inadequate, since the amount of time fathers give to their families may be limited by work commitments or other variables beyond their immediate control. Although there is evidence that fathers who spend more time with their children develop stonger attachments to them, and their children appear to benefit (Ricks, 1985), equally important may be the quality of the interaction (Grossman, Pollack & Golding, 1988). In this latter study, men's autonomy and job satisfaction predicted the amount of playtime they spent with their children, and the quality of those interactions. In addition, they emphasize the role of complementarity in the way mothers and fathers deal with their children. In work with chronically sick children, more emphasis needs to be given to the unique ways in which fathers may contribute to family functioning and child-care, rather than be seen as a reflection of mothers' role.

SIBLINGS

As siblings share a close and interdependent relationship (Sutton-Smith & Rosenberg, 1970) it should not be surprising if chronic disease in one child makes a substantial impact on the life of the remaining healthy siblings. Parents experience a great deal of stress and concern about the sick child, perhaps detracting from time and energy left for other children (Lavigne & Ryan, 1979). The illness can create financial hardship for the family, limiting activities and family resources

(Sieman, 1984; Wallander et al., 1989). In some cases, healthy siblings can develop a pathological identification with the sick child (Featherstone, 1980).

Despite these potential sources of difficulty, research concerned with the impact of chronic disease on healthy siblings has been mixed. There are some indications that healthy children show retarded academic achievement and school progress (McAnarney et al., 1974) and more psychological deficits including lower self-esteem and increased anxiety (Ferrari, 1984; Tew & Laurence, 1973). Others have not reported measurable differences between siblings of chronically sick or handicapped children and controls (Gayton et al., 1977; Dyson & Feurells, in press; Dyson, 1989). Still others have reported both positive and negative consequences (Cleveland & Miller, 1977; Grossman, 1972). In a review of much of this literature, Drotar & Crawford (1985) concluded that:

1. There is no one-to-one correspondence between disease and sibling adjustment
2. Maladjustment is selective and varies with the age, gender and outcome measure employed
3. In interaction with other variables, chronic disease places healthy siblings at increased risk of maladjustment.

More recent work has moved away from this rather deficit-centred model, and emphasizes more qualitative aspects of the sibling relationship. Siblings spend a great deal of time in each others' company, and have a huge influence on socialization generally. They can function to mutual advantage, moderating parental influences and providing a peer-like context for emotional development and power negotiation. Sibling relationships are among the most important precursors of adult relationships (Hartup, 1983; Lamb & Sutton-Smith, 1982), and from this point of view it is unfortunate that the focus of much of this work is on negative aspects of the sibling relationship and frequently, atypical sibling pairs. Outcome measures are invariably in terms of self-esteem or lack of it, aggression or hostility; and the potential of illness experience to promote more empathic and altruistic responses is less understood (Parmalee, 1986). Yet chronic disease can provide opportunities to learn how others feel and offer practical help. Horwitz & Kazak (1990) found that pre-school siblings of cancer patients did not differ in terms of behaviour or social competence from others, but rates of pro-social behaviour were often higher. Neither does much work take account of the interdependence between sibling behaviours and other family factors (Brody & Stoneman, 1986) including family size (Gath, 1974; Kazak & Clark, 1986) and age spacing (Breslau, 1982).

The extent to which healthy children are influenced by, or influence, their siblings remains unclear, partly because of the very complex effect that chronic illness in a child can have for a family (Dunn, 1988).

FAMILY INTERACTION AND COMMUNICATION

Although many factors contribute to a child's attitudes towards chronic disease and consequent adherence to treatment, the family is generally considered to be critical. Characteristics of the family and especially the type and quality of communication appear instrumental in determining children's adherence and cooperation with treatment. Although there is evidence that dimensions of communication and interaction are important in adjustment to many chronic diseases (Chaney & Peterson 1989; Daniels et al., 1986; Levenson et al., 1983; Mulhern, Crisco & Camitta, 1981), most work has focused on families of children with diabetes. Poor family relationships, conflict, lack of cohesion and rigidity have been associated with poorer metabolic control (Anderson et al., 1981; Bobrow, AvEuskin & Siller, 1985; Shouval, Ber & Galatzer, 1982). However, the converse is not necessarily true. Children from well-functioning families are not necessarily those who are also in the best glycaemic control. Baker et al. (1982) reported that family supportiveness, competence and clear communication on diagnosis were associated with improved metabolic control one year later. In a prospective study of 43 newly diagnosed children, Sargent et al. (1985) found that positive family relationships on diagnosis were associated with good control three years later.

Waller et al. (1986) found that good control was dependent on specific aspects of parent behaviour. The importance of warmth and guidance in implementing treatment interacted with the child's age and gender. Good control was related to whether or not parents watched while the child tested blood-sugar levels, wrote down the responses, and if the child had someone in the family to talk to about diabetes. Close family guidance and parental control were related to good metabolic control for boys, but warmth and caring were more important for girls. Although parental guidance and control were associated with better metabolic control for younger children, it was negatively associated with control for older children. Thus, although family conflict and poor communication are fairly consistently associated with poor control in children with diabetes, aspects of family life that contribute to good control are more varied, and at the least change with the child's age and gender.

The processes whereby family relationships may enhance metabolic control have been questioned by Hanson, Henggeler & Burghen (1987). Positive family relationships may operate directly by enhancing physical and mental health, or indirectly by improving adherence and consequently control. In their own research, positive family relationships (assessed by measures of marital satisfaction and family cohesion and adaptability; Olson, 1986), were related to good adherence behaviours but not to metabolic control. Issues of discipline and control may be especially important in family management of diabetes. On the other hand, families are likely to feel considerable warmth and sympathy towards the child, but on the other, concern about the need for vigilance in self-care. Concern that failure to adhere closely to treatment demands will aggravate the possibility of long-term complications may result in parents adopting relatively strict and restrictive approaches to child-rearing. These conflicts are likely to be especially aggravated during adolescence, when moves towards independence may be hampered by parents' wishes to maintain some control over the way in which treatments are implemented. Wertlieb, Hauser & Jacobson (1986) suggest that families of diabetics need to learn new methods of discipline and control, and adopt new rules about behaviour. In newly diagnosed children, Wertlieb, Hauser & Jacobson (1986) found that behaviour problems increased with family conflict and decreased with organization and control. The reverse was found for a comparison group of children treated for acute illnesses: behaviour problems were associated with greater parental control and discipline.

In subsequent work, Hauser et al. (1986) studied the processes of family adaptation, and particularly the roles played by mothers and fathers in maintaining a warm and empathic relationship with their child, while at the same time establishing limits to behaviour and ensuring that treatment demands were satisfactorily implemented. In observations of family interactions, it was found that mothers engaged in more "enabling" speech (problem-solving, active understanding) and fathers more "constraining" speech (indifference, judgement). Further differences between mothers and fathers in their behaviours towards children with diabetes were reported by Eiser et al. (submitted).

Questionnaires were completed by 62 mothers and 45 fathers of children with diabetes to assess their confidence to handle aspects of the treatment, and extent to which they perceived the child to be restricted in different activities. Parents also reported on strategies they themselves used to cope with the condition and methods they used to relate to and discipline their child. Mothers and fathers differed greatly in their reported self-confidence, with mothers being more confident than fathers. They also differed on all measures of coping and reported ways of behaving to their child. Parents agreed only in terms of the extent to which they reported the child was restricted because of diabetes, although fathers tended to see the child as more restricted than mothers.

RELATIONSHIPS IN A WIDER CONTEXT

Children with chronic disease are invariably encouraged to return to school as soon as possible after diagnosis. After the inevitable trauma associated with diagnosis, it is hoped that the child's return to school will facilitate the return to "normal" for the whole family. The fact that the child is able to go to school may signal to the parents that the crisis is past, and that there is some hope for the future. At the same time, it frees the mother from some of the demands of caring for a chronically sick child, and leaves her with some free time, either for herself or other children. It is also assumed that return to normal school is beneficial for the child, both in the short and longer term. In the short term, friendships are hopefully resumed. In participating in as many school-based activities as possible, the child has the best opportunity to make adequate progress in all areas of development. In the longer term, attendance at school and associated academic achievement are essential in order to ensure that the child ultimately has as extensive a choice of career and life-style as others.

Return to normal school is, however, associated with some difficulties for children. Schools are often not at all prepared and teachers ill-informed about how to deal with any medical emergencies, how to explain the illness to other children, or how far chronically sick children should be pushed to participate fully in the curriculum or achieve academically (Eiser & Town, 1987). Part of this problem lies in the lack of communication between medical and teaching staff. Walker (1984) argues that "a lack of realistic information (from the paediatrician) about the child can actually hurt the child's progress through school; since it may result in an inappropriate educational placement, the denial of a necessary related service, or over-protective attitudes and behaviours on the part of uninformed school personnel" (Walker, 1984, p. 222).

Extensive, and often unnecessary, absences have been reported for children with a wide range of chronic conditions. Fowler, Johnson & Atkinson (1985) contacted families of 270 children suffering from 11 different chronic conditions. Mean days absence for these children was 16 days compared with less than 7 days for healthy children over the same period. Those with cystic fibrosis, sickle-cell disease, arthritis, haemophilia or spina bifida averaged the most absences. Extended or frequent absences have also been reported for children with diabetes (Bradbury & Smith, 1983); epilepsy (Holdsworth & Whitmore, 1974); asthma (Hill, Standen & Tattersfield, 1989) and leukaemia (Eiser, 1980; Deasey, Spinetta & Spinetta, 1980). Children with leukaemia are likely to miss a great deal of schooling immediately following diagnosis, but this decreases substantially during the course of the disease. Larcombe et al. (1990) compared 51 children with cancer and 66 with chronic diseases (including renal disease, cardiac and orthopaedic conditions) returning to school after periods of hospitalization. All children experienced some difficulties on return to school, but these were greatest for those with cancer and least for those with orthopaedic conditions. Physical problems (tiredness, mobility, nausea) rather than academic problems, were reported to create difficulties for more children. Several children missed a considerable amount of schooling, especially those with cancer. Absences were generally attributed to episodes of infection or necessitated by trips to hosptial.

It is apparent, however, that school absence is not always predicted from the severity or other medical restrictions associated with the disease. In a study of children with asthma, Anderson et al. (1983) showed that school absence was determined by a variety of variables, including poor maternal health, non-manual occupation of the father, parental separation, more than three children in the family, and lack of access to a car.

Although school absence does not seem to be simply related to academic achievement (Fowler, Johnson & Atkinson, 1985), there are many indications that children with chronic disease function less well in school work compared with healthy children (for reviews see Eiser, 1986; Mearig, 1985). At least for those with leukaemia, this difference in functioning may well continue into adult life (Peckham et al., 1988; Mulhern et al., 1989). However, in the study by

Peckham et al. (1988), there was a very wide range of achievement shown by the children, suggesting that highly supportive environments can do much to overcome the potential disadvantage of chronic disease.

For children with chronic conditions, attendance at normal school can sometimes create difficulties. Lord et al. (1990) looked at the implications of mainstream, combined or special class placement for 31 adolescents with spina bifida and their families. Those in mainstream schools had the most normal scores for academic and social skills, those in combined placements had intermediate scores, and the poorest results were obtained for those in special schools. However, those in combined placements reported least loneliness and those in mainstream education the most. These data may suggest that the normal school placement can be most conducive to good academic standards, but children may be happier in situations where they have some company with other children suffering from similar conditions.

While there is considerable indication that children with chronic disease are at some risk academically, there is as yet no simple explanation as to why it should be so. Hypotheses have involved lower expectations on the part of teachers or parents, over-restrictive parenting (Koocher et al., 1986; Spinetta et al., 1976), learned helplessness on the part of the child, and social isolation and alienation from peers (Chesler & Barbarin, 1986; Wortman & Dunkel-Schetter, 1979). Teachers may be influenced by their own biases in dealing with the child with chronic disease. This has been particularly well documented in relation to childhood cancer (Deasey-Spinetta & Spinetta, 1980; Kaplan, Smith & Grobstein, 1974). The presence of a stereotype about the child with cancer was demonstrated experimentally by Stern & Arenson (1989). Medical students and undergraduates rated children in remission from leukaemia as less sociable, less cognitively competent, less active or well behaved, smaller and less likely to adjust well in the future compared with healthy children. If such a stereotype exists for children well and in remission, it suggests that even more negative stereotypes exist for those undergoing treatment.

It should not be forgotten that some diseases or their treatments alter the physical appearance of children, which can threaten their acceptance within the classroom. Teachers and parents need to work together and handle children's concerns sensitively in order to reduce the potentially negative impact of chronic disease. The problem for many children arises precisely because there is frequently too little contact between hospital, school and home. For any child, successful integration in the school setting is dependent on the establishment of a set of shared beliefs between school and home. In the case of the child with a chronic disease, it is important that these shared beliefs are established, particularly so that teachers are aware of changes in the child's health status that might affect school progress, and so that parents and teachers convey similar messages regarding work and achievement.

SERVICES

Not the least of the difficulties faced by children with chronic disease and their families lies in the need to attend regular clinic appointments, and communicate with medical staff. Differences in the organization of clinics, and the expectations and objectives of staff, may raise difficulties for some families. It is only recently being recognized that service organization and staff attitudes have far-reaching implications for patient management, particularly in relation to clinic attendance and long-term health. Most work has again been conducted in the field of diabetes, and there is evidence that staff attitudes (Hanson et al., 1988; Weinberger, Cohen & Mazzuca, 1984) and the type of clinic (general or specialized) have implications for diabetic control (Bloomfield & Farquhar, 1990). According to Weinberger, Cohen & Mazzuca (1984), staff attitudes (but not knowledge) were predictive of glycaemic control. Patients were in better control where staff emphasized the importance of good control, and worked together as a health-care team. Bloomfield & Farquhar (1990) found that haemoglobin control and days admitted were both lower when children attended specialist rather than general paediatric clinics.

Hanson et al. (1988) interviewed 96 adolescents and their parents about their satisfaction with health-care provision. Satisfaction was assessed from ratings of physicians' personal qualities, professional competence and cost and convenience of care. Generally, family members reported positive attitudes to care and competence, but neutral attitudes about cost and convenience. Adherence to treatment was positively associated with fathers' estimates of staff competence, but only marginally to mothers' and adolescents' perceptions of competence. Adolescents' perceptions of competence was positively associated with metabolic control. These results suggest that adherence and patient comprehension of treatment goals can be enhanced by personal qualities and the perceived competence of medical staff.

Patients and their families do not necessarily perceive clinics or understand the need for regular check-ups in the same way as medical staff. Such differences can create stress between family members, reduce attendance at clinics and result in poor cooperation with advice and treatment. Patient compliance is particularly difficult during adolescence. While many developmental factors can contribute to this behaviour, it is perhaps unfortunate that children are required at the same time to transfer from paediatric to adult services. Attitudes to patient management and treatment objectives differ between paediatricians and adult physicians (Marteau & Baum, 1984), with adult physicians rating the probability of long-term complications to be higher than paediatricians. At present, adolescents may be cared for under one of four general arrangements: paediatric, adolescent, transitional/joint care or adult. Neither paediatric nor adult services alone are likely to meet the needs of the adolescent patient (Wales, 1985). Little support is generally given to patients or their families in order to ease the transition. While paediatricians tend to favour a system of care which includes the whole family, adult physicians encourage independence and direct negotiation between patient and clinic (Cerreto & Travis, 1984). In suddenly restricting the family's role, and excluding them from clinics and treatment management, physicians may unwittingly exaggerate relationships that are in any case strained during adolescence. Much more systematic research is called for to understand patients' perceptions of different clinic organizations and rationale for clinic attendance, and more critically, to assess how clinic organization can affect the immediate and longer-term consequences for patient health.

CONCLUSIONS

Much empirical work is limited in design. There is a tendency to concentrate on one disease group, assuming that all children with diabetes, or asthma, or spina bifida, are much like all other children with these conditions, and at the same time distinct from those who are free of diagnosed disease. There has been a concentration on some conditions, such as cancer or diabetes, and neglect of others, such as asthma, even though the latter is far more prevalent. Lack of attention to specific characteristics or limitations of diseases makes implications from one disease group to another to be problematic.

Methodologically, it is customary to compare children with healthy controls, giving an implicit message that those with chronic disease are somehow deviant or abnormal (Kazak, 1989), rather than children coping with very special circumstances. It is, of course, unlikely that any single parameter of a disease will be identified as critical in determining adjustment of child or family. Diseases vary simultaneously along more than one dimension, and medical agreement about objective indices of severity or restrictiveness of any condition is rare. The more optimistic approach appears to involve greater emphasis on the family's perceptions of the disease, its prognosis and associated limitations. Work within this tradition is relatively rare.

Secondly, work with children with chronic disease necessarily differs from that involving adults because of the relatively rapid developmental changes that take place in the child, family and their relationship (Kazdin, 1989). Despite increasing recognition of this, (Perrin & Gerrity, 1984; Kazdin, 1989), efforts to place empirical work within a firm theoretical footing have almost exclusively adopted "stage" approaches to development and failed to consider problems with these approaches, or alternative theoretical stances (Eiser, 1989). In considering the impact of chronic disease on children and their families, it is necessary that we develop more "child-centred" approaches, attempting to determine how children understand and make sense of their illness experiences.

Thirdly, too much work still is concerned narrowly with the responses of *either* the child or family. New methods of analysis and cooperation across centres are necessary to enable us to unravel the complex interrelationships involved when a child is chronically sick. The essence of understanding and more importantly, promoting patient compliance and health, rests on an analysis of the interdependence between individuals, families and the health-care system.

REFERENCES

Anderson, B. J. (1990). Diabetes and adaptations in family systems. In C. S. Holmes (ed.), *Neuropsychological and Behavioural Aspects of Diabetes*. New York: Springer-Verlag, pp. 85–101.

Anderson, B. J., Miller, J. P., Auslander, W. F. & Santiago, J. V. (1981). Family characteristics of diabetic adolescents: Relationships to metabolic control. *Diabetes Care*, 4, 586–594.

Anderson, H. R., Bailey, P. A., Cooper, J. A., Palmer, J. S. & West, S. (1983). Morbidity and school absence caused by asthma and wheezing illness. *Archives of Disease in Childhood*, 58, 777–784.

Appalone-Ford, C., Gibson, P. & Driefuss, F. E. (1983). Psychosocial considerations in childhood epilepsy. In C. Appalone-Ford (Ed.) *Pediatrics: Epileptology, Classification and Management of Seizures in the Child*. Littleton, MA: PSG Publishing Company.

Baker, L., Rosman, B., Sargent, J., Nogueira, J. & Stanley, C. A. (1982). Family factors predict glycosylated hemoglobin (HbA) in juvenile diabetes: A prospective study. *Diabetes*, 31, (Suppl. 2), 15*a.

Banion, J. R., Miles, M. S. & Carter, M. C. (1983). Problems of mothers in management of children with diabetes. *Diabetes Care*, 6, 548–551.

Barbarin, O., Hughes, D. & Chesler, M. (1985). Stress, coping, and marital functioning among parents of children with cancer. *Journal of Marriage and the Family*, 47, 473–480.

Billings, A. G., Moos, R. H., Miller, J. J. & Gottlieb, J. E. (1987). Psychosocial adaptation in juvenile rheumatic disease: A controlled evaluation. *Health Psychology*, 6, 343–359.

Bloomfield, S. and Farquhar, J. W. (1990). Is a specialist pediatric diabetic clinic better? *Archives of Disease in Childhood*, 65, 139–140.

Bobrow, E. S., AvEuskin, T. W. & Siller, J. (1985). Mother–daughter interaction and adherence to diabetes regimens. *Diabetes Care*, 8, 145–156.

Bradbury, J. A. & Smith, C. W. (1983). An assessment of the diabetic knowledge of school teachers. *Archives of Disease in Childhood*, 58, 692–696.

Breslau, N. (1982). Siblings of disabled children: Birth order and spacing effects. *Journal of Abnormal Child Psychology*, 10, 85–96.

Brody, G. & Stoneman, L. (1986). Contextual issues in the study of sibling socialisation. In J. J. Gallagher & P. M. Vietze (Eds), *Families of Handicapped Persons: Research, Programs and Policy Issues*. Baltimore: Paul H. Brookes.

Bronfrenbrenner, W. (1979). *The Ecology of Human development*. Cambridge, MA: Harvard University Press.

Cadman, D., Boyle, M., Szatmari, P. & Offord, D. R. (1987). Chronic illness, disability, and mental and social well-being: Findings of the Ontario Child Health Study. *Pediatrics*, 79, 805–812.

Cerreto, M. C. & Travis, L. B. (1984). Implications of psychological and family factors in the treatment of diabetes. *Pediatric Clinics of North America*, 31, 689–710.

Chaney, J. M. & Peterson, L. (1989). Family variables and disease management in juvenile rheumatoid arthritis. *Journal of Pediatric Psychology*, 14, 389–404.

Chesler, M. & Barbarin, O. (1986). Parents' perspectives on the school experiences of children with cancer. *Topics in Early Childhood and Special Education*, 5, 36–48.

Cleveland, D. S. & Miller, N. B. (1977). Attitudes and life commitments of older siblings of institutionalised and noninstitutionalised retarded children. *American Journal of Mental Deficiency*, 64, 845–861.

Daniels, D., Miller, J. J., Billings, A. G. & Moos, R. H. (1986). Psychosocial functioning of siblings of children with rheumatic disease. *Journal of Pediatrics*, 109, 379–383.

Deasey-Spinetta, P. & Spinetta, J. (1980). The child with cancer in school: Teachers' appraisal. *American Journal of Pediatric Hematology/Oncology*, 2, 89–94.

Drotar, D. & Crawford, P. (1985). Psychological adaptation of siblings of chronically ill children: Research and practice implications. *Developmental and Behavioural Pediatrics*, 6, 355–362.

Dunn, J. (1988). Sibling influence on childhood development. *Journal of Child Psychology and Psychiatry*, 29, 119–128.

Dyson, L. C. (1989). Adjustment of siblings of handicapped children: A comparison. *Journal of Pediatric Psychology*, 14, 215–230.

Dyson, L. & Feurells, R. R. (in press). A comparison of the self-concept of handicapped children and siblings of nonhandicapped children. *Journal of the Division for Early Childhood*.

Eiser, C. (1980). How leukemia affects a child's schooling. *British Journal of Social and Clinical Psychology*, 19, 365–368.

Eiser, C. (1986). Effects of chronic illness on the child's intellectual development. *Journal of the Royal Society of Medicine*, 79, 2–3.

Eiser, C. (1989). Children's understanding of illness: A critique of the "stage" approach. *Psychology and Health*, 3, 93–101.

Eiser, C. (1990). Psychological effects of chronic disease. *Journal of Child Psychology and Psychiatry*, 1, 85–98.

Eiser, C., Havermans, G., Kirby, R. M. & Eiser, J. R. (submitted). Perceived self-confidence in diabetes management by children and their parents.

Eiser, C. & Town, C. (1987). Teachers' concerns about chronically sick children. Implications for pediatricians. *Developmental Medicine and Child Neurology*, 29, 56–63.

Featherstone, H. (1980). *A Difference in the Family: Life with a Disabled Child*. New York: Basic Books.

Ferrari, M. (1984). Chronic illness: Psychosocial effects on siblings. 1. Chronically ill boys. *Journal of Child Psychology and Psychiatry*, 25, 459–476.

Fowler, M., Johnson, M. & Atkinson, S. (1985). School achievement and absence in children with chronic health conditions. *Journal of Pediatrics*, 106, 683–687.

Gath, A. (1974). Sibling reactions to mental handicap: A comparison of the brothers and sisters of Mongol children. *Journal of Child Psychology and Psychiatry*, 15, 187–198.

Gayton, W. F., Friedman, S. B., Tavormina, J. F. & Tucker, P. (1977). Children with cystic fibrosis; 1. Psychological test findings of patients, siblings and parents. *Pediatrics*, 59, 888–894.

Gortmaker, S. L., Walker, D. K. Weitzman, M. & Sobol, A. M. (1990). Chronic conditions, socioeconomic risks, and behavioural problems in children and adolescents. *Pediatrics*, 85, 267–276.

Grossman, F. K. (1972). *Brothers and Sisters of Retarded Children: An Exploratory Story*. Syracuse, NY: Syracuse University Press.

Grossman, F. K., Pollack, W. S. and Golding, E. (1988). Fathers and children: Predicting the quality and quantity of fathering. *Developmental Psychology*, 24, 82–91.

Hanson, C. L., Henggeler, S. W. & Burghen, G. A. (1987). Model of associations between psychosocial variables and health-outcome measures of adolescents with I.D.D.M. *Diabetes Care*, 10, 752–758.

Hanson, C. L., Henggeler, S. W., Harris, M. A., Mitchell, K. A., Corle, D. L. & Burghen, G. A. (1988). Associations between family members' perceptions of the health care system and the health of youths with insulin-dependent diabetes mellitus. *Journal of Pediatric Psychology*, **13**, 543–554.

Hartup, W. W. (1983). Peer relations. In P. H. Mussen & E. M. Hetherington (Eds), *Handbook of Child Psychology*, Vol. 4, *Socialisation, Personality and Social Development*. New York: Wiley, pp. 103–196.

Hauser, S., Jacobson, A., Wertlieb, D., Weiss-Perry, B., Follansbee, D., Wolfsdorf, J. I., Herkowitz, R. D., Houliban, J. & Rajapark, D. C. (1986). Children with recently diagnosed diabetes: Interactions within their families. *Health Psychology*, **5**, 273–296.

Hill, R. A., Standen, P. J. & Tattersfield, A. E. (1989). Management of asthma in schools. *Archives of Disease in Childhood*, **64**, 246–251.

Hirsch, B. (1980). Natural support systems and coping with major life changes. *American Journal of Community Psychology*, **8**, 263–267.

Hobbs, N. & Perrin, J. M. (Eds) (1985). *Issues in the Care of Children with Chronic Illness*. San Francisco: Jossey-Bass.

Holden, G. W. & Edwards, L. A. (1989). Parental attitudes toward child rearing: instruments, issues and implications. *Psychological Bulletin*, **106**, 29–58.

Holdsworth, L. & Whitmore, K. (1974). A study of children with epilepsy attending ordinary schools. I. Their seizure patterns, progress and behaviour in school. *Developmental Medicine and Child Neurology*, **16**, 746–758.

Horwitz, W. A. & Kazak, A. E. (1990). Family adaptation to childhood cancer: Sibling and family systems variables. *Journal of Clinical Child Psychology*, **19**, 221–228.

Hunt, G. M. (1981). Spina bifida: Implications for 100 children at school. *Developmental Medicine and Child Neurology*, **23**, 160–172.

Johnson, S. B. (1988). Psychological aspects of childhood diabetes. *Journal of Child Psychology and Psychiatry*, **29**, 729–739.

Johnson, S. B., Pollak, T., Silverstein, J. H., Rosenbloom, A. L., Spiller, R., McCallum, M. & Harkavy, J. (1982). Cognitive and behavioural knowledge about insulin dependent diabetes among children and parents. *Pediatrics*, **69**, 708–713.

Kaplan, D., Smith, A. & Grobstein, R. (1974). School management of the seriously ill child. *Journal of School Health*, **44**, 250–254.

Kazak, A. E. (1989). Families of chronically ill children: A systems and social–ecological model of adaptation and challenge. *Journal of Consulting and Clinical Psychology*, **57**, 25–30.

Kazak, A. E. & Clark, M. W. (1986). Stress in families of children with myelomeningocele. *Developmental Medicine and Child Neurology*, **28**, 220–228.

Kazak, A. & Meadows, A. T. (1989). Families of young adolescents who have survived cancer: Social–emotional adjustment, adaptability, and social support. *Journal of Pediatric Psychology*, **14**, 175–192.

Kazak, A. E., Reber, M. & Carter, A. (1988). Structural and qualitative aspects of social networks in families with young chronically ill children. *Journal of Pediatric Psychology*, **13**, 171–182.

Kazak, A. & Wilcox, B. (1984). The structure and function of social support networks in families with a handicapped child. *American Journal of Community Psychology*, **12**, 645–661.

Kazdin, A. E. (1989). Developmental psychopathology: Current research, issues and directions. *American Psychologist*, **44**, 180–187.

Koocher, G., O'Malley, J., Gogan, J. & Foster, D. (1986). Psychological adjustment among pediatric cancer survivors. *Journal of Child Psychology and Psychiatry*, **21**, 163–173.

Lamb, M. E. & Sutton-Smith, D. (Eds) (1982). *Sibling Relationships: Their Nature and Significance across the Life-span*. Hillsdale, NJ: Erlbaum.

Lancaster, S., Prior, M. & Adler, R. (1989). Child behaviour ratings: The influence of maternal characteristics and child temperament. *Journal of Child Psychology and Psychiatry*, 30, 137-150.

Larcombe, I. J., Walker, J., Charlton, A., Meller, S., Morris-Jones, P. & Mott, M. G. (1990). Impact of childhood cancer on return to normal schooling. *British Medical Journal*, 301, 169-171.

Lavigne, J. & Burns, W. J. (1981). *Pediatric Psychology: Introduction for Pediatricians and Psychologists*. New York: Grune & Stratton.

Lavigne, J., Nolan, D. & McLone, D. G. (1988). Temperament, coping, and psychological adjustment in young children with myelomeningocele. *Journal of Pediatric Psychology*, 13, 363-378.

Lavigne, J. & Ryan, M. (1979). Psychologic adjustment of siblings of children with chronic illness. *Pediatrics*, 63, 616-626.

Levenson, P. M., Copeland, D. R., Morrow, J. R., Pfefferbaum, B. & Silberberg, Y. (1983). Disparities in disease-related perceptions of adolescent cancer patients and their parents. *Journal of Pediatric Psychology*, 8, 33-45.

Lipowski, Z. J. (1971). Physical illness, the individual and the coping process. *Psychiatry in Medicine*, 1, 91-98.

Lobato, D., Faust, D. & Spirito, A. (1988). Examining the effects of chronic disease and disability on children's sibling relationships. *Journal of Pediatric Psychology*, 13, 389-408.

Lord, J., Varzos, N., Behrunan, B., Wicks, J. & Wicks, D. (1990). Implications of mainstream classrooms for adolescents with spina bifida. *Developmental Medicine and Child Neurology*, 32, 20-29.

McAlister, R., Butler, E. & Lei, T. (1973). Patterns of interaction among families of behaviourally retarded children. *Journal of Marriage and the Family*, 35, 93-100.

McAnarney, E. R., Pless, I. B., Satterwhite, B. & Friedman, S. (1974). Psychological problems of children with chronic juvenile arthritis. *Pediatrics*, 53, 523.

Marteau, T. M. & Baum, J. D. (1984). Doctors' views on diabetes. *Archives of Disease in Childhood*, 59, 566-570.

Mearig, J. S. (1985). Cognitive development of chronically ill children. In N. Hobbs & J. M. Perrin (Eds), *Issues in the Care of Children with Chronic Illness*. San Francisco: Jossey Bass, pp. 672-697.

Mitchell, R. & Trickett, E. (1980). Social networks and mediators of social support: An analysis of the effects and determinants of social networks. *Community Mental Health Journal*, 16, 27-44.

Mulhern, R. K., Crisco, J. J. & Camitta, B. M. (1981). Patterns of communication among pediatric patients with leukemia, parents, and physicians: Prognostic disagreements and misunderstandings. *Journal of Pediatrics*, 99, 480-483.

Mulhern, R. K., Wasserman, A. L., Friedman, A. G. & Fairclough, D. (1989). Social competence and behavioural adjustment of children who are long-term survivors of cancer. *Pediatrics*, 83, 18-25.

National Centre for Health Statistics. Current estimates from the National Health Interview Survey: United States 1981. *Vital Health Statistics*, series 10, No. 141, Washington, DC: US Government Printing Office, October 1982. (PHS) 83-1569.

Nolan, T., Dresmond, K., Herlich, R. & Hardy, S. (1986). Knowledge of cystic fibrosis in patients and their parents. *Pediatrics*, 77, 229-235.

Olson, D. H. (1986). Circumplex model VII: Validation studies and FACES III. *Family Process*, 25, 337-351.

Panaccione, V. F. & Wahler, R. G. (1986). Child-behavior, maternal depression and social coercion as factors in the quality of child care. *Journal of Abnormal Child Psychology*, 14, 263-278.

Parmelee, A. H. (1986). Children's illnesses: Their beneficial effects on behavioural development. *Child Development*, 57, 1-10.

Peckham, V. C., Meadows, A. T., Bartel, N. & Marrero, O. (1988). Educational late effects in long-term survivors of childhood acute lymphocytic leukemia. *Pediatrics*, 81, 127-133.

Perrin, E. C. & Gerrity, P. S (1984). Development of children with a chronic illness. *Pediatric Clinics of North America*, 31, 19-31.

Perrin, J. M. & MacLean Jr, W. E. (1988). Children with chronic illness: The prevention of dysfunction. *Pediatric Clinics of North America*, 35, 1325-1337.

Perrin, J. M., MacLean, W. E. & Perrin, E. C. (1989). Parental perceptions of health status and psychologic adjustment of children with asthma. *Pediatrics*, 83, 26-30.

Pless, I. B. & Pinkerton, P. (1975). *Chronic Childhood disorder: Promoting Patterns of Adjustment*. London: Henry Kimpton.

Renne, C. M. & Creer, T. L. (1985). Ashmatic children and their families. In C. M. Renne & T. L. Creer (Eds), *Advances in Developmental and Behavioural Politics*, Vol. 6. Greenwich, CT: JAI Press.

Ricks, S. S. (1985). Father–infant interactions: A review of empirical research. *Family Relations*, 34, 505-511.

Sabbeth, B. F. & Leventhal, J. M. (1984). Marital adjustment to chronic childhood illness: A critique of the literature. *Pediatrics*, 73, 762-768.

Sargent, J., Rosman, B., Baker, L., Noguiera, J. & Stanley, C. (1985). Family interaction and diabetic control: A prospective study. *Diabetes*, 34(Suppl. 1), 77A.

Shouval, R., Ber, R. & Galatzer, A. (1982). Family social climate and the length, status and social adaptation of diabetic youth. In Z. Laron (Ed.), *Psychological Aspects of Diabetes in Children and Adolescents*. Basel: Karger.

Sieman, M. (1984). Siblings of the chronically ill or disabled child: Meeting their needs. *Nursing Clinics of North America*, 19, 295-307.

Spinetta, J., Spinetta, P., Kung, F. & Schwartz, D. (1976). *Emotional Aspects of Childhood Cancer and Leukemia: A Handbook for Parents*. San Diego: Leukemia Society of America.

Stern, M. & Arenson, E. (1989). Childhood cancer stereotype: Impact on adult perceptions of children. *Journal of Pediatric Psychology*, 14, 593-606.

Sutton-Smith, B. & Rosenberg, B. C. (1970). *the Sibling*. New York: Holt, Rinehart & Winston.

Tew, B. & Laurence, K. M. (1973). Mothers, brothers and sisters of patients with spina bifida. *Developmental Medicine and Child Neurology*, 15(Suppl. 6), 69-76.

Ungerer, J., Horgan, B., Chaitow, J. & Champion, G. B. (1988). Psychosocial functioning in children and young adults with juvenile arthritis. *Journal of Pediatrics*, 81, 195-202.

Varni, J. W. & Wallander, J. L. (1988). Pediatric chronic disabilities: Hemophilia and spina bifida as examples. In D. Routh (Ed.), *Handbook of Pediatric Psychology*. New York: Guilford Press, pp. 190-221.

Von Bertalanffy, L. (1968). *General Systems Theory: Foundation. Development and Applications*. New York: Braziller.

Waisbren, S. (1980). Parents' reactions to the birth of a developmentally disabled infant. *American Journal of Mental Defficiency*, 84, 356-361.

Wales, J. K. (1985). Adolescent diabetes (A symposium held in March 1985). *Practical Diabetes*, 2, 20.

Walker, D. K. (1984). Care of chronically ill children in schools. *Pediatric Clinics of North America*, 31, 221-233.

Walker, L., Ford, M. B. & Donald, W. D. (1986). Stress in families with cystic fibrosis. Paper presented at the Annual Meeting of the American Psychological Association, Washington, DC.

Walker, S., Ortiz-Valdes, J. A. & Newbrough, J. R. (1989). The role of maternal employment and depression in the psychological adjustment of chronically ill mentally retarded and well children. *Journal of Pediatric Psychology*, 14, 357-370.

Wallander, J. L., Varni, J. W., Babani, L., Banis, H. T. & Wilcox, K. T. (1988). Children with chronic physical disorders: Maternal reports of their psychological adjustment. *Journal of Pediatric Psychology*, **13**, 197–212.

Wallander, J. L. Varni, J. W., Babani, L., DeHeen, C. B., Wilcox, K. T. & Banis, H. T. (1989). The social environment and the adaptation of mothers of physically handicapped children. *Journal of Pediatric Psychology*, **14**, 371–388.

Waller, D. A., Chipman, J. J., B. W., Hightower, M. J., North, A. J., Williams, J. B. & Babick, A. J. (1986). Measuring diabetes specific family support and its relation to metabolic control: a preliminary report. *Journal of the American Academy of Child Psychiatry*, **25**, 415–418.

Weinberger, M., Cohen, S. J. & Mazzuca, S. A. (1984). The role of physicians' knowledge in effective diabetes management. *Social Science and Medicine*, **19**, 965–969.

Wertlieb, D., Hauser, S. T. & Jacobson, A. (1986). Adaptation to diabetes: Behaviour symptoms and family context. *Journal of Pediatric Psychology*, **11**, 463–480.

Wortman, C. & Dunkel-Schetter, C. (1979). Interpersonal relationships and cancer: A theoretical analysis. *Journal of Social Issues*, **35**, 120–155.

Zrebiec, J. F. (1987). Psychosocial commentary on insulin-dependent diabetes mellitus in 5- to 9-year-old children. In S. J. Brink (Ed.), *Pediatric and Adolescent Diabetes Mellitus*. Chicago: Year Book Medical Publishers, pp. 79–88.

7 Doctor–Patient Communication: An Interpersonal Helping Process

HELEN R. WINEFIELD
Department of Psychiatry, University of Adelaide, GPO Box 498, Adelaide, Australia 5001

INTRODUCTION

The goal of this chapter is to provide an interactional perspective on the processes of communication between doctors and patients. The less recent literature will be summarized rather than reiterated: it provided the foundation for developments which currently promise to advance understanding and theory formulation by linking study of the doctor–patient consultation with the wider psychology of helping and empowerment.

The medical consultation is a situation of such richness and complexity that it threatens to overwhelm the observer trying to understand it holistically. Reductionism can provide short-term gains at the risk of selective attention, a similar problem to that being faced by the participants to the consultation. However, because communication inherently implies a dynamic series of exchanges between two or more individuals, it is desirable to keep the level of analysis interactional rather than individual. This chapter adopts the perspective that doctor–patient communication is part of a helping interaction. I will argue that to a greater extent than is often acknowledged, the form of help provided is psychological rather than biological. The tradition of the medical consultation as a problem-solving task for the doctor is valid but narrow; the patient-centred perspective provides a wider view. As will be seen, research evidence for the value of the latter is emerging, although much further work is needed.

Health psychologists have been active in two main relevant areas, namely in conducting research into the process and outcomes of doctor–patient communication, and in the teaching of communication skills to doctors at various educational levels; both will be discussed in detail here. Although the focus of this chapter is specifically on medical communication; many of its considerations also apply to other forms of professional helping.

Communication constitutes the *process* of the medical encounter, and improved health is the desired ultimate *outcome*. The vital question is whether we can specify the form and pattern of communication which raises the

International Review of Health Psychology. Edited by S. Maes, H. Leventhal and M. Johnston
©1992 John Wiley & Sons Ltd

probability of positive changes in health. Everything that transpires during the medical encounter, and every observable characteristic of the participants, has a potential communicative function. Each participant is alert to information from the other in both verbal and non-verbal forms: the physical environment, how the parties are dressed, how and where they sit, look, and what is said and not said (DiMatteo, 1979). As doctoring is a role of central importance to the occupant's identity, and as the patient role is an unwelcome and part-time one, there has been an impetus to prescribe the behaviour of the doctor rather than that of the patient. The burden of responsibility for optimal communication is largely seen as resting with the professional.

Whether the patient's symptoms are reduced or not as a result of the consultation will often be assessed by further communicative behaviours rather than by "objective" measures of somatic function. This chapter assumes that if we grapple with the nature and desirable features of doctor–patient communication, we are in fact grappling with issues of the quality of medical care. Let us begin then by briefly reviewing how the quality of care may be measured.

MEASUREMENT OF THE QUALITY OF HEALTH CARE

In trying to assess the success of a health care intervention, we are trying to quantify the change in health which it causes. The health care intervention seeks to improve health in comparison to its pre-consultation baseline, or in some cases, to prevent its deterioration. The assessment of quality of health care therefore depends upon being able to measure health reliably; however, to the surprise of non-physicians, there are few objective externally validated measures of health.

Measurement of health

The death rate of the patients served by a particular doctor is attractively simple to compute, but a very slow and very contaminated measure of quality of care; more proximate and better-defined outcome measures are necessary. Morbidity, symptoms, and wellness all prove more difficult to quantify. Blood pressure, blood glucose levels, and lung capacity can be measured with reasonable (though imperfect) reliability and validity; thus some aspects at least of the control of hypertension, diabetes, and asthma can relatively easily be assessed. In other diseases the assessment of severity is more dependent on levels of reported (ie subjective) pain or dysfunction, particularly if we seek measures which are not intrusive, invasive, or needful of expensive machinery and analyses.

Beyond measuring the extent of illness, how can physical well-being be quantified? Health defined in positive terms rather than by the absence of symptoms seems to include reasonable energy levels and enjoyment of life, and the capacity to participate in normal social activities such as seeing friends and working at one's usual tasks (paid or not). Such descriptions of physical well-being, or quality of life, sound very similar to the usual definitions of emotional well-being, also expressed in terms of satisfying social relationships, self-confidence, energy for living, and sense of mastery and competence (Strupp, 1989, p. 723).

Other assessable outcomes of health care

Compliance

The level of compliance or patient adherence to recommendations is a popular outcome measure in medicine, often with the implication that compliance and health benefits are highly correlated (DiMatteo & DiNicola, 1982). Compliance is difficult to measure reliably without active patient cooperation, is variable, and is always less than perfect particularly when complicated or long-term behaviour change is recommended. As an outcome or quality-of-care measure, compliance suffers too from the fact that it may be determined by many other factors such as cost in addition to the quality of care.

One prerequisite for compliance is the patient's recall of the doctor's instructions, and recall in turn is facilitated by specific and comprehensible terms, lack of jargon, repetition, and hearing the most important parts of the message first (Ley, 1988). Recall of information has sometimes been used as an indicator of the success of the consultation, although it is obviously an indirect measure of the quality of care.

Patient satisfaction

Patient satisfaction, loyalty, and failure to sue must be accorded some credibility as indicators of the quality of medical practice, even though they may be biased by the patients' lack of professional judgment. As individuals by and large decide to seek entry to the sick role by consulting the socially recognized healer, they are also in the best position to seek exits from the sick role by defining themselves as recovered. Thus there is inescapably an element of subjectivity in health assessment, which means that the perceptions of the patient must be sought. A variety of scales is available to do so, and satisfaction shows some correlation with both compliance and symptom relief (Fitzpatrick, 1984; Hall & Dornan, 1988). Although measures of patient satisfaction with medical care are always positively skewed, the two areas most frequently noted to cause dissatisfaction are the doctor's lack of skill in communicating (a) information, and (b) respect for the patient.

Patient satisfaction may have direct and independent effects on perceived/reported well-being. Rather than being beneficial only as a step on the way to greater compliance, the patient's sense of being respected and cared for may reduce anxieties, encourage coping efforts, and supportively buffer him or her against the isolation, stigma, and daily practical difficulties of illness. The immunological correlates of hopefulness, although in the infancy of quantitative study, are clearly more beneficial than those of chronic stress, depression, and social deprivation (O'Leary, 1990).

Doctor's satisfaction

The doctor's satisfaction with the consultation can also provide valuable information about the quality of the helping interaction. Doctors have described the problems caused by "difficult" patients: the power struggles which can develop (Ross & Phipps, 1986), malignant dependency (Ryle, 1987), O'Dowd's (1988) heartsink patients, and the thick chart syndrome (John et al., 1987). Schwenk et al. (1989) found that both complex medical problems, and frustrating responses to doctor advice, needed to occur for the patient to be regarded as difficult.

In a later section of this chapter the links between the communication during the consultation and these various consultation outcomes will be explicitly reviewed. Now I shall proceed to examine in more detail, the process by which doctors seek to achieve the outcomes reviewed above.

THE PROCESS OF HELPING IN DOCTOR–PATIENT ENCOUNTERS

The help which medical practitioners provide has both similarities and differences from that expected from other sources of help in the patient's life. Unlike confidants and family members, doctors do not make the patient feel loved and needed, and do not offer general practical assistance such as loans, transport, babysitting, or doing household chores. The physical procedures they may perform are skilled, and the advice they offer is expert rather than experiential; on the other hand, unlike specialist psychotherapists they do not routinely aim to achieve patient insight and self-understanding (Winefield, 1987). What is common to expert medical help and to effective informal support, is the demonstration of respect and care for the help-seeking person. How to express these attitudes has therefore become a component of the communication skills training of medical students by psychologists, as will be discussed below.

Other perspectives which apply to the medical consultation include its function as a medium of exchange, both of information and of influence, and its political role to legitimize some expressions of malaise and distress as disease and thus allow entry of the sufferer to the sick role upon which considerable social benefits depend (Parsons, 1951). These perspectives will be treated as incorporated in the helping viewpoint rather than being explored independently. They all form real but restricted subsets of the dominant social function of medical care which is the relief of suffering.

The professional role in medical care

The help which doctors offer is based on their professional role rather than on a history of personal attachment to the recipient. The detachment of the professional role requires doctors to express care and respect for individuals who might be regarded as difficult, or actively unlikeable, in ordinary social interactions. Difficult patients may be angry, passive, complaining, denying, overly affectionate, or schizophrenic; the violent, the disfigured, the dying, and the addicted also need high-quality care (Lipp, 1986). The patient can in principle expect conscientious medical treatment regardless of his or her personal charm, appearance, or responsiveness to treatment. Recalcitrant and unresponsive patients pose problems for physicians if they arouse feelings of hostility or rejection. There is some exploration in the literature of physician burnout (Maslach & Jackson, 1982) and the consequences of that depersonalizing, emotionally exhausted state. For example, Melville (1980) reported an association between job dissatisfaction and risky prescribing habits. However, the possible emotional stress to the professional of providing egalitarian care, and the appropriate coping techniques, have received relatively little research attention.

The role of communication in medical care

Although medical textbooks express considerable optimism about the health benefits of advances in pharmacology, surgery and diagnostic technology, in fact a large proportion of patient illness and disease remains undiagnosable, in practice unpreventable, and increasingly in Western societies, incurable. Effective help for many health problems depends upon effective doctor–patient communication, as exemplified by the following:

1. Many symptoms presented to doctors, such as headaches, sleeping difficulties, weight loss, nausea, and pain can signify either organic or emotional dysfunction
2. The decision to present symptoms of a minor or self-limited kind (such as respiratory infections) for medical treatment can signify emotional distress (eg work dissatisfaction)
3. Positive response to medical treatment may not be a specific consequence of the drug or procedures used, but may show the power of the placebo effect (Shepherd & Sartorius, 1989)
4. Some patients will present physical symptoms to seek solutions for interpersonal inadequacies. In fact our society provides many reinforcements to express psychological pain and fear in somatic terms, with focus on the physiological manifestations and consequences. Foss & Rothenberg (1987, p. 8) have argued that "the biomedical model is pathology-inducing in its own right by virtue of its systematic exclusion of extrasomatic etiological factors"
5. Often medical care can consist mainly of emotional support, neither effective treatment nor cure being available for the increasing proportion of chronic illnesses suffered by patients in industrialized countries
6. Permanent self-care regimes for chronic illnesses such as asthma, diabetes, hypertension, epilepsy, arthritis, and drug abuse, the sexually transmitted

diseases, and recovery from acute illnesses and surgery, require emotional and informational support (Ben-Sira, 1984; Neuling & Winefield, 1988; Taylor, 1986)

7. Interpersonal stress (loss, disappointment, and conflict) can aggravate sensitivity to physical dysfunctions, and chronic physical conditions can be exacerbated by anxiety or depression, sometimes because these lead to poor compliance with control regimes

8. Most medical care for psychological symptoms is provided by non-psychiatrist general physicians (Shepherd et al., 1966). This includes marital and sexual counselling, coping with grief and bereavement, child and adolescent behaviour disorders, and the strains of caring for aged or handicapped family members, as well as the more clearly psychiatric disorders of anxiety states, depression, and chronic mental illness.

Lipp (1986, p. x) after describing three-quarters of a century of efforts to "humanize" medical care, claimed that the psychological aspects of medical practice are often clinically inconsequential—but that they make a difference to the doctor's self-esteem and sense of mastery. This must be the ultimate doctor-centred justification of such skills!

Applying the psychotherapy model to all health care

There are benefits to individual sufferers of advances in pharmacology, surgery, and diagnostics, and both life expectancy and quality of life for many with chronic illness have been increasing. However, because of the highly psychological nature of medical care as outlined above, it seems relevant to explore what findings from psychotherapy research may be applicable to all health care, as psychotherapy is the speciality of reducing distress by psychological means. Psychologists have put much effort in recent years into delineating the critical elements of psychotherapy, and as shown above, the goals of both enterprises (psychotherapy and general medical care) converge on improved patient well-being.

Methods

The major methodological conclusion from psychotherapy research is the need to describe the process of helping very precisely, for example with exact records of the communicatory behaviours, then to link these variables to outcomes assessed as reliably and validly as possible (Greenberg, 1986). Recent calls for increased sophistication in conceptualizing the health care process resonate with similar conclusions applied to both specialist psychotherapy and to social support. For example, Inui & Carter (1985) and other reviewers have called for more attempts to disaggregate the process of communication in health care, with more attention to context and changes over time, and with sequential analyses rather than frequency counts of relevant behaviours. Although research following these recommendations is extremely difficult, some interesting findings are emerging which will be discussed more fully below.

Conclusions

The main substantive finding of psychotherapy research is the "overriding significance of the interpersonal relationship between patient and therapist as the vehicle for therapeutic change" (Strupp, 1989, p. 723). Early and continuous assessment of patient satisfaction is very valuable. Luborsky et al. (1985) found that patients' ratings of their attitude to their therapist after the third session predicted the outcome of psychotherapy better than did any other patient, therapist, or interaction variable, and there is much supporting evidence (Greenberg, 1986). The parallel in health care might be patient attitudinal indicators assessed during the consultation, or soon after a chronic illness has been diagnosed.

While the health care literature stresses the importance of the doctor–patient relationship in a general way, actual training in how to develop, measure, and use it therapeutically is usually absent. The informed and deliberate cultivation and use of the affective relationship between the parties which defines psychotherapy (Strupp, 1986) means that the therapist must pay attention to his or her emotional responses to the patient, and use that information to increase the patient's self-understanding. The implied requirement to give signficance to feelings contrasts with the traditional conceptualization of the doctor's task in non-affective, problem-solving terms (see below).

In applying these insights from the research on psychological helping, doctors would not only express empathy and understanding about their patients' emotional responses to life events, but also recognize, monitor, and make constructive use of their own feelings towards the patient. They would need to learn to regard the relationship as powerfully therapeutic in its own right rather than as just a means to enhance patient compliance with advice (Berg, 1987). It would be helpful to doctors if researchers could specify the language patterns which indicate how the therapeutic relationship is developing, so that doctors could assess its progress from interactional information available to them during the course of the consultation. Efforts to do so will be reviewed towards the end of the chapter.

DOCTORS' VIEWS OF DOCTOR–PATIENT COMMUNICATION

The consultation process represented in standard medical texts could perhaps be summarized as:
1. Doctor systematically elicits all the necessary information from patient, applies professional knowledge, and reaches a diagnostic decision
2. Doctor tells patient enough to motivate compliance with expert advice, ideally checking that message is understood and drawing diagrams or writing it down if necessary

3. Doctor may arrange to check patient health progress at suitable follow-up.

The doctor assumes professional responsibility for the patient's health care, and with this, a high level of control of both the consultation and the patient's future health-related behaviours. This biomedical focus sees the doctor's communication skills as an *adjunct* to effective health care delivery, in contrast to the conceptualization above of helpful communications as the *vehicle* of medical care.

There are many influences upon the communicatory style of the doctor. Leaving aside individual differences in personality among members of the medical profession, other influences include formal courses in communication during undergraduate and postgraduate education, informal learning by modelling from the clinical consultants who teach and examine bedside medicine in the large teaching hospitals, peer reinforcements, and a host of other economic and socio-political influences, from cultural expectations of the doctor's role to the payment arrangements, which frequently encourage spending minimum time with each patient. Most information is available about the first of these influences: educational input.

Communication training for doctors

Behavioural science courses in undergraduate medical curricula teach psychological perspectives on human health and illness and a basic appreciation of the possible contribution of the social sciences to medical practice. Such courses frequently include, or are followed by, intensive study and rehearsal of skills relevant to doctor–patient communication. The principles of behavioural change have been applied to this educational task, with specification of the desirable target behaviours, individualized assessment of skills, informational feedback on progress and so on, and there is considerable evidence that in the short term at least, students acquire new abilities to ask open-ended questions, make reflective summaries of what the other has said, and express emotional support. They reach criterion levels of skill as determined by their teachers and assessed by ratings, with or without videotaped interviews and simulated patients (Maguire, 1984; McAvoy, 1988; Pendleton et al., 1984; Thompson, 1984). Long-term outcomes of such teaching have not often been assessed, as the difficulties in doing so independently of other influences on the student make that a formidable task. However Maguire, Fairbairn & Fletcher (1986a) were able to show that young doctors who as students had been randomly allocated to video feedback training in interviewing, maintained their superiority over conventionally trained peers after five years. Both groups, however, performed poorly in using open questions and asking about the psychosocial impact of health problems.

Information exchange in interview training

The primary focus of standard texts on medical interviewing/history-taking is information extraction, with the implication that doctors need "the facts, all the facts, and nothing but the facts" relevant to the disease, as decided by themselves (see Tuckett et al., 1985, pp. 168–9). Patient ideas about what information is relevant to the doctor's decision-making may not coincide with the doctor's: Waitzkin (1989) described how doctors use questions, interruptions, and topic changes to shift patient discourse away from psychosocial sources of distress ("the voice of the lifeworld") and back to "the voice of medicine". Even in that arena of discourse, doctors often decide very quickly what they want to hear from the patient and move from open-ended to directive questioning. Beckman & Frankel (1984) found that in 69% of primary care visits in their sample, the doctor interrupted the patient's initial statement of concerns, and only one of the 51 patients so treated subsequently finished their statement about why they had come to the clinic.

Information-giving is the next task discussed in medical texts. Because patients lack training in the specialist medical vocabulary, there are many hazards to their understanding, let alone their recall, of what the doctor tells them. Therefore doctors have to be able to choose comprehensible terms as a first step to persuading patients towards recommended actions. The translation problems of medical versus everyday language have been described by many authors, including Scott & Weiner (1984) and Gibbs, Gibbs & Henrich (1987). Bourhis, Roth & MacQueen (1989) made the further point that use of specialist jargon also has affective significance: efforts by doctors to converge to the language style of their patients will be perceived as signs of liking and respect. In their study, doctors reported using everyday language with their patients, but this was not how either the patients or the nurses reported the situation.

Danziger (1978) described how doctors and patients may have matching or mismatched expectations of the control to be exercised by the doctor, and how this control takes the form primarily of control of information-giving. Numerous studies attest to the unfavourable effects on patients of inadequate information-giving by doctors. For example, Mason (1985) found that patients with diabetes were often confused and anxious, and uninformed about their own self-care, after supposedly having everything explained by the doctor and dietitian. As patients are usually of lower social status than their doctors, and are in any case likely to lack assertiveness because they feel ill, they commonly do not challenge incomprehensible explanations or instructions. Even when they depart the consultation with unanswered questions, which happens more frequently than doctors estimate, patients may not express dissatisfaction with the consultation (Shapiro et al., 1983). They are likely to attend very closely to the doctor's non-verbal communicatory behaviours for clues, and if in hospital, to seek information later from nurses (Mathews, 1983).

Tuckett et al. (1985) concluded none the less that the difficulties which patients have in understanding and remembering instructions have been overplayed in medical texts. After careful study of a large number of British general practice consultations, these authors decided that the traditional stereotype of the patient as too ignorant to recall or make sense of what the doctor has said, is grossly misleading, but that it persists because it is compatible with the doctor's reluctance to share expertise or to accord the patient's ideas any status. In practice, patients' ideas were not systematically sought during the general practice consultations they studied, and tended to be devalued on the few occasions that they were offered.

Maguire, Fairbairn & Fletcher (1986b) in the follow-up study described above were clearly disappointed to report that both groups of young doctors (specially versus conventionally trained in interviewing) gave inadequate information: specifically they failed to discover the patients' own views, expectations, and responses to the treatment plan, or to mention prognosis.

Advice-giving may be counter-productive if the initial expression of the problem is incomplete or confused. Advice-giving rather than empathy is, however, the usual response to a problem statement, even by students faced with trigger statements of psychosocial and emotional problems (Winefield, 1982). Patients are likely to feel more committed to action which is arrived at by examining the alternatives rather than by passively accepting the doctor's opinions, especially about psychosocial rather than purely biomedical concerns. It is worth noting at this point that Smits et al. (1991) found a positive correlation between behavioural (interpersonal) skills and medical (diagnostic and treatment) skills, in 75 Dutch general practitioners.

Many doctors want to learn how to give information more effectively and how to counsel patients with psychosocial problems; this was the most frequently chosen area where South Australian general practitioners expressed the need for extra training, in a state-wide survey ($N = 966$ and return rate $= 78\%$; Gill, 1988). The psychotherapeutic concept of letting the patient's frame of reference dominate the interaction, while the professional refrains from direct advice in favour of fostering the patient's confidence in achieving a resolution, is under-emphasized in medical texts. The doctor's need to be perceived as in control, perhaps with the justification that the doctor's self-assurance potentiates the placebo effect, is deeply ingrained and warrants further discussion later.

The therapeutic relationship in interview training

Training in how to maximize the therapeutic potential of the help-seeking interaction would include much more than getting the relevant facts, checking that the patient can understand and remember the doctor's instructions, and making the right percentage of reflections. Yet a practical apprenticeship in cultivation of a helping relationship is much less often included in interviewing training compared with the information-exchange aspects.

Balint (1964, p. 1) is often quoted that "the most frequently used drug in primary health care was the doctor himself"—a finding quickly followed by the worrying discovery that no pharmacology existed for this important drug, ie no textbooks on the correct dosage, or possible hazards of the drug's use, and no explanations for unsatisfactory outcomes of apparently conscientious administrations of it. Balint groups, which have a psychoanalytic orientation, now meet in many centres to discuss cases, especially those where the patient's or doctor's emotions and motivations have a critical role in treatment outcomes. However, these groups are voluntary extras, and probably attract doctors who already have a particular interest in and sensitivity to the psychological aspects of practice.

Although doctors are not routinely trained with supervision, feedback, and formal assessment to use the relationship therapeutically, there are some descriptions in the non-psychiatric medical literature of how to cultivate and use a therapeutic alliance. Stein (1987, p. 7), for example, wrote that "The self of the physician—of any clinician—is a powerful diagnostic and therapeutic tool". Reiser & Rosen (1984) advocated "following the affect", in other words, keeping track of the emotions experienced by both parties to the interview; workshops for communication teachers by the Task Force on the Medical Interview and Related Skills are very much focused on dealing with the doctor's feelings towards the patient (Novack, 1989). Smith (1984) showed how unrecognized feelings interfered with student interviewing competence. Micro-analyses of recorded consultations enable the doctor's feelings about the patient to be acknowledged during training, using methods like Elliott & Shapiro's (1988) Brief Structured Recall or Kagan's (1979) Interpersonal Process Recall. These teaching approaches are compatible with psychotherapy-derived views of medical care as a mutual endeavour, but incompatible with the current technocractic emphasis in medicine on new drugs and physical procedures.

The teachers

Early in the medical course, psychosocially oriented teaching is often provided by non-doctors (including psychologists) and/or by psychiatrists. Later-year students have additional opportunities to learn from numerous informal observations of the behaviour of their clinical teachers. Where there are discrepancies between the teachings from different sources, students probably identify with teachers of higher status, or those who best match their own career aspirations. For psychotherapeutic insights to be incorporated into compulsory medical training, they must therefore be seen to be accepted by the senior consultants who act as clinical teachers. Surgeons, gastro-enterologists, and cardiologists would need to demonstrate their commitment to this mode of communication as well as the psychiatrists and family physicians who may well be already persuaded.

PATIENT VIEWS OF DOCTOR–PATIENT COMMUNICATION

To sample the perspective of the help-seeker/patient requires consideration of how people, having assessed themselves as suffering a health problem and obtained medical attention, interpret and respond to the doctor's helping efforts. Patients vary in their level of help-elicitation skills (Winefield, 1984), they undergo no formal training in how to be effective as patients, may have learned maladaptive expectations by observation or from past experiences, and are likely to be feeling anxious and depressed about their illness. Shame and humiliation are common experiences for them (Lazare, 1987). None the less patients have ideas about proper behaviour towards and by the doctor, and what their own goals are for the interaction.

Salmon & Quine (1989) found that primary care patients' intentions in seeking help could be summarized as wanting explanations, emotional support, medical advice, or more general information. As Calnan (1988) has pointed out, patients' assessments of the quality of care are likely to be affected by several interrelated factors: their reasons for seeking care (eg wanting technical help, diagnosis, advice, or counselling), their past direct and indirect experiences of health care, the socio-political values of the health care system, and their own images of health. Demographic factors such as age mediate all these: greater patient age is consistently associated with greater willingness to express satisfaction (Fitzpatrick, 1984; Hall & Dornan, 1990). Other individual differences such as in expectations (Ditto & Hilton, 1990) and coping techniques (Miller, Leinbach & Brody, 1989; Pruyn et al., 1985) also moderate patient responses to different symptoms, forms of treatment, and doctor style.

It would be paradoxical to expect people who have been exhorted in mass media campaigns to take responsibility for health by changing their diet, getting regular exercise, applying sunscreen and stopping smoking, to abrogate this responsibility for active participation when illness occurs, and be satisfied with unquestioning acceptance of medical instruction. As well as wishing to become a non-patient as quickly as possible, patients may also want to salvage their dignity in the medical consultation and remind the doctor of their other, non-patient life. The patient-centred movement within medicine stresses the need for patient–doctor mutuality rather than doctor control, in exploration of options and in formulation and negotiation of plans (eg Tuckett et al., 1985; Pendleton et al., 1984). There is evidence that increased (not absolute) patient control of conversational content is associated with better response to treatment, as will be reviewed below.

PROCESS–OUTCOME STUDIES OF MEDICAL COMMUNICATION

A number of researchers have demonstrated by careful analyses of the recorded discourse and a variety of outcome measures, the benefits of enhanced patient control, or decreased patient powerlessness, in the consultation. In an early study Stiles et al. (1979) found that patients were more satisfied when their conceptual framework rather than the doctor's was dominant in the concluding segment of the consultation, in which the doctor gave information and advice. Weinberger, Greene & Mamlin (1981) used discrminant analysis to show that encounters satisfactory to patients had been characterized by physician non-verbal encouragement, questions about family and social situations, and expressions of continuity from previous visits. At the same time the doctors felt most satisfied with consultations where patients were seen as compliant and where humour and non-verbal encouragement were used during the interaction.

Stewart (1984) defined patient-centred behaviour by the doctor as statements in a number of interactional categories which included greetings, friendly comments, encouragement, jokes and laughter, agreement, requests for opinion and direction, and expressions of tension or anxiety. Patient compliance was associated with higher rates of these doctor behaviours. Similarly Rost, Carter & Inui (1989) found that compliance with new medication regimes was superior where patients had volunteered information (including sometimes, comments on non-health-related "social" topics), rather than just answering the doctor's questions. However, Robinson & Whitfield (1988) found that patients who volunteered information during the consultation made more errors or omissions in their subsequent accounts of what they had been told by the doctor. These also tended to be patients who presented a new problem to the doctor, leading to the possibility that the information-processing demands of presenting, receiving, and integrating new ideas during one brief consultation can become excessive.

A meta-analysis (Hall, Roter & Katz, 1988; Roter & Hall, 1989) grouped provider behaviours into the process super-categories of information-giving, questions, competence, partnership building, and socio-emotional behaviour. Patient satisfaction was more closely related to provider behaviours than was either recall or compliance, and it was rather more closely related to amount of information provided (including opinions, advice, explanations, instructions, discussion of diagnosis and prognosis, etc.; average correlation 0.33) than to partnership building (including reflections, interpretations, patient-centred statements, requests, questions, etc.; average $r = 0.27$). The authors concluded that "patients *interpret* good task performance, such as informativeness, as reflecting the providers' caring disposition and positive regard. . . . A provider's merely being nice or caring, in the absence of positive or negative indications of task performance, does not supply the evidence on competence that a patient needs" (p. 668).

Whitcher-Alagna (1983) offered a three-part explanation for the often observed relationship between patients' satisfaction and both the amount of information they have received, and the affective tone of the consultation. Firstly, information may enhance the patient's sense of control (and reduce the sense of helplessness); secondly, the doctor's efforts to provide information conscientiously convey care and concern; thirdly, patients know that it takes time for the doctor to explain things clearly and that for the doctor, time is money, and "help that is costly to the donor produces more positive recipient-responses" (p. 138).

In a study distinguished by its use of physiological as well as self-report measures of health, Kaplan, Greenfield & Ware (1989) found that patients experienced better outcomes when consultations had contained more expression of affect, especially negative affect, by both parties. They surmised that some friction between patient and doctor might indicate a higher level of engagement between the two, and/or that greater patient control has independent biochemical benefits.

Henbest & Stewart (1989) defined patient-centredness in terms of responses by the doctor which enabled patients to express all their reasons for coming, including symptoms, thoughts, feelings and expectations. Each such utterance by a patient was noted, and the patient-centredness of the doctor's response (ignore, closed question, open question, or specific facilitation) was simply scored. There was a high correlation between patient-centredness scores for the first two minutes and for the whole consultation. Subsequently Henbest & Stewart (1990) found an association between the patient-centredness of the doctor's response to their main symptom, and the patients' decreased concern about that symptom after the consultation, but not with patient satisfaction, or with symptom reduction two weeks afterwards. This second study also suggested the need to revise the scoring for patient-centredness, in that outcomes were poorer after open-ended than closed responses, although responses which specifically facilitated expression of expectations, thoughts, or feelings, were consistently associated with the best outcomes. More work on this measure would be justified by the desirability of developing an index of patient-centredness which could be used not only by researchers everywhere, but also by medical practitioners and those teaching interviewing skills to them.

Winefield & Murrell (1991) returned to the idea that different patterns of doctor response might be required to facilitate patient engagement at different stages of the consultation. They divided transcripts of consultations into diagnostic and prescriptive phases, using as the borderline the first piece of expert advice by the doctor, then related the verbal interaction features of each stage to the satisfaction of both participants. While the ideal consultation from the doctor's point of view was one with more open-ended questions in the first phase and more predictions in the second, patients' satisfaction was associated with being allowed or encouraged to discuss their own ideas, including negative attitudes, in the second or prescriptive phase of the consultation. Thus doctors preferred consultations which followed a fairly predictable path from problem statement to resolution in a way which assured the doctor of his or her competence. Anxiety about not being able to help seemed to constitute the worst source of dissatisfaction for doctors, as found by Schwenk et al. (1989). At the same time the patients' agenda seemed to be somewhat different: they preferred consultations where they had the opportunity to discuss their reactions to the doctor's recommendations after hearing them. Sometimes they wanted to add extra information, and sometimes to express hesitations or anxieties. It is as though the patients were adherents of the Szasz & Hollender (1956) "mutual participation" model of doctor–patient roles, while the doctors were worrying about their capacity to fill the "active" role.

Barriers to the patient-centred view

The available research thus suggests some possible modifications to the traditionally doctor-centred view of how medical communication should best proceed. In contemplating how such findings might be applied within medical education, it is necessary to recognize the potential barriers to their acceptance. Similar ideas have been proposed in the past, albeit without a comparable empirical base, and have had little impact on the way medicine is practised. For example, Tuckett et al. (1985) noted that although the doctors they studied all seemed devoted to the welfare of their patients, they were extremely reluctant to cede control to them. Medical school faculties collectively make policy decisions about funding for teacher salaries and equipment, and use of student curriculum time, such that in practice the medical education system has considerable inertia. The view of the doctor's role which patient- and relationship-centredness imply, is potentially an unbalancing innovation. Can students be taught to do effective patient-centred consultations and still fit the examiner's model of the properly trained doctor?

Reiser & Rosen (1984) highlighted the disturbing tendency for students to compartmentalize their thinking about the goals and techniques of interviewing, and to do perfect holistic, patient-centred interviews on the psychiatric round, then perfect biomedical, symptom-focused interviews everywhere else. As previously noted, patient-centredness is unlikely to be accepted while it is advocated only by psychiatrists and psychologists, because of their marginal status within the medical establishment (Engel, 1982).

Kagan (1979), discussing learning to use the process as content, observed that "students to not 'naturally' discuss with a patient their mutual relationship. Even when given direct instruction in the skill, students seldom are able to use it" (p. 482). He felt that students fear the time commitment—but they often waste time in asking questions to which they know the answers, or in giving recommendations which fit so badly with the patient's ideas that they will never be followed. Patient dissatisfaction can of course lead to time-wasteful repeat visits, where medical care is pre-paid, and coping with these "redundant" complaints causes doctor dissatisfaction (Ben-Sira, 1990).

Students also fear not being capable of psychotherapeutic influence without very extensive training. Putnam et al. (1988) had in previous research found benefits from high rates of patient information-giving other than in yes/no form. However, when these authors tried to train interns to listen without asking questions, the interns "expressed great discomfort at allowing patients to talk about their illnesses in their own words because they were afraid patients would bring up emotionally charged issues which they could not handle" (p. 44). Tuckett et al. (1985) substantially agreed, in their discussion of the pressures upon doctors to make serious decisions quickly, mediate between the patient, relatives, and medical service, and cope with doubt, failure, and a sense of helplessness. They accordingly suggested that doctor-centredness was as much related to doctors' anxieties as to their wish to retain economic and social status, and furthermore that acknowledging the patients' different but relevant expertise, as in patient-centred communication, could reduce the stresses upon doctors.

FUTURE DIRECTIONS AND RESEARCH NEEDS

Knowledge of how and which interactional features are related to outcomes such as patient satisfaction with the helping relationship may help doctors to re-evaluate the significance of behaviours which they might otherwise regard as time-wasting or threatening. For example, if doctors were trained to recognize it as a positive indicator when patients raised questions or expressed their ideas about the suggested treatment, they might prize the occurrence of such behaviours. Further intervention studies are required.

Situations where patient-centredness is not appropriate would include those, relatively rare overall in medical practice, where the patient is unconscious or extremely cognitively disabled. In other situations too, there may be limitations on the extent to which patient-centredness is helpful. For example, the relationship between patient control and satisfaction may well be non-linear over the whole range of both variables. As previously noted, some patients may be more responsive to this attitude by the doctor than others, either in general or in particular medical situations, perhaps depending on how they appraise their degree of threat (Nerenz & Leventhal, 1983). The disappointing yield of efforts to distinguish patient attributes associated with good or poor compliance, suggests some caution in this regard. Monitoring of the interaction, rather than screening patients with a personality questionnaire, is likely to remain the doctor's best guide to the development of the therapeutic alliance.

Research difficulties and needs

A major methodological difficulty with research in this area, exemplified by Winefield & Murrell's (1991) study, has been the unwillingness of randomly chosen doctors to allow tape- or video-recordings of their consultations. Only a minority who were already particularly interested in communication agreed to take part, therefore many variables including attitudes to the psychosocial aspects of care are likely to differ systematically in participants compared with non-participants in research projects.

As doctors characteristically want to provide the best of care, the most reliable way to overcome resistance to a more patient-centred view would be to prove empirically that it leads to better patient health. Such data are as yet meagre, and more research is badly needed. As pointed out by Inui & Carter (1985), research needs to control for pre-encounter variables such as past familiarity of the doctor with the patient and the symptom, and the goals of the consultation. We need measures of patient-centredness which are interactional in nature rather than individual-oriented, such as the Henbest & Stewart (1989) formula and its successors. Descriptive systems for the interactional process must be comprehensive, reliable to apply, and usable in clinical settings; for maximum usefulness the sequences of behaviour must be captured rather than merely the overall frequencies with which each occurs (Roter & Hall 1989). A flexible combination of pragmatic and content methods of discourse analysis may be needed: is patient-initiated speech on any subject equally valuable, or is that related to the doctor's advice the most beneficial?

One possible approach would be to include patients in the reviews of videotaped interviews which characterize Kagan's (1979) Interpersonal Process Recall training, as Arborelius, Bremberg & Timpka (1991) did with doctors. Direct feedback about the patient's interpretation of, and affective response to, the process of communication could be illuminating for the doctor who, during the consultation, was preoccupied with the problem-solving task posed by the patient's symptoms. The multivariate statistics required are increasingly accessible via computer packages; unfortunately the interpretation of their results can be far from straightforward. Joint research, with psychologists and medical practitioners working collaboratively, seems likely to be productive.

Other research difficulties concern the likely non-linear relationship between patient control and satisfaction, and the need to measure the possible mediating role of third factors such as patient self-esteem, social class, or severity of illness. Intervention studies are needed to explore these parameters. Whether certain interactional features are causes or reflections of good process is not yet clear: the communication pattern and the health benefits may both result from some third factor. An explanation which Kaplan, Greenfield & Ware (1989) tried to eliminate was that patients who feel less ill, or who are more assertive or self-confident beforehand, are the ones who speak up more and also the ones who recover faster. Other possibilities are:

1. That consultations where the therapeutic relationship develops well, give patients confidence to speak up and simultaneously make them feel better, or
2. That a good relationship encourages patients to take more control which in turn improves health.

Therefore it may be an over-simplification to aim only to train doctors to speak differently (eg allow or encourage patients to assume greater control of the conversation), if their basic skills at cultivating and using the therapeutic relationship remain underdeveloped.

Public awareness of and interest in preventive health issues will in theory improve the acceptability to patients of expressing their ideas and actively seeking comprehensive biopsychosocial health care. We may hope that this same spirit of mutuality will provide a context in which the research which needs to be done will be acceptable to the potential doctor subjects.

Doctor–patient communication is a subject upon which much has been written, and its critical importance is currently being re-recognized. The task for health psychologists now is to transmute clinical wisdom and fragmentary research results into a coherent body of scientific knowledge, suitable for application to both medical education and professional practice. Our training in quantification and hypothesis-testing has much to offer this endeavour; at the same time we can make important contributions to psychology in the process.

REFERENCES

Arborelius, E., Bremberg, S. & Timpka, T. (1991). What is going on when the general practitioner doesn't grasp the situation? *Family Medicine*, **8**, 3–9.

Balint, M. (1964). *The Doctor, his Patient and the Illness*. London: Pitman.

Beckman, H. B. & Frankel, R. M. (1984). The effect of physician behavior on the collection of data. *Annals of Internal Medicine*, **101**, 692–696.

Ben-Sira, Z. (1984). Chronic illness, stress and coping. *Social Science and Medicine*, **18**, 725–736.

Ben-Sira, Z. (1990). Primary care practitioners' likelihood to engage in a bio-psychosocial approach: An additional perspective on the doctor–patient relationship. *Social Science and Medicine*, **31**, 565–576.

Berg, M. (1987). Patient education and the physician–patient relationship. *Journal of Family Practice*, **24**, 169–172.

Bourhis, R. Y., Roth, S. & MacQueen, G. (1989). Communication in the hospital setting: A survey of medical and everyday language use amongst patients, nurses and doctors. *Social Science and Medicine*, **28**, 339–346.

Calnan, M. (1988). Towards a conceptual framework of lay evaluation of health care. *Social Science and Medicine*, **27**, 927–933.

Danziger, S. K. (1978). The uses of expertise in doctor–patient encounters during pregnancy. *Social Science and Medicine*, **12**, 359–367.

DiMatteo, M. R. (1979). A social–psychological analysis of physician–patient rapport: Toward a science of the art of medicine. *Journal of Social Issues*, **35**, 12–33.

DiMatteo, M. R. & DiNicola, D. D. (1982). *Achieving Patient Compliance: The Psychology of the Medical Practitioner's Role*. New York: Pergamon.

Ditto, P. H. & Hilton, J. L. (1990). Expectancy processes in the health care interaction sequence. *Journal of Social Issues*, **46**, 97–124.

Elliott, R. & Shapiro, D. A. (1988). Brief structured recall: A more efficient method for studying significant therapy events. *British Journal of Medical Psychology*, **61**, 141–153.

Engel, G. L. (1982). The biopsychosocial model and medical education. Who are to be the teachers? *New England Journal of Medical Education*, **306**, 802–805.

Fitzpatrick, R. (1984). Satisfaction with health care. In R. Fitzpatrick, J. Hinton, S. Newman, G. Scambler & J. Thompson (Eds), *The Experience of Illness*. London: Tavistock, p. 154–175.

Foss, L. & Rothenberg, K. (1987). *The Second Medical Revolution: From Biomedicine to Infomedicine*. Boston: Shambhala.

Gibbs, R. D., Gibbs, P. H. & Henrich, J. (1987). Patient understanding of commonly used medical vocabulary. *Journal of Family Practice*, **25**, 176–178.

Gill, D. (1988). *Review of General Medical Practice in South Australia*. Adelaide: Joint Working Party of Royal Australian College of General Practitioners, South Australian Health Commission, and Australian Medical Association.

Greenberg, L. S. (1986). Change process research. *Journal of Consulting and Clinical Psychology*, **54**, 4–9.

Hall, J. A. & Dornan, M. C. (1988). What patients like about their medical care and how often they are asked: A meta-analysis of the satisfaction literature. *Social Science and Medicine*, **27**, 935–939.

Hall, J. A. & Dornan, M. C. (1990). Patient sociodemographic characteristics as prediction of satisfaction with medical care: A meta-analysis. *Social Science and Medicine*, **30**, 811–818.

Hall, J. A., Roter, D. L. & Katz, N. R. (1988). Meta-analysis of provider behavior in medical encounters. *Medical Care*, **26**, 657–675.

Henbest, R. J. & Stewart, M. (1989). Patient-centreness in the consultation. I: A method for measurement. *Family Practice*, **6**, 249–253.

Henbest, R. J. & Stewart, M. (1990). Patient-centreness in the consultation. II: Does it really make a difference? *Family Practice*, **7**, 28–33.

Inui, T. S. & Carter, W. B. (1985). Problems and prospects for health services research on provider–patient communication. *Medical Care*, **23**, 521–538.

John, C., Schwenk, T.L., Roi, L.D. & Cohen, M. (1987). Medical care and demographic characteristics of "difficult" patients. *The Journal of Family Practice*, **24**, 607–610.

Kagan, N. (1979). Counseling psychology, interpersonal skills, and health care. In G. C. Stone, F. Cohen & N. E. Adler (Eds), *Health Psychology: A Handbook*. San Francisco: Jossey-Bass, p. 465–485.

Kaplan, S. H., Greenfield, S. & Ware, J. E. (1989). Assessing the effects of physician–patient interactions on the outcomes of chronic disease. *Medical Care*, **27**, S110–S127.

Lazare, A. (1987). Shame and humiliation in the medical encounter. *Archives of Internal Medicine*, **147**, 1653–1658.

Ley, P. (1988). *Communicating with Patients: Improving Communication, Satisfaction and Compliance*. London: Croom Helm.

Lipp, M. R. (1986). *Respectful Treatment: A Practical Handbook of Patient Care*, 2nd edn. New York: Elsevier.

Luborsky, L., McLellan, A. T., Woody, G. E., O'Brien, C.P. & Auerbach, A. (1985). Therapist success and its determinants. *Archives of General Psychiatry*, **42**, 602–611.

McAvoy, B. R. (1988). Teaching clinical skills to medical students: The use of simulated patients and videotaping in general practice. *Medical Education*, **22**, 193–199.

Maguire, P. (1984). Interviewing skills. *Medical Teacher*, **6**, 128–133.

Maguire, P., Fairbairn, S. & Fletcher, C. (1986a). Consultation skills of young doctors: I Benefits of feedback training in interviewing as students persist. *British Medical Journal*, **292**, 1573–1576.

Maguire, P., Fairbairn, S. & Fletcher, C. (1986b). II—Most young doctors are bad at giving information. *British Medical Journal*, **292**, 1576–1578.

Maslach, C. & Jackson, S. E. (1982). Burnout in health care professions: A social psychological analysis. In G. Sanders & J. Suls (Eds), *Social Psychology of Health and Illness*. Hillsdale, NJ: Erlbaum, pp. 227–251.

Mason, C. (1985). The production and effects of uncertainty with special reference to diabetes mellitus. *Social Science and Medicine*, **21**, 1329–1334.

Mathews, J. J. (1983). The communication process in clinical settings. *Social Science and Medicine*, **17**, 1371–1378.

Melville, A. (1980). Job satisfaction in general practice: Implications for prescribing. *Social Science and Medicine*, **14A**, 495–499.

Miller, S. M., Leinbach, A. & Brody, D. S. (1989). Coping style in hypertensive patients: Nature and consequences. *Journal of Consulting and Clinical Psychology*, **57**, 333–337.

Nerenz, D. R. & Leventhal, H. (1983). Self-regulation theory in chronic illness. In: T. G. Burish and L. A. Bradley (Eds), *Coping with Chronic Illness*. New York: Academic Press, pp. 13–37.

Neuling, S. J. & Winefield, H. R. (1988). Social support and recovery after surgery for breast cancer: Frequency and correlates of supportive behaviours by family, friends, and surgeon. *Social Science and Medicine*, **27**, 385–392.

Novack, D. H. (Ed.) (1989). *Medical Encounter: A Newsletter on the Medical Interview and Related Skills*. Vol. 6. Task Force on Doctor and Patient of the Society of General Internal Medicine. Providence, RI.

O'Dowd, T. C. (1988). Five years of heartsink patients in general practice. *British Medical Journal*, **297**, 528–530.

O'Leary, A. (1990). Stress, emotion, and human immune function. *Psychological Bulletin*, **108**, 363–382.

Parsons, T. (1951). *The Social System*. New York: Free Press.

Pendleton, D., Schofield, T., Tate, P. & Havelock, P. (1984). *The Consultation: An Approach to Learning and Teaching*. Oxford: Oxford University Press.

Pruyn, J. F. A., Rijckman, R. M., van Brunschot, C. J. M. & van den Borne, H. W. (1985). Cancer patients' personality characteristics, physician–patient communication and adoption of the Moerman diet. *Social Science and Medicine*, **20**, 841–847.

Putnam, S. M., Stiles, W. B., Jacob, M. C. & James, S. A. (1988). Teaching the medical interview: An intervention study. *Journal of General Internal Medicine*, **3**, 38–47.

Reiser, D. E. & Rosen, D. H. (1984). *Medicine as a Human Experience*. Rockville, Md: Aspen.

Robinson, E. J. & Whitfield, M. J. (1988). Contributions of patients to general practitioner consultations in relation to their understanding of doctor's instructions and advice. *Social Science and Medicine*, **27**, 895–900.

Ross, J. L. & Phipps, E. (1986). Physician–patient power struggles: Their role in noncompliance. *Family Medicine*, **18**, 99–101.

Rost, K., Carter, W. & Inui, T. (1989). Introduction of information during the initial medical visit: Consequences for patient follow-through with physician recommendations for medication. *Social Science and Medicine*, **28**, 315–321.

Roter, D. L. & Hall, J. A. (1989). Studies of doctor–patient interaction. *Annual Review of Public Health*, **10**, 163–180.

Ryle, A. (1987). Problems of patients' dependency on doctors: Discussion paper. *Journal of the Royal Society of Medicine*, **80**, 25–26.

Salmon, P. & Quine, J. (1989). Patients' intentions in primary care: Measurement and preliminary investigation. *Psychology and Health*, **3**, 103–110

Schwenk, T. L., Marquez, J. T., Lefever, R. D. & Cohen, M. (1989). Physician and patient determinants of difficult physician–patient relationships. *Journal of Family Practice*, **28**, 59–63.

Scott, N. & Weiner, M. F. (1984). 'Patientspeak': An exercise in communication. *Journal of Medical Education*, **59**, 890–893.

Shapiro, M. C., Najman, J. M., Chang, A., Keeping, J. D., Morrison, J. & Western, J. S. (1983). Information control and the exercise of power in the obstetrical encounter. *Social Science and Medicine*, **17**, 139–146.

Shepherd, M., Cooper, B., Brown, A. C. & Kalton, G. W. (1966). *Psychiatric Illness in General Practice*. London: Oxford University Press.

Shepherd, M. & Sartorius, N. (Eds) (1989). *Non-specific Aspects of Treatment*. Toronto: Hans Huber.

Smith, R. C. (1984). Teaching interviewing skills to medical students: The issue of countertransference. *Journal of Medical Education*, **59**, 582–588.

Smits, A. J. A., Meyboom, W. A., Mokkink, H. G. A., van Son, J. A. J. & van Eijk, J. (1991). Medical versus behavioural skills: An observation study of 75 general practitioners. *Family Practice*, **8**, 14–18.

Stein, H. F. (1987). One's self in clinical relationships. *Family Medicine*, **19**, 7–8.

Stewart, M. A. (1984). What is a successful doctor–patient interview? A study of interactions and outcomes. *Social Science and Medicine*, **19**, 167–175.

Stiles, W. B., Putnam, S. M., James, S. A. & Wolf, M. H. (1979). Dimensions of patient and physician roles in medical screening interviews. *Social Science and Medicine*, **13A**, 335–341.

Strupp, H. H. (1986). The nonspecific hypothesis of therapeutic effectiveness: A current assessment. *American Journal of Orthopsychiatry*, **56**, 513–520.

Strupp, H. H. (1989). Can the practitioner learn from the researcher? *American Psychologist*, **44**, 717–724.

Szasz, T. S. & Hollender, M. H. (1956). A contribution to the philosophy of medicine: The basic models of the doctor–patient relationship. *Archives of Internal Medicine*, **97**, 585–592.

Taylor, S. E. (1986). *Health Psychology*. New York: Random House.

Thompson, J. (1984). Communicating with patients. In R. Fitzpatrick, J. Hinton, S. Newman, G. Scambler & J. Thompson (Eds) *The Experience of illness*. London: Tavistock, p. 87–108.

Tuckett, D., Boulton, M., Olson, C. & Williams, A. (1985). *Meetings between Experts: An Approach to Sharing Ideas in Medical Consultations*. London: Tavistock.

Waitzkin, H. (1989). A critical theory of medical discourse: Ideology, social control, and the processing of social context in medical encounters. *Journal of Health and Social Behavior*, **30**, 220–239.

Weinberger, M., Greene, J. Y. & Mamlin, J. J. (1981). The impact of clinical encounter events on patient and physician satisfaction. *Social Science and Medicine*, **15E**, 239–244.

Whitcher-Alagna, S. (1983). Receiving medical help: A psychosocial perspective on patient reactions. In A. Nadler, J. D. Fisher & B. M. DePaulo (Eds), *New Directions in Helping*, Vol. 3., *Applied Perspectives on Help-seeking and -receiving*. New York: Academic Press, p. 131–161.

Winefield, H. R. (1982). Subjective and objective outcomes of communication skills training in first year. *Medical Education*, **16**, 192–196.

Winefield, H. R. (1984). The nature and elicitation of social support: Some implications for the helping professions. *Behavioural Psychotherapy*, **12**, 318–330.

Winefield, H. R. (1987). Psychotherapy and social support: Parallels and differences in the helping process. *Clinical Psychology Review*, **7**, 631–644.

Winefield, H. R. & Murrell, T. G. C. (1991). Speech patterns and satisfaction in diagnostic and prescriptive stages of general practice consultations. *British Journal of Medical Psychology*, **64**, 103–115.

Part IV

PRACTICAL AND PROFESSIONAL ISSUES

8 Health Psychology in Africa South of the Sahara

KARL PELTZER
(formerly Department of Mental Health, Faculty of Health Sciences,
Obafemi Awolowo University, Ile-Ife, Nigeria)
Amani Counselling Society, Box 41738, Nairobi, Kenya

INTRODUCTION

Sub-Saharan Africa has a population of 491 million and it is expected to have 666 million by the year 2000, with 40% living in urban areas. The African region is economically the poorest in the world. The crude death rate per thousand population decreased from 22 in 1965 to 17 in 1985, whereas the crude birth rate remained the same with 48 per thousand population. The result is an annual growth of population of 3.3% (1985–2000) (World Bank, 1988). The population growth has effects on the health situation so that reproductive psychology should be considered as a priority area of health psychology in Africa.

Characteristic for the economically poor African region are diseases of poverty (acute infections, parasitic diseases, malnutrition and other killing diseases) which continue to produce a low average life expectancy at birth. At the same time, death-postponing medical technology is already resulting in increased rates of chronic non-communicable disorders as well as diseases of modern life. For example, the expectation of life at birth in Nigeria is only 37 years compared with 72 in the United Kingdom, but for those who have survived to age 65 the expectation of life in both countries is 75 years (WHO, 1981, pp. 23ff.).

Economic dependency and hardship, problems of hunger and starvation, the result of wars (one-third of all the 132 wars, since the end of the Second World War in 1945, have been fought in Africa), political oppression, deportation, over 6 million refugees, hostile environments (like fear of armed robbers), child labour (10 million regularly employed and 16 million working), the accelerated growth of the population, the disorderly urbanization and the urban–rural imbalance, massive labour migration, crowded cities, traffic jams, pollution, unemployment, stress of poor functioning of basic structural facilities (water supply, electricity, telephone), the predominance of young people, and in general, of the population in a situation of cultural deprivation, and the lack of adequate public services, are factors that generate problems with important psychosocial repercussions

International Review of Health Psychology. Edited by S. Maes, H. Leventhal and M. Johnston
©1992 John Wiley & Sons Ltd

(WHO, 1980; Ebigbo, 1989a; Lamontague, 1971; Osuntokun, 1986; Peltzer, 1989a; Rahim & Cederblad, 1986; Wober, 1975, pp. 198ff; Adegbola, 1987).

The growing importance of psychosocial problems and the failure of public health programmes that had not taken into account psychosocial factors determining people's behaviour led to a relatively new programme of the World Health Organization (WHO) on behavioural aspects of health and health care (Dasen, Berry & Sartorius, 1988, p. 15). Such behavioural aspects have become more important with the shift towards primary care and the delivery of health services (often integrated with other development programmes) at the community level. Community-oriented programmes depend on the coordinated efforts of practitioners at all levels (parents, village health workers, medically trained experts), for example for the GOBI (growth monitoring, oral rehydration/breast feeding promotion/immunization strategy) programmes. In addition, there is a growing recognition of the importance of understanding the social and cultural factors that influence patterns of health and disease, the recognition of illness, and the search for cures (Harkness, Wyon & Super, 1988, p. 241).

Despite the relevance of behavioural medicine and health psychology for Africa, a systematic review of medical, psychological and anthropological literature has only identified a few reports incorporating psychological, cultural or social dimensions into the design of research or intervention projects on disease prevention and control in Africa (Awaritefe, 1977; Chrisman & Maretzki, 1982; Dasen, Berry & Sartorius, 1988; DeCola & Shoyinka, 1984; Dressler, 1984; Dunn, 1979; Ebigbo & Kumaraswamy, 1984; Elder, 1987; Fabrega, 1974; Gatchel, Baum & Singer, 1982; Green, 1985; Harkness, Wyon & Super, 1988; Holtzman et al., 1987; ICAA, 1985; Krantz, Grunberg & Baum, 1985; Lamping, 1985; Lipkin & Kupka, 1982; Lipowski & Hanover, 1972; Matarazzo et al., 1984; Millon, Green & Meagher, 1982; Peltzer & Ebigbo, 1989a; Perlean & Brady, 1979; Sanson-Fisher et al., 1988; Stone, Cohen & Adler, 1979; Temoskok, Van Dyke & Zegans, 1984; Weiss & Weiss, 1981; WHO, 1980; Williams & Gentry, 1977; Winefield & Peay, 1980). Dasen, Berry & Sartorius (1988) have concluded that while there is much in Western psychological literature that is relevant to issues of health, there is little that is immediately and directly applicable to the promotion of health in African countries. That is, much of psychology is culture-bound, and because of this many potential applications have to be tried out in African cultures, for example, since lessons from cross-cultural psychology, transcultural psychiatry and ethnomedicine remind us that culturally insensitive health care may be of no help at all (cf Holtzman et al., 1987).

In the following an attempt is made to give a review of the most important issues of health psychology in Africa south of the Sahara (excluding South Africa):
1. Diseases (tropical diseases, diarrhoeal diseases, malnutrition, AIDS, psychological factors affecting physical conditions, other diseases)
2. Health-related behaviours (accidents, addiction and smoking, reproductive psychology)

3. Health psychology assessments
4. Health psychology interventions.

DISEASES

Tropical diseases

Common tropical diseases in Africa are malaria, schistosomiasis, filariasis, African trypanosomiasis and leprosy. Apart from the WHO Special Programme for Social and Economic Aspects of Tropical Disease Research, the important area of psychosocial aspects in tropical diseases is entirely under-researched (see also WHO, 1980).

Malaria

Collier-Jackson (1985) and Kloos (1975) investigated the malaria concept of illness compared with clinical evidence and preventive measures used (chloroquine, going to clinic, spraying DDT, traditional preventives). Weiss (1985, p. 177) has suggested that psychopathology arising from social stressors or mental disorder may function as an antecedent potentiating typical somatic symptoms of malaria. This relationship between social stressors, anxiety and malaria should be more researched. Harkness, Wyon & Super (1988, pp. 245, 249) have pointed out that behavioural sciences could contribute to better understanding of human factors in the control of malaria through research on local ideas about illness and healing, interactions between clients and practitioners in the context of malaria control, and relationships between the behaviour of human hosts and mosquito vectors. Unlike the study of vector or parasite behaviour, the study of human behaviour must include not only what people do but what they see themselves as doing and why.

Schistosomiasis

The behavioural aspects of schistosomiasis transmission and the implications for control have been recognized by several researchers (Dalton, 1976; Kloos, 1975; Rosenfield, Smith & Wolman, 1977).

Filariasis and African trypanosomiasis

Kenney and Hewitt (1950) have reported on psychoneurotic disturbances in filariasis. With regard to African trypanosomiasis, the author is only aware of psychological research conducted at the Tropical Diseases Research Unit in Ndola, Zambia.

Leprosy

Several authors (eg Emeharole, 1987) reported on the compelling role of psychosocial stressors, shame and social stigma in leprosy patients. Even in the absence of infection, leprophobia is a significant clinical entity. Depression following admission for leprosy treatment and other psychological and psychosomatic aspects have been documented (Weiss, 1985, pp. 184ff.; Bekere, 1981; Verghese et al., 1971).

Generally, according to Weiss (1985, p. 184), it is reasonable to argue that the high prevalence of widespread tropical diseases enhances both somatic distress and the somatic idiom; the former facilitates psychologization and the latter facilitates somatization; hence, endemic tropical diseases may facilitate both (see also German, 1979). Thus one may consider a class of psychiatric disorders associated with tropical diseases which arise in the absence of infection or other specific pathophysiological processes affecting the identified cases, for example patients with delusions of parasitosis (Peltzer & Hossain, in press) or phobic states like venereophobia (Peltzer & Hossain, 1988/89). The relevant antecedents often include the presence of parasitic disease or infection in the environment at large, rather than actual infection, in a patient who may be susceptible by virtue of predisposing psychological factors (Weiss, 1985, p. 183).

Diarrhoeal diseases

The mainstay of treatment of acute diarrhoea is fluid replacement, particularly oral rehydration therapy (ORT). In order to be successful an ORT programme may require behaviour change at many levels; for example, mothers may need to overcome their beliefs which lead to the practice of witholding fluids from babies with diarrhoea (Namboze, 1983).

The mechanisms of delayed treatment after home treatment and those of traditional healers have been described by Green (1985), and Van Binsbergen (1979) analysed an extended case on the interrelationship between diarrhoea and kinship ties. In a wider context, UNICEF (1985) has emphasized health behaviour in water and sanitation programmes, and Harkness, Wyon & Super (1988, p. 248) want to promote child health and growth by modifications in the physical setting, customs of care (eg carrying the infant) and parental psychology (eg understanding of germ theory) which are acceptable and desirable to the parents and the community.

Malnutrition

Protein–energy malnutrition (PEM) is an important cause of child death in Africa. For example, in Lusaka multiple malnutrition has been identified in 35% of child deaths. In a Lusaka-based study (Peltzer, Bhat & Chanda, in press) psychosocial factors playing a significant role in the causation of PEM have been identified and included in health psychological counselling as follows:

1. Wrong budgeting pattern, no financial support by the (legal) father of the child
2. Lack of maternal care (change of the carer, unwanted pregnancy)
3. Maternal, familial and community stress
4. Concept of illness and health-seeking pattern
5. Early and abrupt weaning
6. Behavioural problems of the child
7. Poverty and ignorance.

As a result, psychosocial aspects should be considered in the management of PEM. For example, the admitting staff can utilize the psychosocial assessment profile as above. After the child has overcome the acute stage of PEM the health worker can provide the carer including the head of household with counselling in the identified psychosocial problem areas.

Furthermore, Geber & Dean (1967) have described psychological aspects accompanying kwashiorkor, and Izuora & Ebigbo (1988) highlighted the attitudes and reactions towards PEM by the child, the carer and the attending medical staff.

AIDS and other sexually transmitted diseases

The acquired immunodeficiency syndrome (AIDS) is a serious health problem in many African countries. Literature on Africa suggests that it is primarily a heterosexually transmitted disease with a male : female ratio of 1 : 1 and more than 80% of the cases occurring between 20 and 40 years. Considering the Zambian cultural context, a psychosocial counselling concept for asymptomatic patients with HIV infection and AIDS related complex (ARC)/AIDS patients was developed (Peltzer et al., 1989a).

As a result of psychosocial counselling with HIV infected patients, behaviour can be changed especially in regard to further transmission of the HIV infection to others and the reduction of alcohol intake. In strengthening psychosocial services for HIV patients psychiatric clinical officers can be trained. Moreover, the role of (healing) churches and other social service (community) organizations including traditional healers will probably (have to) expand tremendously in psychosocial support and care especially for the AIDS patient. Therefore, the latter institutions should also be involved in AIDS training courses.

Sajiwandani & Baboo (1987) reported that sexually transmitted diseases (STDs) are the second largest public health problem in Zambia, with a rate of 30.4 per thousand population, and they suggest psychological guidelines in using the STDs control strategem model, for example:

1. Seeing patients in private and not in long queues
2. Recognizing that the already poor self-image may get worse if the patient is not carefully handled by rudeness or showing no respect.
3. Confidentiality of all reports in locked files
4. When it is important to refer the case or community to colleagues with more experience in interviewing and counselling skills.

Psychological factors affecting physical conditions

Major disorders are cardiovascular disorders, peptic ulcer, bronchial asthma and diabetes mellitus and minor ones are eating disorders and premenstrual tension.

Cardiovascular disorders (CVDs)

Most studies indicate that coronary heart disorders, hypertension and stroke have, although low before, increased considerably. Especially among urban Africans the rates have become similar to those in industrial societies (Beiser et al., 1976; Collomb, 1973; Akinkugbe, 1980; Dressler, 1984; Falase, Basile & Osuntokun, 1973; Osuntokun, 1977; Osuntokun et al., 1979). Possible explanations for the increased rate of CVDs are mental, environmental and acculturation stress, higher salt intake, obesity and smoking, (Lambo, 1963; Eferakeya & Imasuen, 1985; Osuntokun et al., 1979).

Peptic ulcer

For instance, Lewis & Aderoju (1978) found ulcer most prevalent in Southern Nigerians belonging to the lower socio-economic class (see also Payet et al., 1965). Stress (domestic, financial, exams) and dietary factors were found to be major agents in the precipitation of exacerbations and recurrences of symptoms of chronic duodenal ulcer in Ibadan. The bulkiness of Nigerian food has been considered to predispose to ulcer formation by reason of the sheer weight of the stomach. On the dietary agents, chillies and cassava preparations were potent ulcerogenic food substances. Asparin, alcohol and smoking also contributed to the worsening of the condition but were not major factors.

Bronchial asthma

Sofowora (1970) found that bronchial asthma in the Nigerian patient does not differ significantly in incidence or presentation from that seen in Europe. Psychological factors as precipitants of bronchial asthma were encountered in all age groups, especially the pampered only child or childless wives. Other precipitating factors encountered included occupational hazards, strong odours and inhalants.

Diabetes mellitus

Ebigbo & Oli (1985) found that many Nigerian diabetics had a life history of significant stressful situations (like early loss of father, being first-borns). In addition, 37% had somatic symptoms which were indicative of psychiatric disturbance (see also Olatawura, 1972). Famuyiwa, Edozien & Ukoli (1985) found that diabetic patients showed greatest concern over their ability to work and extreme difficulty in getting their medications regularly.

Premenstrual pain and eating disorders, especially anorexia nervosa and to a lesser extent obesity, are considered as newly emerging diseases of the affluent class. The particular psychodynamics and personality factors involved in these conditions have been reported (Brown & Konner, 1987; Buchan & Gregory, 1984; Ebigbo & Okunna, 1986/87; Hooper, Malcolm & Garner, 1986; Olatawura, Ayorinde & Ogunlesi, 1977).

Other diseases of relevance are epilepsy, cancer, sickle cell disease, suicide, rubella, poliomyelitis and iodine deficiency.

Epilepsy

Jilek-Aall & Jilek (1989, p. 355) wrote that it is the general view among experts that epilepsy is more common in Africa than in the Western world. The general attitudes of the public towards epilepsy are very negative which makes identification and management difficult (Awaritefe, Long & Awaritefe, 1985; Jilek-Aall & Jilek, 1989). Another problem is that in spite of the relatively meagre results of traditional medicine in the treatment of epilepsy, a popular belief in many African countries holds that epilepsy is not amenable to modern medical therapy, but belongs to the realm of idigenous healing. This seems to be a relevant area of public health psychology (Jilek-Aall & Jilek, 1989, p. 362).

Cancer

Cancer has become an increasingly important problem in Africa (Solanke et al, 1982). Johnson & Dada (1984, p. 29) found that Nigerian cancer patients were significantly angry, depressed and frightened in relation to the people's lack of knowledge regarding the nature of cancer. Ebigbo, Ukabam & Ojukwu (1985) pointed out the link between cancer and stress in diagnosis, etiology and treatment of the cancer patient in Nigeria.

Sickle cell disease

Olatawura (1976) found that sickle cell disease in children can lead to neurotic behaviour disorders because of its chronic nature, a resultant poor self-esteem and general unhappiness. In the relatively few victims who survive to adulthood, it generates various psychological problems which range from poor self-esteem, inadequate personality disorders through unhappy marital life to paranoid illness. Since no cure is available, public education and genetic counselling appear to be the only approach to the problem.

Suicidal behaviour only rarely occurred in the traditional African because of relative integration into the group. However, there is an increase in the transitional/modern African; for example, males in Lusaka had a suicide rate of 11.2 per 100000 (Collomb & Collignon, 1974; Gueye, Collignon & M'Bousson, 1984; Tousignant & Mishara, 1981; Asuuni, 1962; Bohannon, 1960). Jeffreys (1944) reported highest suicide rates during seasonal environmental stressors like failure of the individual's crops/harvest.

HEALTH-RELATED BEHAVIOURS

Accidents

Ayeni (1980) has reported that motor vehicle accidents are at 14.03% the major cause of death in Lagos city; second comes influenza and pneumonia at 9.6% and third enteritis and diarrhoeal diseases at 8.16%. Among adults, death from motor vehicle accidents accounted for 26% of deaths in the age group 15 years and above. Peltzer (1989c) found that from 353 children in surgical admissions at a teaching hospital in Zambia 78% were admitted because of accidents. Four major potential causes could be identified: lack of supervision by parent or teacher, environmental hazards, attention seeking, cultural conflict or lower socio-economic class.

Some contributing aspects of accidents in drivers have been described by Ilechukwu (1985, p. 188); for example, drivers take alcohol and believe in it as a boost to driving, or use non-prescribed amphetamines or kola nuts to keep awake without having any idea of negative consequences. Psychological aspects of accidents have been further reported on by Mulindi (1988) in Kenya.

The important area of accident research is certainly under-researched.

Addiction and smoking

Obot (1989, p. 329) pointed out that one of the most disturbing health-related problems in contemporary Africa is the use and abuse of chemical substances. In both popular and scientific periodicals, there has been a recognition of a trend in the use and abuse of alcohol, tobacco products, stimulants, cannabis, sedative–hypnotics and narcotics. This is also reflected in 292 relevant studies between 1965 and 1984. Alcohol seems to be the most important problem and to a lesser extent cannabis, amphetamines and smoking. For example, the manufacturing sector to which the breweries belong, recorded an annual average growth of 15% between 1970 and 1984 in Nigeria (see also Asuni & Pela, 1986; Derek, 1986; Ebie & Tongue 1988; Géralin, 1954; African Psychiatric Association, 1974; Obot, 1989; Verbeke & Corin, 1976). Most studies have described the various problems associated with substance abuse but only a few try to consider the cultural context in the causation, intervention methods and control mechanisms. For example, Peltzer (1989b, p. 82) found as causative factors in alcohol and cannabis abuse in Malawi a number of factors responsible, for example:

1. Some elder person in the family, especially the father or uncle, had passed away and the (first-born) son is still too young (often during adolescence) to take over adult and father role responsibilities
2. A loose and vague family hierarchy
3. Peers had a bad influence.

Intervening factors were, for example, direct punishment, reasoning of an elder relative, physical side effects of the drug.

Yach (1986, p. 279) shows that smoking represents an important current and future health risk to people in Africa. The consumption of tobacco is increasing; for example, in Kenya tobacco sales are growing by 8% per annum; 14% of Nigerian schoolchildren and 71% of 11–20-year-olds in Senegal smoke. There is evidence that the highest tar and nicotine cigarettes are smoked by people from the lowest social classes (Yach, 1986, p. 286). D'Hondt & Vandewiele (1983, p. 333) found the following reasons for smoking in school-going adolescents in Senegal:

(a) economic (the intensive advertisement campaigns in favour of tobacco smoking)
(b) cultural (the ambivalence of traditional attitudes of Western urbanization, and the attractiveness of the Western way of life)
(c) psychological (the traumas of modernism on a basically poor developing country).

Reproductive psychology

Most African countries have rates of national increase in excess of 3%, with a total fertility rate of 6.7 children per woman (1985) in subSaharan Africa (World Bank, 1988), and it is now becoming clear to most countries that population growth is a serious issue and that poor family spacing is affecting health (Bennett, 1986, p. 739). According to Elder (1987, p. 338), currently most lacking in African countries are appropriate incentives and behavioural technologies needed for the implementation of these incentives to control population growth.

Brand (1989) has investigated the psychodynamics of fertility regulation in Benin; for example, the concept that "Every coitus gives birth to a human being". Thus society has to find means of controlling sexual life by integrating it into the religious sphere, that of the voodoo: this will control life and abnormalities from frequent, complete sexual relationships. The desire to have children is mollified by the fear of creating abnormal "beings" who, on the one hand, could be born and enter the world of man, and on the other, could populate the invisible universe of "beings" and as a result, affect humans and create instability. This fear makes the Wéménou space every coitus (p. 122).

Other authors have researched specific aspects of reproductive psychology, for example child spacing (Ebigbo & Chukudebelu, 1980), family planning (Ali, 1979), reproduction motives, for example 80% of the villagers felt that limiting the number of children was against God's will (Peltzer, 1988b), the relationship of breast-feeding with postpartum amenorrhea and postpartum sexual abstinence (Oni, 1987), reproductive behaviour (Batia, 1978), psychosocial aspects of unwed adolescent pregnancy (Peltzer & Likwa, in press).

HEALTH PSYCHOLOGY ASSESSMENTS

Only a few culturally adopted health psychology assessment instruments exist, for example the Awaritefe Psychological Index (Awaritefe, 1982), the Enugu Somatization Scale (Ebigbo, 1982), recording health problems triaxially (Freund & Kalumba, 1982), the Crown Crisp Experiential Index (Mgbemema, 1989, p. 204), and some culture-fair tests (Famuyiwa, 1989, p. 198). Studies on psychometric characteristics and validity have been conducted by Morakinyo (1979) on the Cornell Medical Index and General Health Questionnaire and by Jegede (1977) on the Health Opinion Survey. No studies are known on Type A behaviour, anger-in, or methods for measuring social support (Dressler, 1984; Heitzman & Kaplan, 1988). It could be useful to utilize research findings like psychological tests of cerebral malaria patients in the Vietnam War (Kastle et al., 1968).

The specific African aspects of psychological defence mechanisms in relation to health psychological problems have been described by Peltzer & Ebigbo (1989b). Dimensions of personality and smoking behaviour were researched by Sijuwola (1989). Maes, Vingerhoets & Van Heck (1987, pp. 571, 575) found that infectious diseases have a strong association with stress. Thus research on mediating or modifying stressor–disease relationship including coping styles, personality traits and social support are relevant.

HEALTH PSYCHOLOGY INTERVENTIONS

Drug and prescription compliance is a very important area of health psychology in Africa. For example, Olowu & Lamikaura (1986, p. 158 found a high percentage of drug non-compliers—56% of students and 61% of junior staff used native medicines as a substitute for or together with pharmaceutical drugs. Awaritefe (1984) has pointed out that on the other hand drug taking is becoming an epidemic and people have learnt the wrong lesson that seeing a doctor is synonymous with taking a drug. The need for more information and communication on the importance of drugs is emphasized (Olowu & Lamikaura, 1986; Smith, 1984).

Little is known about effective psychosocial intervention strategies for tropical diseases (see also Kamwendo, Chiotha & Kandawire, 1985).

In the case of diarrhoeal diseases, positive reinforcement can be used for reinforcing appropriate disposal of human waste, keeping water clean and/or cleaning it before use (Elder, 1987, p. 342). Patel, Eisemon & Arocha (1988) have suggested using cognitive psychology by introducing new technology in a manner that continues to provide coherence with people's beliefs rather than isolated facts (see also Zoysa et al., 1984).

For the treatment of malnutrition, Elder (1987, p. 341) has described the importance of positive reinforcement for increasing appropriate nutritional behaviour; for example, mothers were given coupons for appropriate behaviour: breast-feeding until at least the age of 12–15 months, supplementing breast milk adequately beginning at about the fourth month, planting green, leafy vegetables near the home, striving for a weight gain each month, and returning to the health centre for medical checks on health, diet and progress. These coupons were used for lottery draws every three months in which prizes were sacks of corn or rice provided by the government.

Peltzer et al. (1989a) described a psychosocial counselling concept for HIV positive patients which included the following aspects: information transfer of HIV positive diagnosis and illness concept, initial reactions like denial and psychosocial management, subsequent reactions and counselling (denial, anger or fear, bargaining and depression, acceptance and resignation), and complications in the counselling process (within a married couple, one partner is HIV positive and the other partner is negative, childless couple, pregnant patient, children of parents who both have AIDS/ARC, patient suffering from a mental disorder).

Little research has been done on the psychological management of patients with CVDs and complications (Peltzer, 1987, pp. 233–240). Awa (1984, p. 372) described a hypno-behavioural approach in the treatment of hypertension and Ihenacho & Ebigbo (in press) reported on psychological aspects of a cardiac pacemaker. Furthermore, Akinkugbe (1980, p. 58) sees the problem compounded by the fact that relatively few in Africa fully recognize the importance of regular uninterrupted treatment once a firm diagnosis of hypertension has been made.

Intervention strategies for addiction seem no longer to be effective on a social and community level in transitional African societies. however, some African healing churches (Peltzer, 1985) and "born again" Christian movements (Peltzer, 1989d) seem to offer an effective life-style change including addictive behaviour. Also, not much is known about behaviour therapy (Morakinyo, 1983) and psychosocial counselling with substance abuses or self-help groups (AA) in Africa. Therefore more should be done on the prevention, therapy and rehabilitation of drug addicts in Africa including African healing churches and other religious groups (Awaritefe & Ebie, 1975; Peltzer, 1988a).

Positive reinforcement for increasing control of population growth was used with Ghanaian women and health workers/recruiters for attending family planning clinics. The health workers gave various target women coupons which made them eligible for tins of powdered milk upon presentation to clinic staff. Workers themselves were on a point system whereby one point was awarded for a referral (ie the distribution of one coupon) and three points for subsequent attendance of the target woman, etc. (Perkin, 1970).

Specific intervention techniques cannot be described further here, for example, behaviour therapy (Awaritefe, 1989), hypnosis and relaxation therapies (Ebigbo, 1989d) or family therapy (Ebigbo, 1989b).

CONCLUSION

Highlighting what is different about health psychology in Africa in contrast to industrial societies, the following issues are dealt with: demography, diseases, health-related behaviour, health psychology assessments, health psychology interventions, tracing and organization of services.

The African region has the highest population growth and urbanization rate in the world. Being the economically poorest region, diseases of poverty like acute infections, parasitic diseases, malnutrition and other killing diseases produce a low average life expectancy at birth. In addition, after the Second World War most of the wars have been fought in Africa leading to a number of health-devastating consequences.

Prevalence rates on the 10 most common diseases in Africa could not be identified, since only African countries like Mauritius reports statistics to WHO, which are totally unrepresentative for the region of sub-Saharan Africa. However, some figures seem to indicate that the following diseases are more prevalent in the African than in other regions of the world: malaria, schistosomiasis, filariasis, African trypanosomiasis, diarrhoeal diseases, malnutrition, poliomyelitis, AIDS and other STDs, epilepsy and sickle cell disease. Especially the psychosocial and behavioural aspects of these diseases and their interrelationship with psychological factors and disorders have not been studied enough.

The enormous increase in chronic non-communicable diseases, especially in urban settings, needs urgent health psychological attention. This is particularly so since these diseases often present themselves in a cultural context not accessible to Western techniques.

Health-related behaviour like "accidents", addiction and smoking is also becoming increasingly important, calling for special attention. Reproductive psychology seems to be one of the highest priorities, considering the high population growth rate in the African region.

Health psychological assessment instruments and intervention methods are hardly used, mostly not adapted to the particular cultural context, and are most needed. As an example of health psychological interventions, Ebigbo (1989c, p. 706) has described his functions in a Nigerian teaching hospital:

> I was consulted to help in the following cases: helping a cardiac patient to accept a pace maker, to prepare the anxious patient for an operation, to prepare the cancer patient in the acute stage for death, to help the anxious pregnant females prepare for labour, to help the worried, amputated patient to accept his amputation, to help detect emotional disturbance in suspected cases in internal medicine, to help desensitize venereal diseases phobic

patients, to motivate cases of tricotillomania to stop hair pulling, to motivate cases of hysteric laming and extreme obsessional tic, to come out of the laming escapism and leave the tic, to help women who cannot get pregnant as a result of poor communication with their husbands, to get pregnant.

In organizing health psychological services experiences like the above in Nigeria and from other developing countries like the Cuban public health model can be utilized, for example, where in the polyclinic public health psychology service there is at least one psychologist and one psychometrist for every 10 000 inhabitants. The goals of the service are to promote health, well-being and the development of the individual, to improve public satisfaction with medical services, to promote an understanding of the role played in health by life-style and personality, and to improve links between the health team and the community (Averasturi, 1988, p. 292).

Generally, health psychology in the African continent has been neglected for too long and the potential insights that it provides have not been used in efforts to improve health care and induce new initiatives for socio-economic development (Sartorius, 1989, p. iii). Since only a very few health psychologists are available in African countries, he/she has to take over more teaching and supervisory functions than in a Western context. It should be remembered that most of the population in African nations is less than 20 years of age. Therefore special importance should be given to child and adolescent health psychology. Although by the year 2000 40% of the population in Africa south of the Sahara will be living in urban areas, health psychology should by no means be concentrated in the urban centres but emphasis should be laid on the rural population and the concept of primary health care (Peltzer et al., 1989b, p. 721). Some authors (Paltiel, 1987, p. 233) speak of the feminization of poverty in Africa and emphasize the health psychological consequences of that adverse status which should be addressed.

Although some of the studies have described detrimental habits and behaviour, very little is known on behavioural and psychosocial counselling skills which are adapted to African cultural contexts. Certainly, the vast area of traditional and faith healing with regard to health psychology has to be seriously researched and more effectively utilized.

Unfortunately, health psychology research in Africa has often been oriented to research interests of the metropoles on non-communicable chronic diseases rather than communicable and tropical diseases.

Generally, research and teaching of health psychology in Africa need urgently to be promoted. For example, only 10 psychologists are working in health psychology education in Nigeria, which has a population of more than 100 million (Obot, 1988). Efforts should be undertaken to promote research and training in health psychology in Africa, for example with the establishment of regional centres or the promotion of publications in the field (*African Journal of Behavioural Sciences* discontinued publication in 1981, *PLURALE: Revue Africaine des Sciences Sociales et Médicales pour la Santé, Journal of African Psychology*).

REFERENCES

Adegbola, O. (1987). The impact of urbanization and industrialiszation on health conditions: The case of Nigeria. *World Health Statistics Quarterly*, **40**, 74–84.

African Psychiatric Association (1974). *Alcohol and Drug Dependence in Africa*. Proceedings of a workshop, Nairobi. Lausanne: ICAA.

Akinkugbe, O. O. (1980). High blood pressure in the African context. *Tropical Doctor*, **10**, 56–58

Ali, M. R. (1979). *A Study of Knowledge about Attitude Towards and Practice of Family Planning in Zambia*. Lusaka: University of Zambia.

Asuni, T. (1962). Suicide in Western Nigeria. *British Medical Journal*, **2**, 1091–1097.

Asuni, T. & Pela, O. A. (1986). Drug abuse in Africa. *Bulletin on Narcotics*, **38**, 55.

Averasturi, L. G. (1988). Psychosocial factors and health: the Cuban model. In P.R. Dasen, J. W. Berry & N. Sartorius (Eds), *Health and Cross-cultural Psychology: Towards Applications*. London: Sage, pp. 281–297.

Awa, A. E. (1984). Hypno-behavioural approach: An adjunct to medication in the treatment of essential hypertension. In C. A. Onwuzurike & E. Enekwechi (Eds) *Clinical Psychology and the Nigerian Society*, pp. 372–389. Jos: Nigerian Association of Clinical Psychologists.

Awaritefe, A. (1977). Clinical psychology in the African context. *International Journal of Psychology*, **12**, 231–239.

Awaritefe, A. (1982). The Awaritefe Psychological Index (API). *Nigerian Journal of Clinical Psychology*, **1**, 42–53.

Awaritefe, A. (1984). Psychology in medical practice. In P.O. Ebigbo & N. Kumaraswamy (Eds) *Psychology in Medicine*. Proceedings of a one-day symposium, Enugu Medical Society, Enugu, 11 May, pp. 9–18.

Awaritefe, A. (1989). Behaviour therapy. In K. Peltzer & P.O. Ebigbo (Eds), *Clinical Psychology in Africa*. Enugu: Working Group for African Psychology, pp. 586–602.

Awaritefe, A. & Ebie, J. C. (1975). On the strategy for the prevention of drug abuse. *African Journal of Psychiatry*, **2**, 139–144.

Awaritefe, A., London, A. C. & Awaritefe, M. (1985). Epilepsy and psychosis: A comparison of societal attitudes. *Epilepsia*, **26**, 1–9.

Ayeni, O. (1980). Causes of mortality in an African city. *African Journal of Medicine and Medical Sciences*, **9**, 139–149.

Batia, C. (1978). An analysis of reproductive norms and behaviour in rural Ghana. Ph.D thesis, University of California.

Beiser, M., Collomb, H., Ravel, H. & Nafziger, C. (1976). Systemic blood pressure studies among the Serer of Senegal. *Journal of Chronic Diseases*, **29**, 371–380.

Bekere, P. B. (1981). Psychological reactions to leprosy. *Leprosy in India*, **53**, 266–272.

Bennett F.J. (1986). Health revolution in Africa? *Social Science and Medicine*, **22**, 737–740.

Bohannon, P. (Ed.) (1960). *African homicide and Suicide*. Evanston: Princeton University Press.

Brand, R. (1989). Fertility and anthropological significance of coitus in the Wemenou society (Benin). In K. Peltzer & P. O. Ebigbo (Eds), *Clinical Psychology in Africa*, pp. 119–129. Enugu: Working Group for African Psychology.

Brown, P.J. & Konner, M. (1987). An anthropological perspective on obesity. In R. J. Wurtman & J. C. Wurtman (Eds), *Human Obesity*. New York: New York Academy of Sciences, pp. 29–56.

Buchan, T. & Gregory, L. D. (1984). Anorexia nervosa in a black Zimbabwean. *British Journal of Psychiatry*, **145**, 326–330.

Chrisman, N. J. & Maretzki, T. W. (Eds) (1982) *Clinically Applied Anthropology*. Dordrecht/Holland: D. Reidel.

Collier-Jackson, L. (1985). Malaria in Liberian children and mothers: Biocultural perceptions of illness vs clinical evidence of disease. *Social Science and Medicine*, 20, 1287.

Collomb, H. (1973). Médecine psychosomatique au Sénégal. Presented at the Second Congress of the International College of Psychosomatic Medicine, Amsterdam, June.

Collomb, H. & Collignon, R. (1974). Les conduites suicidaires en Afrique. *Psychopathologie Africaine*, 10, 55–113.

Dalton, P. R. (1976). A socio-ecological approach to the control of Schistosoma mansoni in St. Lucia. *Bulletin of the World Health Organization*, 54, 587–595.

Dasen, P. R., Berry, J. W. & Sartorius, N. (Eds) (1988). *Health and Cross-cultural Psychology: Towards Applications*. London: Sage.

DeCola, F. D. & Shoyinka, P. H. (Eds) (1984). *Three Decades of Medical Research at the College of Medicine Ibadan, Nigeria, 1948-1980*. Ibadan: Ibadan University Press.

Derek, Y. (1986). The impact of smoking in developing countries with special reference to Africa. *International Journal of Health Services*, 16, 279–293.

D'Hondt, W. & Vandewiele, M. (1983). Attitudes of Senegalese schoolgoing adolescents towards tobacco smoking. *Journal of Youth and Adolescence*, 12, 333–353.

Dressler, W. W. (1984). Social and cultural influences in cardiovascular disease: A review. *Transcultural Psychiatric Research Review*, 21, 5–42.

Dunn, F. L. (1979). Behavioural aspects of the control of parasitic diseases. *Bulletin of WHO*, 57, 499–512.

Ebie, J. C. & Tongue, E. J. (Eds) (1988). *Handbook of the African Training Courses on Drug Dependence*. Lausanne: ICAA.

Ebigbo, P. O. (1982). Development of a culture specific (Nigeria) screening scale of somatic complaints indicating psychiatric disturbance. *Culture, Medicine and Psychiatry*, 6, 29–43.

Ebigbo, P. O. (1989a). Psychosocial aspects of child abuse and neglect in Africa. In K. Peltzer & P.O. Ebigbo (Eds), *Clinical Psychology in Africa*. Enugu: Working Group for African Psychology, pp. 401–424.

Ebigbo, P. O. (1989b). The practice of family therapy in the University of Nigeria Teaching Hospital, Enugu. In K. Peltzer & P. O. Ebigbo (Eds), *Clinical Psychology in Africa*. Enugu: Working Group for African Psychology, pp. 551–574.

Ebigbo, P.O. (1989c). The clinical psychologist among doctors: A personal experience. In K. Peltzer & P. O. Ebigbo (Eds), *Clinical Psychology in Africa*. Enugu: Working Group for African Psychology, pp. 698–713.

Ebigbo, P.O. (1989d). The role of hypnosis and relaxation therapies in the management of the mentally ill. In K. Peltzer & P. O. Ebigbo (Eds) *Clinical Psychology in Africa*. Enugu: Working Group for African Psychology, pp. 620–647.

Ebigbo, P. O. & Chukudebelu, W. O. (1980). Child spacing and child mortality among Nigerian Igbos. *International Journal of Gynaecology and Obstetrics*, 18, 372–374.

Ebigbo, P. O. & Kumaraswamy, N. (1984). *Psychology in Medicine*. Proceedings of a one-day symposium, Enugu Medical Society, Enugu, 11 May.

Ebigbo, P. O. & Okunna, E. N. (1986/87) Anorexia nervosa resulting from family rejection. *Psychopathologie Africaine*, 21, 177–183.

Ebigbo, P. O. & Oli, J. M. (1985). Stress im Leben nigerianischer Diabetiker. *Zeitschrift für Psychosomatische Medizin und Psychoanalyse*, 31, 267–283.

Ebigbo, P. O., Ukabam, S. O. & Ojukwu, J. O. (1985). Family therapy in the management of a dying Nigerian cancer patient. *International Journal of Family Psychiatry*, 6, 83–95.

Eferakeya, A. E. & Imasuen, E. J. (1985). Menopausal hypertension in the Nigerian female: Role of psychosocial stress. *Public Health*, 99, 235.

Elder, J. P. (1987). Applications of behavior modification to health promotion in the developing world. *Social Science and Medicine*, **24**, 335–349.

Emeharole, P. O. (1987). Stigmatized illnesses in Africa. *Journal Royal Society Health*, **7**, 23–27.

Fabrega, H. J. (1974). *Disease and Social Behaviour: An Interdisciplinary Perspective*. Cambridge, Mass.: MIT.

Falase, A. O., Basile, O. & Osuntokun, B. O. (1973). Myocardial infarction in Nigerians. *Tropical and Geographical Medicine*, **25**, 147–150.

Famuyiwa, O. O. (1989). Psychometric and personality assessment. In K. Peltzer & P. O. Ebigbo (Eds) *Clinical Psychology in Africa*. Enugu: Working Group for African Psychology, pp. 193–199.

Famuyiwa, O. O., Edozien, E. M. & Ukoli, C. O. (1985). Social, cultural and economic factors in the management of diabetes mellitus in Nigeria. *African Journal of Medicine and Medical Sciences*, **14**, 145–154.

Freund, P. J. & Kalumba, K. (1982). Zambia's participation in the WHO collaborative project on recording health problems triaxially: The physical, psychological and social components of primary health care. *Medical Journal of Zambia*, **16**, 76–79.

Gatchel, R. J., Baum, A. & Singer, J. E. (Eds) (1982). *Handbook of Psychology and Health*. Hillsdale, New Jersey: Erlbaum.

Geber, M. & Dean, R. F. A. (1967). The psychological changes accompanying kwashiorkor. In F. R. Wickert (Ed.) *Readings in African Psychology: From French Language Sources*. East Lansing, Michigan: Michigan State University.

Géralin, H. (1954). L'alcoolisme en Afrique Noire. *Revue de Psychologie des Peuples*, **9**, 405–414.

German, G. A. (1979). The psychiatric aspects of tropical disorders. *Bulletin of WHO*, **57**, 359–371.

Green, E. C. (1985). Traditional healers and childhood diarrhoeal disease in Swaziland: The interface of anthropology and health education. *Social Science and Medicine*, **20**, 277–285.

Gueye, M., Collignon, R. & M'Bousson, M. (1984). Suicid und Depression im Senegal und in Afrika. *Psyche*, **8**, 696–709.

Harkness, S., Wyon, J. B. & Super, C. M. (1988) The relevance of behavioural sciences to disease prevention and control in developing countries. In P. R. Dasen, J. W. Berry & N. Sartorius (Eds), *Health and Cross-cultural Psychology: Towards Applications*. London: Sage, pp. 239–255.

Heitzman, C. A. & Kaplan, R. M. (1988). Assessment of methods for measuring social support. *Health Psychology*, **75**, 109.

Holtzman, W. H., Evans, R. I., Kennedy, S. & Iscoe, I. (1987). Psychology and health: Contributions of psychology to the improvement of health and health care. *Bulletin of the World Health Organisation*, **65**, 913–935.

Hooper, B. Malcolm, S. H. & Garner, D. M. (1986). Application of the eating disorders inventory to a sample of black, white, and mixed race schoolgirls in Zimbabwe. *International Journal of Eating Disorders*, **5**, 161.

ICAA (1985). *Bibliography on Drug and Alochol-related Issues in Africa*. Lausanne: ICAA.

Ihenacho, H. & Ebigbo, P. O. (in press). The African patient with cardiac pace maker. *Tropical Cardiologist*.

Ilechukwu, S. C. (1985). Psychological constraints in the minimization of motor vehicle accidents in Nigeria. In E. Okpara (Ed.), *Psychologial Strategies for National Development*. Enugu: Nigerian Psychological Association, pp. 184–194.

Izuora, G. I. & Ebigbo, P. O. (1988). Emotional reactions of Africans to children with severe kwashiorkor. *International Journal of Child Abuse and Neglect*, **7**, 351–356.

Jeffreys, M. D. W. (1944). African suicides in the Bamenda Division; British Cameroons. *Transactions of the Royal Society of South Africa*, 30, 135–141.

Jegede, R. O. (1977). Psychometric characteristics of the Health Opinion Survey. *Psychological Reports*, 40, 1160–1162.

Jilek-Aall, L. & Jilek, W. G. (1989). Epilepsy and its psychosocial implications in Africa. In K. Peltzer & P. O. Ebigbo (Eds), *Clinical Psychology in Africa*. Enugu: Working Group for African Psychology, pp. 353–382.

Johnson, C. A. & Dada, I. B. O. (1984). An attitudinal survey of the psychological reactions to cancer. *Nigerian Journal of Clinical Psychology*, 3, 29–40.

Kamwendo, A., Chiotha, S. & Kandawire, J. A. K. (1985). Factors affecting schistosomiasis transmission in two rural villages in Malawi. Zomba: Chancellor College Staff Seminar Paper No. 49.

Kastle, A. J. et al. (1968). Psychological testing of cerebral malaria patients. *Journal of Nervous and Mental Disease*, 147, 553–561.

Kenney, M. & Hewitt, R. (1950). Psychoneurotic disturbances in filariasis, and their relief by removal of adult norms or treatment with Hetrazan. *American Journal of Tropical Medicine and Hygiene*, 30, 895–899.

Kloos, H. (1975). Disease concepts and medical practices in relation to malaria among fever cases in Addis Ababa. In S. Paul (Ed.), *Ethnomedicine and Social Science in Tropical Africa*. Munich: Klaus Renner, pp. 209–234.

Krantz, D. S., Grunberg, N. E. & Baum, A. (1985). Health psychology. *Annual Review of Psychology*, 36, 349–383.

Lambo, T. (1963). *Psychosomatic Disorders in West Africa* (WHO Technical Reports Series 275). Geneva: WHO.

Lamontague, Y. (1971). Psychological problems of Biafran children. *Psychopathologie Africaine*, 7, 225–383.

Lamping, D. L. (1985). Assessment in health psychology. *Canadian Psychology*, 26, 121–139.

Lewis, E. A. & Aderoju, E. A. (1978). Factors in the etiology of chronic duodenal ulcer in Ibadan. *Tropic and Geographical Medicine*, 30, 75–79.

Lipkin, M. & Kupka, W. (Eds) (1982). *Psychosocial Factors Affecting Health*. New York: Praeger.

Lipowski, Z. J. & Hanover (1972). *Psychosocial Aspects of Physical Illness*. Basel: Karger.

Maes, S., Vingerhoets, A. & Van Heck, G. (1987). The study of stress and disease: Some developments and requirements. *Social Science and Medicine*, 25, 567–578.

Matarazzo, J. D., Weiss, S. M., Herd, J. A., Miller, N. E. & Weiss, S. M. (Eds) (1984). *Behavioural Health: A Handbook of Health Enhancement and Disease Prevention*. New York: Wiley.

Mgbemena, N. J. (1989). Some current methods of psychological assessment in Nigeria. In K. Peltzer & P. O. Ebigbo (Eds), *Clinical Psychology in Africa*. Enugu: Working Group for African Psychology, pp. 200–207.

Millon, T., Green, C. J. & Meagher, R. (Eds) (1982). *Handbook of Clinical Health Psychology*. London: Sage.

Morakinyo, V. O. (1979). The sensitivity and validity of the Cornell Medical Index and the General Health Questionnaire in an African population. *African Journal of Psychiatry*, 5, 1–8.

Morakinyo, V.O. (1983). Aversion therapy of cannabis dependence in Nigeria. *Drug and Alcohol Dependence*, 12, 287–293.

Mulindi, A. Z. S. (1988). Psychological aspects of accidents. *The Nairobi Journal of Medicine*, 14, 7–9; 58–59.

Namboze, J. M. (1983). Health and culture in an African society. *Social Science and Medicine*, 17, 204.

Obot, I. S. (1988). Social science and medical education in Nigeria. *Social Science and Medicine*, 26, 1191–1196.

Obot, I. S. (1989). Alcohol and drug-related disorders in Africa. In K. Peltzer & P. O. Ebigbo (Eds), *Clinical Psychology in Africa*. Enugu: Working Group for African Psychology, pp. 329–344.

Olatawura, M. O. (1972). The psychiatric complications of diabetes mellitus in children. *African Journal of Medicine and Medical Sciences*, 3, 231–240.

Olatawura, M. O. (1976). Sickle cell disease: The psychological aspects. *African Journal of Psychiatry*, 3, 373–377.

Olatawura, M. O., Ayorinde, A. & Ogunlesi, S. A. (1977). The premenstrual syndrome in Nigerians. *Nigerian Medical Journal (Lagos)*, 7, 57–65.

Olowu, A. A. & Lamikaura, A. (1986). Compliance and drug use. Some Nigerian data. *Journal of Social and Administrative Pharmacy*, 3, 157–159.

Oni, G. A. (1987). Breast feeding: Its relationship with postpartum amenorrhea and postpartum sexual abstinence in a Nigerian community. *Social Science and Medicine*, 24, 255–262.

Osuntokun, B. O. (1977) Stroke in the Africans. *African Journal of Medical Science*, 6, 39–53.

Osuntokun, B. O. (1986). Behaviour and health. In E. B. Wilson (Ed.), *Psychology and Society*. Ile-Ife: Nigerian Psychological Association, pp. 1–20.

Osuntokun, B. O., Bademosi, O., Oyediran, A. B. O., Akinkugbe, O. O. & Carlisle, R. C. (1979). Incidence of stroke in an African city. *Stroke*, 10, 205–208.

Paltiel, F. L. (1987). Women and mental health: A post-Nairobi perspective. *World Health Statistics Quarterly*, 40, 233–266.

Patel, V. L., Eisemon, T. O. & Arocha, J. F. (1988). Causal reasoning and the treatment of diarrhoeal disease by mothers in Kenya. *Social Science and Medicine*, 27, 1277–1286.

Payet, M., Saukalé, M., Collomb, H., Moulanier, M., Pene, P. & Sow, A. M. (1965). Les facteurs psychosomatiques dans le déterminisme de l'ulcère gastroduodénal chez le Noir africain. *Le Progrès Médical*, 2, 45–60.

Peltzer, K. (1985). The therapy of alcoholics and cannabis smokers in the Zion Christian church in Malawi. *Transcultural Psychiatric Research Review*, 22, 252–255.

Peltzer, K. (1987) *Some Contributions of Traditional Healing Practices towards Psychosocial Health Care in Malawi*. Eschborn: FBP.

Peltzer, K. (1988a). Psychosocial counseling of persons with substance related disorders in Subsaharan Africa. In J. C. Ebie & E. J. Tongue (Eds), *Handbook of the African Training Courses on Drug Dependence*. Lausanne: ICAA, pp. 163–172.

Peltzer, K. (1988b). Reproduction motives in married Malawians. *Journal of African Psychology*, 1, 92–101.

Peltzer, K. (1989a). Assessment and intervention of psychosocial problems in refugees in Lusaka, Zambia. *International Journal of Mental Health*, 17, 113–121.

Peltzer, K. (1989b). Causative and intervening factors of harmful alcohol consumption and cannabis use in Malawi. *International Journal of Addictions*, 24, 79–85.

Peltzer, K. (1989c). Psychosocial aspects of accidents/injuries of children in surgical admissions at the University Teaching Hospital in Lusaka, Zambia. *The Central African Journal of Medicine*, 36, 317–323.

Peltzer, K. (1989d). The impact of "born again" Christians on psychosocial services in Lusaka, Zambia. In K. Peltzer & P. O. Ebigbo (Eds), *Clinical Psychology in Africa*. Enugu: Working Group for African Psychology, pp. 607–611.

Peltzer, K., Bhat, G. J. & Chanda, D. (1990). Psychosocial assessment, counseling, and follow-up of patients with severe protein-energy malnutrition in Lusaka, Zambia. *Journal of African Psychology*, **2**, 77–87.

Peltzer, K. & Ebigbo, P. O. (1989a). *Clinical Psychology in Africa*. Enugu: Working Group for African Psychology.

Peltzer, K. & Ebigbo, P. O. (1989b). The (group) Ego and (collective) defence mechanisms. In K. Peltzer & P. O. Ebigbo (Eds), *Clinical Psychology in Africa*. Enugu: Working Group for African Psychology, pp. 154–165.

Peltzer, K., Hira, S. K., Wadhawan, D., Kamanga, J., Ferguson, D. C. E. & Perine, P. L. (1989a). Psychosocial counseling of patients infected with human immunodeficiency virus (HIV) in Lusaka, Zambia. *Tropical Doctor*, **19**, 164–168.

Peltzer, K. & Hossain, M. Z. (in press). Psychosocial factors in dermatology patients at a Nigerian teaching hospital. *International Journal of Mental Health*.

Peltzer, K. & Hossain, M. Z. (1988/89). Venereophobia as seen in a sexually transmitted diseases clinic at a Nigerian teaching hospital. *Psychopathologie Africaine*, **22**, 203–222.

Peltzer, K. & Likwa, R. (in press). Psychosocial aspects of unwed adolescent pregnancy in Lusaka, Zambia. *International Journal of Mental Health*.

Peltzer, K., Stubbe, H., Ebigbo, P. O. & Madu, S. (1989b). Training of clinical psychology in Africa. In K. Peltzer & P. O. Ebigbo (Eds), *Clinical Psychology in Africa*. Enugu: Working Group for African Psychology, pp. 714–722.

Perkin, G. (1970). Known monetary commodity incentives in family planning programmes: A preliminary trial. *Studies in Family Planning*, **57**, 12–15.

Perlean, D. F. & Brady, J. P. (Eds) (1979). *Behavioural Medicine: Theory and Practice*. Baltimore: Williams & Wilkins.

Rahim, S. D. A. & Cederblad, M. (1986). Effects of rapid urbanization on child behaviour and health in a part of Khartoum, Sudan II: Psychosocial influences on behaviour. *Social Science and Medicine*, **22**, 723–730.

Rosenfield, P. L., Smith, R. A. & Wolman, M. G. (1977). Development and verification of a schistosomiasis transmission model. *The American Journal of Tropical Medicine and Hygiene*, **26**, 505–516.

Sajiwandani, J. J. & Baboo, K. S. (1987). Sexually transmitted diseases in Zambia. *Journal Royal Society Health*, **5**, 183–186.

Sanson-Fisher, R. W., Webb, G. R., Donovan, K. & Byles, J. E. (1988). The health of people in developing countries: A challenge for behavioural medicine. Paper presented at the XXIV International Congress of Psychology, Sydney, September.

Sartorius, N. (1989). Preface to clinical psychology in Africa. In K. Peltzer & P. O. Ebigbo (Eds), *Clinical Psychology in Africa*. Enugu: Working Group for African Psychology, pp. iii–iv.

Sijuwola, O. A. (1989). Dimensions of personality and smoking behaviour. *African Journal of Medicine and Medical Sciences* **18**, 105–108.

Smith, D. L. (1984). The informational needs of the patient. *Nigerian Journal of Pharmacology* **15**, 17–24.

Sofowora, E. A. (1970). Bronchial asthma in the tropics: A study of 250 Nigerian patients. *East African Medical Journal*, **47**, 434–439.

Solanke, T. F., Osunkoya, B. O., Williams, C. K. O. & Agboola, O. O. (1982). *Cancer in Nigeria*. Ibadan: Ibadan University Press.

Stone, G. C., Cohen, F. & Adler, N. E. (1979). *Health Psychology*. San Francisco: Jossey-Bass.

Temoskok, L., Van Dyke, C. & Zegans, L. S. (1984). *Emotions in Health and Illness*. Orlando, FL: Grune & Stratton.

Tousignant, M. & Mishara, B. L. (1981). Suicide and culture: A review of the literature (1969–1980). *Transcultural Psychiatric Research Review*, **18**, 5–23.

UNICEF (1985). *Promoting Health Behaviour in Water and Sanitation Programmes*. Report of a Working Group, New York, 25–29 March 1985.

Van Bisbergen, W. M. J. (1979). The infancy of Edward Shellonga: An extended case from the Zambian Nkoya. In S. Van der Geest & K. W. Van der Veen (Eds), *In Search of Health: Essays in Medical Anthropology*. Amsterdam: University of Amsterdam, Vakgroep CANSA.

Verbeke, R. & Corin, E. (1976). The use of Indian hemp in Zaire: A formulation of hypotheses on the basis of an inquiry using a written questionnaire. *British Journal of Addiction*, **71**, 167–74.

Verghese, A. et al. (1971). Psychosomatic aspects of rehabilitation of leprosy patients. *International Journal of Leprosy* **39**, 842–847.

Weiss, M. G. (1985). The interrelationship of tropical disease and mental disorder. *Culture, Medicine and Psychiatry*, **9**, 121–200.

Weiss, S. M. & Weiss, J. A. (Eds) (1981). *Perspectives in Behaviour Medicine*. New York: Academic Press.

WHO (Special Program for Research and Training in Tropical Diseases) (1980) *Report of the Second Scientific Working Group on Social and Economic Research: Guidelines to Assess the Social and Economic Consequences of the Tropical Diseases*, Geneva, 22–27 October 1980, TDR/SER/SW 6 (2)/80.3.

WHO (1981). *Social Dimensions of Mental Health*. Geneva: WHO.

Williams, R. B. & Gentry, W. D. (1977). *Behavioural Approaches to Medical Treatment*. Cambridge, MA: Ballinger.

Winefield, H. R. & Peay, M. Y. (1980). *Behavioural Science in Medicine*. London: George Allen.

Wober, M. (1975). *Psychology in Africa*. London: International African Institute.

World Bank (1988). *World Development Report 1988*. Oxford: Oxford University Press.

Yach, D. (1986). The impact of smoking in developing countries with special reference to Africa. *International Journal of Health Services*, **16**, 279–292.

Zoysa, I. de, Carson, D. et al. (1984). Perceptions of childhood diarrhoea and its treatment in rural Zimbabwe. *Social Science and Medicine*, **19**, 727–734.

9 Australian Health Psychology

NEVILLE OWEN
Department of Community Medicine, University of Adelaide, PO Box 498, Australia 5001

BRIAN OLDENBURG
Department of Public Health, University of Sydney, Australia

INTRODUCTION

Over the past decade there have been many new developments in behavioural medicine, preventive health programmes, treatment programmes and prevention of drug and alcohol problems, preventing HIV transmission, and more general health-policy initiatives in Australia. Psychologists have been active in many of these areas (see Oldenburg & Owen, 1990; Taylor & Owen, 1989). There are many individual researchers and groups who are active and productive in health psychology. Rather than attempt to provide a comprehensive account of the field, we have opted to give examples from the work of four major Australian centres concerned with different aspects of health psychology research. We have selected a university department of psychology with a health psychology research programme, a behavioural science department within a university medical school, a behavioural science research centre concerned with cancer prevention, and a psychology unit in a large teaching hospital. As well as being representative of the range of work in Australia, these four groups are generally regarded to be the largest and most productive in their particular fields.

AUSTRALIAN PSYCHOLOGY

Australia has a population of approximately 17 million people, about 80% of whom reside in the coastal capital cities of the seven Australian states. Sydney and Melbourne are the most populous cities, with over 4 million people each; there are six other major urban areas with smaller populations. The continent of Australia is about 3500 km from east to west and about 2500 km from north to south.

Australia was occupied by the British in the late eighteenth century, initially as a penal colony, and then by free settlers. The Aboriginal people suffered the

International Review of Health Psychology. Edited by S. Maes, H. Leventhal and M. Johnston
©1992 John Wiley & Sons Ltd

usual effects of colonisation, and now represent a very small and generally disadvantaged portion of the total population. For much of its recent history, Australia was a geographically isolated British colony with some migrants from northern Europe. Since the 1940s, our predominantly British cultural mores have increasingly been influenced by the fact that many immigrants from southern Europe and from Asia have settled here. Australia is a more cosmopolitan and culturally diverse country than might be suggested by the content of some of the television soap operas we export, or by the television-advertising promotions used to attract tourists to Australia.

Australia's health system has some of the features of a strongly nationalised system such as those found in Scandinavian countries, but also some of the features of a privatised system such as that found in the USA (Sax, 1984). The profession of psychology is well established and active in Australia. The Australian Psychological Society (APS) was a branch of the British Psychological Society until 1966. The APS has a membership of some 5200, and is the major body representing the professional interests of psychologists in Australia. The Society publishes two peer-reviewed national journals, and various state and national newsletters are published regularly.

Most of the seven Australian states now have legislation which prescribes who may identify themselves as a psychologist. Registration as a psychologist generally requires a four-year degree with major studies in psychology, plus two years of experience under the supervision of a registered psychologist. The APS has boards of clinical neuropsychologists, clinical psychologists, community psychologists, counselling psychologists, educational and developmental psychologists, forensic psychologists and organizational psychologists, but there is not, as yet, a specific board of health psychologists. An APS Working Party on Health Psychology has recently made recommendations to the Society on how health psychology may best be supported and developed.

There are about 18 Australian universities which have departments of psychology, but with recent institutional restructuring and amalgamations of a number of tertiary-education institutions, it is difficult at the present time to give accurate estimates. Many psychology students now complete a two-year master's degree, in addition to a four-year bachelor's degree in psychology. New psychology master's programmes are currently being developed in many institutions, and doctoral programmes in specialised areas of the discipline are being developed and planned. Training opportunities in psychology in Australia are expanding rapidly at present, with the prospect of much greater specialisation and diversity in training and professional practice emerging over the next few years.

It has been estimated that 70–90% of psychologists employed in Australia are in the public sector, but there are increasing numbers in private practice. Of those psychologists providing clinical services in the public sector, most are employed in community mental health or traditional psychiatric settings. But with the trend towards de-institutionalisation of psychiatric services, there has been a significant shift in Australia towards transferring inpatient psychiatric facilities away from the traditionally large psychiatric hospitals to smaller inpatient units in general hospitals.

Prior to these changes there were few psychologists engaged in clinical activities within general hospital settings, other than in some of the larger university teaching hospitals. A recent survey of the current activities of psychologists in acute general hospitals in Australia showed that although there were a large number of potential roles for psychologists in this setting, they were most often restricted to five major treatment areas—neurology, psychosomatic medicine, death and dying, paediatrics and substance abuse (Groth-Marnat, 1988). Psychologists also work in community health centres, which were established under the community health programme in the 1970s (Sax, 1984).

HEALTH PSYCHOLOGY ACTIVITIES IN AUSTRALIA

Other accounts of some of the different aspects and areas of Australian health psychology may be found in Martin (1988), Oldenburg & Owen (1990) and Taylor & Owen (1989). The latter two papers deal mainly with the public-health and primary-prevention aspects of health psychology (see also Best & Proctor, 1988). Two of the earliest accounts of the potential contributions of psychologists in community and preventive health care can be found in Clarke (1974) and Viney (1974). Martin (1988) has surveyed and discussed the teaching of health psychology, and Innes & Owen (1980) describe one of the first health-psychology courses taught in Australia. Sanson-Fisher (1984a) has considered some of the issues and difficulties for psychologists and other social scientists working in the health field. Dadds (1988) deals with the development of behaviour modification in Australia, and includes a discussion of trends in a number of areas of behavioural health research.

In a recent survey of individuals involved in health-behaviour research in the Western Pacific region (Sanson-Fisher, 1984b), psychology was found to be the discipline with the greatest representation (32%), followed by medicine (23%) and sociology (14%). The majority of respondents were located in universities and other centres of tertiary education (70%). Most Australian respondents indicated they had postgraduate qualifications, with 47% stating they had acquired a PhD. As the context, or target for research, the community was the favoured setting for study (26%), followed by hospital outpatients (15%) and hospital inpatients settings (14%).

The first major Australian conference in the health and behaviour field took place in August 1980 convened by the Monash University Department of Psychological Medicine (Tiller & Martin, 1980). Later that year, Cumberland College of Health Sciences in Sydney hosted the first of a number of behavioural medicine conferences (Sheppard, 1982–87). Health psychology research was strongly represented at a National Symposium on Behavioural Research in Cancer in 1988, and at meetings of the Health Promotion Special Interest Group of the Australian Public Health Association in 1988 and 1990. There are also more generalist conferences at which health psychologists present their work: APS, the Australian Behaviour Modification Association, the Public Health Association of Australia and New Zealand, the Australian and New Zealand College of Psychiatrists, the Australian Society of Psychiatric Research, and other medical conferences.

Within the discipline of psychology itself, there have, until recently, been only a small number of departments which have strongly encouraged health-psychology research. For example, Lovibond at the University of New South Wales in Sydney has supported a number of health psychology projects (eg Lovibond, Birrell & Langeluddecke, 1986). Much of the community and preventive work in health psychology has developed out of the concerns for social activism which was implicit in early work on behaviour modification in Australia (Winkler, 1976; Winkler & Krasner, 1987).

King and Remenyi's (1986) book, *Health Care: A Behavioural Approach* gives an overview of much of the behavioural health-psychology research done in Australia up to the mid-1980s. The strong influence which North American psychology has had on work in Australia is apparent in this volume. While British and European influences are sometimes apparent, a major influence seems to be that of behaviour modification and social-learning theory, and behavioural medicine research from the USA.

In the following sections, we describe some of the work of four centres concerned with different areas of health psychology. In doing so, we also comment on some of the general issues which their work illustrates, and attempt to show some of the contributions of this work to health psychology in Australia, and internationally.

A UNIVERSITY DEPARTMENT OF PSYCHOLOGY

There is a strong and well-established programme of health-psychology research based in the Department of Psychology at the University of Wollongong, a relatively new and rapidly growing university in a regional centre situated 80 km south of Sydney, the capital city of the state of New South Wales. The Wollongong research programme has a strong emphasis on phenomenological studies concerned with patients' perceptions and interpretations of the meanings which they attach to health, building on Kelly's (1955) personal-construct theory and methods (see Viney, 1980, 1988). Currently, there are eight PhD students involved in research projects related to this general area, and there are five large external grants which fund a set of interrelated studies.

While a great deal of Australian health psychology has a behavioural emphasis, the Wollongong programme is more phenomenological in its orientation. There is a current research project examining psychological and social health and their interrelationships, which is being conducted in collaboration with colleagues in the public health and nutrition area of the University's new Faculty of Health and Behavioural Sciences. Personal-construct theory and methods have also been applied to important social and health issues such as unemployment (Viney, 1985), and reactions to knowledge of HIV infection (Viney et al., 1989).

As well as studies concerned with the understanding of the meanings which people attach to health, illness and other life circumstances, Viney and her associates have conducted studies on the effect of psychological interventions (eg Viney et al., 1985), on interventions to influence how people understand health, illness and illness-related behaviour patterns (Viney, 1987a,b), and on patients' interactions with health-care providers (eg Viney & Westbrook, 1982). Viney and her associates have also made contributions focusing on the health-care system more generally, which have been influential in raising the awareness of psychologists of opportunities and issues which arose as part of the implementation of the Australian federal government's Community Health Programme (Viney, 1974; Clarke, 1974).

The Wollongong programme has been very active in developing and promoting a "constructivist" approach in Australian psychology in general, and in health psychology in particular (Viney, 1987b, 1988). Viney's pheno-menological research strategies are in contrast to much of the other work in health psychology in Australia, which generally has a more behavioural theoretical orientation. The work of Viney's group has promoted some theoretical diversity in Australian health psychology. Health psychology is likely to develop a large and diverse constituency, as it becomes more involved in a number of areas of medicine, health services and community-health and preventive programmes. The other disciplines involved in these areas include sociologists, anthropologists and social psychiatrists, many of whom may be more comfortable with phenomenological theories and methods. Health-psychology research is often, of necessity, interdisciplinary in nature, and our discipline needs to be able to draw on a wide range of different psychological theories and methods, in order to be able to contribute to different research areas and problems which arise in the health field.

A BEHAVIOURAL SCIENCE DEPARTMENT IN A MEDICAL SCHOOL

The Department of Behavioural Science in Relation to Medicine at the University of Newcastle (160 km north of Sydney) has developed a number of major research lines in health psychology and behavioural medicine. These include studies of doctor–patient interaction, diabetes care, screening for various types of cancer, and problems associated with substance use. This department has recently been awarded a programme grant by the Cancer Council of the state of New South Wales, and is investigating behavioural and psychological aspects of cancer prevention, with some studies in collaboration with the Melbourne Centre for Behavioural Research in Cancer, which we also describe in this chapter.

A major line of research of the group in Newcastle has been in the study of doctor–patient interaction (eg Feletti, Firman & Sanson-Fisher, 1986), with a particular emphasis on counselling and preventive activities. These studies have also dealt with the detection of psychological disturbance (Sanson-Fisher & Hennrikus, 1988), with detection of patients' smoking status (Dickinson et al., 1989), and with the evaluation of the performance of medical interns (Gordon, Saunders & Sanson-Fisher, 1989) and methodological issues in the study of doctor–patient interactions (Redman et al., 1989).

Preventive aspects of automobile safety have also been examined (Bowman, Sanson-Fisher & Webb, 1989; Redman, Sanson-Fisher & Cockburn, 1988), as well as analyses of women's health needs (Redman et al., 1988), quality of life in cancer patients (Donovan, Sanson-Fisher & Redman, 1989), the cost-effectiveness of heart-disease prevention strategies (Hall et al., 1988) and aspects of secondary-preventive interventions with diabetics (Sanson-Fisher et al., 1989).

The University of Newcastle Department of Behavioural Sciences in Relation to Medicine has a well-established research programme, the most notable characteristic of which is the extent to which the studies which have been conducted have been in traditional medical-care settings. There has been very productive cooperation between psychologists, medical researchers and medical practitioners in the areas in which these studies have been conducted. The studies of doctor–patient interactions are in an area where members of the medical profession are often understandably sensitive to objective observation of their practice by non-medical researchers, and it is a tribute to the professional and diplomatic skills of the Newcastle researchers that they have been so successful in carrying out these studies.

The results of the wide range of studies carried out by members of the Newcastle programme show how it is possible for health psychologists to carry out research in a way that is closely integrated into clinical aspects of medical practice. The conduct of this research has no doubt been facilitated by a number of factors related to the Newcastle setting. The University of Newcastle Medical School was established in the early 1970s, with the goal of integrating behavioural science strongly into the medical school curriculum, and into research. Also, Newcastle is a relatively small city, and informal communication between health psychologists and medical researchers has created a climate conducive to collaboration and goodwill. These factors aside, the Newcastle programme shows that health psychologists can achieve a great deal in working closely with medical researchers and practitioners, although such collaboration and involvement of psychologists have by no means been universally successful in Australia (Sanson-Fisher, 1984a).

A BEHAVIOURAL RESEARCH CENTRE CONCERNED
WITH CANCER PREVENTION

The Centre for Behavioural Research in Cancer (CBRC) of the Anti-Cancer Council of Victoria in Melbourne has carried out studies of the behavioural epidemiology of smoking, based on data collected nationally (Hill, 1988; Hill, White & Gray, 1988), and has a strong association with the anti-smoking campaigns being conducted in the state of Victoria. Smoking-prevalence studies, and studies on smoking cessation conducted by the Centre, provide access to large data sets which have been used in a range of studies on the stability and change of smoking behaviour. The Centre is staffed by three PhD-level psychologists (the director, and two senior behavioural scientists). There also are three research officers, and eight support staff, including an executive officer trained in medical records administration, representing a well-developed administrative infrastructure. The CBRC is one of three divisions of the Anti-Cancer Council of the state of Victoria; the other two divisions are Programmes, and the Cancer Epidemiology Centre.

The CBRC is a specialised research centre located virtually inside a large and well-funded health promotion endeavour. Its own budget in 1989 was close to $700 000. The research staff of the CBRC are closely involved with the health education and health promotion staff of the Anti-Cancer Council's programmes, which overall have a budget of some $6 million. These programmes include a quit smoking campaign, a general anti-cancer public education campaign, and a solar radiation protection campaign. The CBRC is closely involved in message formulation, evaluation and a range of other consultative and advisory activities in relation to these large-scale preventive-health campaigns.

A major focus of the research of the CBRC has been on population studies of behavioural risk factors for cancer. It now works with population-prevalence data sets on smoking prevalence for children and adults; prevalence of skin-protection behaviour in summer; prevalence of Pap-smear tests, breast self-examination and skin self-examination; and prevalence of screening mammography. These data sets provide baselines for future studies of the stability and change in these behaviour patterns and cancer-screening activities.

As well as conducting studies which provide important population-prevalence data on behaviours related to cancer and cancer prevention, the CBRC is also involved in studies on coping and psychological adjustment to cancer diagnosis and treatment, and on aspects of behaviour change related to cancer prevention. For example, there have been studies on controlled smoking as a treatment outcome (Hill et al., 1988a); on the determinants of child and adolescent smoking behaviour (Hill et al., 1987); on trends in the population prevalence of aspects of smoking behaviour (Hill, 1988; Pierce et al., 1987); on the outcomes of breast self-examination (Hill et al., 1988b); on relationships of colon-cancer screening behaviour and health beliefs (Macrae et al., 1984); on factors influencing taking precautions against skin cancer (Hill, Rassaby & Gardner, 1984); and on patient perceptions of cancer treatment (Rassaby & Hill, 1983).

In addition to evaluation research, prevalence studies and other work in descriptive behavioural epidemiology, the CBRC has also had a strong focus on basic and applied theoretical studies. For example, the introduction of workplace smoking bans in Australia has been treated as a natural experiment, and has been used to examine theoretical questions about the relationships between environmental change, attitudes and behaviour change. A collaborative study with researchers from Sydney and Adelaide is testing a number of hypotheses about the effects of environmental and social determinants of smoking behaviour (Borland et al., 1989, 1990, in press).

The CBRC collaborates with other groups with basic behavioural research interests, and also with bodies concerned with community interventions and health campaigns. It conducts practical evaluation studies, applied research and theoretically focused research. This mix of practical and theoretical interests has been important in generating a diverse, energetic and highly productive research environment in this centre; the CBRC now has a national and international reputation as a centre of excellence in behavioural research in cancer. Its staff collaborate with a number of other preventive-health research groups, including the Newcastle group described earlier, and they are planning to do studies in conjunction with a new cancer prevention research centre currently being established at the University of Queensland.

One of the particular strengths of these Australian cancer prevention centres is the focus on skin-cancer prevention (eg Hill, Rassaby & Gardner, 1984). This is an important area of cancer prevention which has not yet been examined to any great extent, and behavioural studies currently in progress in Australia are likely to be innovative and illuminative.

A TEACHING-HOSPITAL PSYCHOLOGY DEPARTMENT

In Australia, psychology departments in general hospitals have not been large nor have they been active in research, apart from a small number of departments based in large teaching hospitals. Groth-Marnat (1988) surveyed psychologists in these settings: he argues that while there are many potential roles for psychologists, these roles, in general, have not been strongly developed. The work of psychologists in hospitals tends to be restricted to the areas of neurology, psychosomatic medicine, death and dying, paediatrics, and substance abuse. Groth-Marnat argues that psychologists have the potential to contribute to other areas in the primary and secondary prevention of chronic disease, and to work on psychological and behavioural aspects of disease and its treatment in virtually all of the major medical specialities.

The Department of Clinical Psychology at Westmead Hospital differs in a number of respects from the general state of hospital health psychology described by Groth-Marnat—it is an example of a general-hospital psychology department which has begun to expand its clinical roles and research activities beyond what might be considered to be the traditional boundaries of the discipline in the hospital setting.

Westmead Hospital is in the populous and sprawling western suburbs of Sydney, a city of more than 4 million people. The catchment area for the hospital has a population of around 1 million; it is an area of relatively high unemployment, has many recent immigrants, and has higher than average rates of cardiovascular disease and other health problems (Cumming et al., 1989). Four of the 21 staff of the Westmead Psychology Department work in psychiatry; the remainder are placed elsewhere in a number of specialist departments and services throughout the general hospital. There are five clinical neuropsychologists who work with adults and children, and with a wide range of neurological conditions.

The broad objectives of the Westmead Psychology Department are to apply psychological principles and methods to the problems of patients, their families and staff within the general hospital setting, and to increase the awareness and understanding of psychological factors in the development and prevention of illness and in rehabilitation. More specifically, staff of the department are concerned with contributions throughout the hospital which involve the improvement of methods of patient care, the evaluation of outcomes, and research to improve assessment and treatment procedures. Training and educational services are provided for other hospital departments.

Currently, there are 15 full-time and 6 part-time psychologists who work in the department, and 4 research staff. While the department has considerable demands placed on it for service provision and training, it also has a range of health-psychology research projects around clinical problem areas, and also has studies on more general preventive-health problems. For example, studies of worksite-based smoking-cessation interventions have been conducted (DiGuisto, 1987). These have taken clinical behaviour-therapy methods into a community setting, and have also examined some basic methodological issues in the biological validation of verbal reports of smoking behaviour (DiGuisto, 1986).

Other studies conducted by staff of the Westmead Psychology Department have had a more clinical focus, and there has been a strong line of research into eating disorders, particularly bulimia and anorexia (O'Connor, Touyz & Beumont, 1989; Touyz et al., 1989). Staff have developed practical guidelines on how psychological assessment may be employed in medical settings (Touyz & Byrne, 1989), and have worked on analyses of the consequences of cancer treatment (Cousens et al., 1988). Recently, the department has also begun to develop a reputation as a centre of expertise in the treatment of gambling.

The Westmead Hospital Psychology Department is the largest general-hospital psychology department in Australia, and is therefore not representative of the majority of work in hospital-based health psychology in this country. However, it is likely that as the field develops in Australia, there will soon be a number of hospital-based psychology departments which begin to rival Westmead in size, and in the range of innovative research and health-psychology service provision which is offered.

The Westmead department has some links with psychiatry, but has always been independent of that particular medical specialty. It has concentrated on developing relationships with the hospital more generally, and with a range of medical specialties, emphasising the use of the research skills of the discipline, and a preventive and educational focus. Many other hospital-based psychology services in Australia have not been so successful in developing such links and an independent status. As Groth-Marnat (1988) has argued, we should begin to see more departments operating in Australian hospital settings in a manner similar to the Westmead department.

CONCLUSIONS

The Australian health-psychology activities which we have discussed are those which we, with the advice of colleagues in the health psychology field in this country, have selected as examples of interesting and productive centres, and which exemplify a range of different aspects of health psychology. These four are probably also the largest and most productive centres in the field in this country. Other active and innovative centres also exist—for example, the postgraduate programme at the University of Western Australia (see Wilson, 1987), and the Health Psychology Centre in the Lincoln School of Health Sciences at LaTrobe University. These other centres, as well as many individual researchers, clinicians, and also educators in Australian psychology departments and medical schools (eg Winefield & Peay, 1980), are also doing some very good work in health psychology. For example, psychological research on a number of aspects of the management and prevention of HIV (eg Ross, 1988) is a rapidly developing area; there has been a strong line of research at the University of Western Australia on behavioural aspects of headache (eg Martin, 1986).

One area which we have not discussed here are the postgraduate health psychology and public health training programmes which recently have been established at a number of Australian universities (see Oldenburg & Owen, 1990), and some of the population-focused behavioural research in Australia (see Taylor & Owen, 1989) which has not been included in this discussion. Another approach which we might have taken is to describe the range of specific health-oriented projects which many Australian psychology researchers are currently conducting with recently awarded funding support from bodies like the National Heart Foundation and the National Health and Medical Research Council. These currently funded projects are now too numerous to list in detail here: the two research funding bodies mentioned above do provide such details in recent reports.

Many of the studies in the research centres we have described are supported by these relatively new funding sources such as the National Heart Foundation's education and prevention research grants, behavioural medicine and intervention-study research grants from the Public Health Research and Development Committee of the National Health and Medical Research Council, programme development grants from the Commonwealth Department of Health, and Commonwealth AIDS-prevention research funds. Various other health research funding bodies such as the Victorian Health Promotion Foundation and state anti-cancer bodies are now providing increasing proportions of their research budgets for behavioural research.

Health-psychology research, and a range of related clinical, community and other activities are becoming well established in Australia. We have described the work of four of the most productive groups, and have tried to convey some of the flavour of local research and practice. The Working Party on Health Psychology is currently making some strong recommendations to the APS about formalising and supporting the field in this country. Over the next 5–10 years, we expect to see the further expansion of high-quality research and many new practical applications of Australian health psychology.

ACKNOWLEDGEMENTS

The head of each of the units whose research activities we discuss has kindly provided us with representative published material and recent reports of their activities. We express our thanks to the following individuals and to the staff of their units for providing this information: Linda Viney, University of Wollongong; Rob Sanson-Fisher, University of Newcastle; David Hill, Centre for Behavioural Research in Cancer; and Stephen Touyz, Westmead Hospital.

REFERENCES

Best, J. A. & Proctor, S. (1988). Behavioural medicine training from a public health perspective. *Annals of Behavioral Medicine*, 10, 19–22.

Borland, R., Chapman, S., Owen, N. & Hill, D. J. (1990). Effects of workplace smoking bans on cigarette consumption. *American Journal of Public Health*, 80, 178–180.

Borland, R., Chapman, S., Owen, N. & Hill, D. J. (in press). Changes in acceptance of workplace smoking following their implementation: A prospective study. *Preventive Medicine*.

Borland, R., Owen, N., Hill, D. J. & Chapman, S. (1989). Acceptance of workplace bans on smoking in Commonwealth Government Offices. *Medical Journal of Australia*, 151, 525–528.

Bowman, J. A., Sanson-Fisher, R. W. & Webb, G. R. (1989). Interventions in preschools to increase the use of safety restraints by pre-school children. *Pediatrics*, 79(1), 103–109.

Clarke, A. M. (1974). Community health care: implications for psychologists and for society. *Australian Psychologist*, 9 (Suppl. 1).

Cousens, P., Walters, B., Said, J. & Stevens, M. (1988). Cognitive effects of cranial irradiation in leukemia: A survey and meta-analysis. *Journal of Child Psychology and Psychiatry*, 29, 839–852.

Cumming, R. G., Barton, G. E., Fahey, P., Wilson, A. & Leeder, S. (1989). Cardiovascular disease-related knowledge and attitudes in a high-risk Australian population. *Medical Journal of Australia*, 150, 551–558.

Dadds, M. R. (1988). Behaviour modification in Australia: A quantitative review of the last decade. *Behaviour Change*, 5, 147–153.

Dickinson, J. A., Wiggers, J., Leeder, S. R. & Sanson-Fisher, R. W. (1989). General practitioners' detection of patients' smoking status. *Medical Journal of Australia*, 150, 420–426.

DiGuisto, E. (1986). Some properties of saliva cotinine measurements in indicating exposure to tobacco smoking. *American Journal of Public Health*, 76, 1245–1246.

DiGuisto, E. (1987). A workplace smoking cessation programme—a strategy with potential for mass application. *Community Health Studies*, 11 (Suppl.), 45–52.

Donovan, K., Sanson-Fisher, R. W. & Redman, S. (1989). Measuring quality of life in cancer patients. *Journal of Clinical Oncology*, 7, 959–968.

Feletti, G., Firman, D. & Sanson-Fisher, R. (1986). Patient satisfaction with primary-care consultations. *Journal of Behavioural Medicine*, 9, 389–400.

Gordon, J. J., Saunders, N. A. & Sanson-Fisher, R. W. (1989). Evaluating interns' performance using simulated patients in a casualty department. *Medical Journal of Australia*, 151, 18–21.

Groth-Marnat, G. (1988). A survey of the current and future directors of professional psychology in acute general hospitals in Australia. *Australian Psychologist*, 23, 127–135.

Hall, J., Heller, R., Dobson, A., Lloyd, D., Sanson-Fisher, R. & Leeder, S. (1988). A cost effectiveness analysis of alternative strategies for the prevention of heart disease. *Medical Journal of Australia*, 148, 273–277.

Hill, D. J. (1988). Australian patterns of tobacco smoking in 1986. *Medical Journal of Australia*, 149, 6–12.

Hill, D., Rassaby, J. & Gardner, G. (1984). Determinants of intentions to take precautions against skin cancer. *Community Health Studies*, 9, 205–208.

Hill, D., Weiss, D. J., Walker, D. L. & Jolley, D. (1988a). Long-term evaluation of controlled smoking as a treatment outcome. *British Journal of Addiction*, 83, 203–207.

Hill, D. J., White, V. M. & Gray, N. J. (1988). Measures of tobacco smoking in Australia 1974–1986 by means of a standard method. *Medical Journal of Australia*, 149, 10–12.

Hill, D., White, V., Jolley, D. & Mapperson, K. (1988b). Self-examination of the breast: Is it beneficial? Meta-analysis of studies investigating breast self-examination and extent of disease in patients with breast cancer. *British Medical Journal*, 297, 271–275.

Hill, D., Willcox, S., Gardner, G. & Houston, J. (1987). Tobacco and alcohol use among Australian secondary schoolchildren. *Medical Journal of Australia*, 146, 125–130.

Innes, J. M. & Owen, N. (1980). Social and behavioural dimensions of community health: An introductory course on psychology in health-care settings. *Australian Psychologist*, 15, 169–180.

Kelly, G. A. (1955). *The Psychology of Personal Constructs*, Vols 1 and 2. New York: Norton.

King, N. J. & Remenyi, A. G. (1986). *Health Care: A Behavioural Approach*. Sydney: Grune and Stratton.

Lovibond, S. H., Birrell, P. C. & Langeluddecke, P. (1986). Changing coronary heart disease risk factor status: The effects of three behavioral programs. *Journal of Behavioral Medicine*, 9, 415–438.

Macrae, F. A., Hill, D. J., St, John, D. J. B., Ambikapthy, A & Garner, J. F. Ballarat General Practitioner Research Group (1984). Predicting colon cancer screening behaviour from health beliefs. *Preventive Medicine*, 13, 115–126.

Martin, P. R. (1986). Headaches. In N. J. King & A. Remenyi (Eds), *Health Care: A Behaviour Approach*. Sydney: Grune & Stratton, pp. 145–158.

O'Connor, M., Touyz, S. W. & Beumont, P. J. V. (1989). Practice guidelines: Dietary management of patients with bulimia nervosa. *Australian Journal of Nutrition and Dietetics*, 46(3), 72–73.

Oldenburg, B. & Owen, N. (1990). Health psychology in Australia. *Psychology and Health*, 4, 73–81.

Pierce, J. P., Aldrich, R. N., Hanratty, S., Dwyer, T. & Hill, D. (1987). Uptake and quitting smoking trends in Australia 1974–1984. *Preventive Medicine*, 16, 252–260.

Rassaby, J. & Hill, D. (1983). Patient's perceptions of breast reconstruction following mastectomy. *Medical Journal of Australia*, **2**, 173–176.

Redman, S., Dickinson, J. A., Hennrikus, D. J. & Sanson-Fisher, R. W. (1989). The assessment of reactivity in direct observation studies of doctor–patient interactions. *Psychology and Health*, **3**, 17–28.

Redman, S., Hennrikus, D., Bowman, J. & Sanson-Fisher, R. (1988). Assessing women's health needs. *Medical Journal of Australia*, **148**, 123–127.

Redman, S., Sanson-Fisher, R. & Cockburn, J. (1988). Rehabilitation programmes for drink drivers: A critical appraisal. *Community Health Studies*, **12**, 418–427.

Ross, M. W. (1988). Prevalence of risk factors for AIDS infection in the Australian population. *Medical Journal of Australia*, **149**, 362–365.

Sanson-Fisher, R. (1984a). Commentary: Behavioural science and its relation to medicine—a need for positive action. *Community Health Studies*, **9**, 275–283.

Sanson-Fisher, R. (1984b). *Health Behaviour Research in Australia, New Zealand and Papua New Guinea: An Overview.* Geneva: World Health Organization.

Sanson-Fisher, R. W., Campbell, E. M., Redman, S. & Hennrikus, D. J. (1989). Patient–provider interactions and patient outcomes. *The Diabetes Educator*, **15**, 134–138.

Sanson-Fisher, R. W. & Hennrikus, D. J. (1988). Why do primary care physicians often fail to detect psychological disturbance in their patients? In S. Henderson & G. D. Burrows (Eds), *Handbook of Social Psychiatry.* Canberra: Elsevier Science.

Sax, S. (1984). *A Strife of Interests.* Sydney: Allen & Unwin.

Sheppard, J. L. (1982–87). *Advances in Behavioural Medicine*, Vols 1–4. Sydney: Cumberland College of Health Sciences.

Taylor, C. B. & Owen, N. (1989). Behavioural medicine: Research and development in disease prevention. *Behavioural Change*, **6**, 3–11.

Tiller, J. W. & Martin, P. R. (Eds) (1980). *Proceedings of the Geigy Psychiatric Symposium on Behavioural Medicine.* Sydney: Ciba-Geigy.

Touyz, S. W. & Byrne, D. G. (1989). Psychological assessment. In P. J. V. Beumont & R. Hampshire (Eds), *Textbook of Psychiatry.* Melbourne: Blackwell.

Touyz, S. W., Gertler, R., Brigham, S., Sommerville, B. & Beumont, P. J. V. (1989). Anorexia nervosa in a patient with multiple sclerosis: A case report. *International Journal of Eating Disorders*, **8**, 231–234.

Viney, L. L. (1974). The role of the psychologist in community health care. *Australian Psychologist*, **9** (Suppl. 2).

Viney, L. L. (1980). *Transitions.* Sydney: Cassell.

Viney, L. L. (1985). "They call you a dole bludger": Psychological reactions to unemployment. *Journal of Community Psychology*, **13**, 31–45.

Viney, L. L. (1987a). A sociophenomenological approach to lifespan development complementing Erikson's psychodynamic approach. *Human Development*, **30**, 125–136.

Viney, L. L. (1987b). Images of illness: A model of patients' psychological reactions to physical illness. *Psychiatric Medicine*, **5**, 15–23.

Viney, L. L. (1988). Which data collection methods are appropriate for a constructivist psychology? *International Journal of Personal Construct Psychology*, **1**, 191–203.

Viney, L. L., Clarke, A. M., Bunn, T. A. & Benjamin, Y. N. (1985). An evaluation of three crisis intervention programmes for general hospital patients. *British Journal of Medical Psychology*, **58**, 75–86.

Viney, L. L., Henry, R., Walker, B. M. & Crooks, L. (1989). The emotional reactions of HIV antibody positive men. *British Journal of Medical Psychology*, **62**, 153–161.

Viney, L. L. & Westbrook, M. T. (1982). Coping with chronic illness: The mediating role of biographic and illness-related factors. *Journal of Psychosomatic Medicine*, **26**, 595–605.

Wilson, P. H. (1987). In memory of Robin Winkler: His contribution to behaviour modification in Australia. *Behaviour Change*, **4**, 3–10.

Winefield, H. R. & Peay, M. Y. (1980). *Behavioural Science in Medicine*. London: Allen & Unwin/Beaconsfield.

Winkler, R. C. (1976). New directions for behaviour modification in homosexuality, open education and behavioural economics. In P. W. Sheehan & K. D. White (Eds), "Behaviour modification in Australia". *Australian Psychologist*. **11**, Monogr. Suppl. No.3, pp. 70–84.

Winkler, R. C. & Krasner, L. (1987). A social history of behaviour modification in Australia. *Behaviour Change*, **4**, 11–25.

Index

SUBSCRIPTION NOTICE

This Wiley product is updated annually to reflect important developments in the subject field.

If you purchased this copy directly from John Wiley & Sons, we will have already recorded your subscription and will inform you of new volumes.

If, however, you purchased this product from a bookseller and wish to be notified of future volumes, please fill in your details and return to Wiley (address printed overleaf).

NAME: _____

ADDRESS: _____

_____

_____

COUNTRY: _____

TELEPHONE: _____

Bookseller where purchased

_____

WILEY
Publishers Since 1807

REPONSE PAYEE
GRANDE-BRETAGNE

Sarah Stevens (MARKETING)
John Wiley & Sons Ltd.
Baffins Lane
CHICHESTER
West Sussex
GREAT BRITAIN
PO19 1YN